CLARENDON ARISTOTLE SERIES

General Editor: J. L. ACKRILL

CLARENDON ARISTOTLE SERIES

CATEGORIES and *DE INTERPRETATIONE*
J. L. ACKRILL

DE ANIMA, Books II and III
D. W. HAMLYN

DE GENERATIONE ET CORRUPTIONE
C. J. F. WILLIAMS

EUDEMIAN ETHICS, Books I, II, and VIII
MICHAEL WOODS

METAPHYSICS, Books Γ, Δ, E
CHRISTOPHER KIRWAN

METAPHYSICS, Books M and N
JULIA ANNAS

PHYSICS, Books I and II
W. CHARLTON

POSTERIOR ANALYTICS
JONATHAN BARNES

ARISTOTLE'S
PHYSICS

BOOKS III AND IV

Translated with Notes
by
EDWARD HUSSEY
Fellow of All Souls College
Oxford

CLARENDON PRESS · OXFORD
OXFORD UNIVERSITY PRESS · NEW YORK
1983

Oxford University Press, Walton Street, Oxford OX2 6DP

London Glasgow New York Toronto
Delhi Bombay Calcutta Madras Karachi
Kuala Lumpur Singapore Hong Kong Tokyo
Nairobi Dar es Salaam Cape Town
Melbourne Auckland
and associated companies in
Beirut Berlin Ibadan Mexico City Nicosia

Oxford is a trade mark of Oxford University Press

British Library Cataloguing in Publication Data
Hussey, Edward
Aristotle's Physics: books III and IV. – (Clarendon
Aristotle Series)
1. Aristotle – Physics
I. Title
110   Q151.A7
ISBN 0-19-872068-8
ISBN 0-19-872069-6 Pbk

Library of Congress Cataloging in Publication Data
Aristotle.
Aristotle's Physics, books III and IV.
(Clarendon Aristotle series)
Translation of: Physics.
Bibliography: p.
Includes index.
1. Science, Ancient.   2. Physics – Early works
to 1800.   I. Hussey, Edward.   II. Title.   III. Se-
ries.
Q151.A7913 1983   500.2   82-18996
ISBN 0-19-872068-8 (U.S.)
ISBN 0-19-872069-6 (U.S.: pbk.)

Set by Hope Services, Abingdon
Printed in Great Britain
at the University Press, Oxford
by Eric Buckley
Printer to the University

PREFACE AND DEDICATION

This volume offers guidance to a reader who wishes to explore books III and IV of Aristotle's *Physics*. The translation and the notes follow the common pattern of the Clarendon Aristotle Series. The translation aims to be literal, in the sense that it tries to beg as few questions of interpretation as possible. The notes give a step-by-step discussion of the text.

In the Introduction, I have tried to give a more connected account of what Aristotle is about in these books. Two fundamental, and controversial, topics that arise are (*i*) Aristotle's philosophy of mathematics; and (*ii*) Aristotle's mathematical or other 'laws' of motion and of change in general. On these, I have provided fairly systematic treatments, but ones which are in some degree unorthodox. These topics, therefore, I have relegated to Additional Notes at the end of the volume.

It is a pleasure to acknowledge the various kinds of help I have received in preparing this book. I must record particularly my gratitude to the Editor of the Clarendon Aristotle Series, Professor John Ackrill, for his sympathetic patience and valuable comments and advice at all stages. To David Charles, David Fowler, Jennifer Hornsby, Gavin Lawrence, Christopher Peacocke, Malcolm Schofield, and David Wiggins I am variously indebted for conversation, guidance and encouragement. I thank Edna Laird and Diane Burden for their efficient typing, and Derek Parfit for the generosity with which he allowed me the use of his electronic word-processing equipment.

To Gwil Owen, who died when the manuscript of this book was already in the hands of the publisher, I owe in common with many others a less easily defined, but deeper debt for his teaching and example in the study of ancient philosophy. I dedicate this book to his memory, and to that of another friend early dead, R. C. ('Prof') Zaehner.

All Souls College, Oxford   E.L.H.
July 1982

CONTENTS

INTRODUCTION   ix

TRANSLATION   1

NOTES   55

ADDITIONAL NOTES   176
   (A) Aristotle's Philosophy of Mathematics   176
   (B) Aristotelian Dynamics   185

EXPLANATION OF REFERENCES   201

LIST OF DIVERGENCES FROM THE TEXT OF ROSS   208

GLOSSARY   210

INDEXES   215

INTRODUCTION

1. *PHYSICS* III AND IV AND THEIR INTERPRETATION

(a) Contents, aim, and method

Books III and IV of Aristotle's *Physics* consist of five essays, on the subjects of *change* (III.1–3), the *infinite* (III.4–8), *place* (IV.1–4), *void* (IV.5–9), and *time* (IV.10–14). It is clear that they were composed fairly early in Aristotle's career as an independent thinker. Probably they were originally written soon after the *Topics* was completed, and not (except for the essay on time) much reworked later. Some clues to the history of their composition are pointed out in the notes. For the understanding of the text, though, questions of relative and absolute chronology are not of importance.[1]

Aristotle's aim is to arrive at a correct general theory about each of the subjects under discussion. His method is the method of dialectic, by which (in theory at least) the philosophical inquirer started from the accumulated material of common-sense intuitions, previous opinions of philosophers, and observed facts relevant to the subject, and ascended by a process of rational criticism and generalization to the correct account of the subject, which would usually be enshrined in a definition of the central term. The practice of Aristotelian dialectic is codified in the *Topics*, and *Physics* III and IV provide one of the earliest surviving examples of its application.[2]

Dialectic is a formalization of the ordinary processes of rational reflection, and most of the time the modern reader will not be far out if he takes Aristotle to be doing in these essays much what a modern physicist or philosopher does when discussing certain very general topics, such as the nature of time or space, in general terms. The peculiarities of Aristotle's discussions derive not so much from a

---

[1] On the date and composition of the *Physics* see esp. Ross (1), 1–11.
[2] On dialectic in general: Index of subjects (under 'Dialectical Method'); and Owen (3), Wieland (2).

peculiar method of thought as from the fact that Aristotle starts out with a particular set of assumptions or philosophical commitments, of which the influence is often manifest and everywhere present. It would be impossible, and pointless, to state all these assumptions. In the later sections of this Introduction, and in the notes, some of them are identified and elucidated. Two in particular it may be useful to mention here, because they are so alien to our ways of thinking, and not only mistaken but disastrously so: the assumptions (a) that all the sciences are, not merely essentially finite and completable, but in principle deducible from principles which are in some sense self-evident; (b) that the essential truths about physics, at any rate the physics of inanimate matter, lie more or less 'on the surface' in the sense that there is no 'micro-structure' of matter, and no physical agent not directly observable, by the unaided senses, as such.

Besides such assumptions there is Aristotle's general metaphysical position, and this is one that is fairly familiar, and even fashionable, at the present time: essentialist, realist,[1] and anti-Platonist. As an exponent of this kind of position Aristotle has had (at least until recently) no serious rival. These essays are in the end important, if they are so at all, not only as almost the earliest but also as classic expressions of a durable philosophical treatment of the problems under discussion.

(b) Obstacles to understanding

For the innocent modern reader, the obstacles that lie in the way of understanding and appreciating these books, or any work of Aristotle, are many and serious.

(1) The language barrier. Aristotle's Greek, even when perfectly clear in its own terms, is full of words and phrases for which there is no English equivalent. Even the most faithful translation needs to be supplemented by a commentary.

(2) The presentation is often repellent and difficult. It is obvious that these writings were never prepared for any 'publication' or

---

[1] Aristotle's realism is severely qualified in certain directions; see below, secs 3(c) 3 and 6 (g).

literary presentation by Aristotle; they reek of the lecture-room, though the first editors of the Aristotelian corpus may have tidied them up a little. The language is sometimes sloppy and ambiguous, or clumsy and obscure. There is some confusing arrangement of materials, some repetition, and a few short passages which can hardly be authentic.

(3) The exposition is in any case esoteric and allusive. Essential components of the positions taken up may be left out as understood by Aristotle's original audiences. Aristotle's thought as a whole being highly systematic, this entails a constant risk of simply failing to see the whole of what is intended. This is particularly true where the underlying assumptions are strange to modern ways of thinking (see (a) above).

(4) Even when obstacles (1), (2), and (3) have been overcome, there is still left the intrinsic difficulty of grasping the nature and implications of Aristotle's doctrines on an inherently difficult subject-matter.

(5) Less serious, by far, but still occasionally irritating is our ignorance of the historical background. Independently of Aristotle we know sadly little about what his predecessors and contemporaries thought on the subjects discussed, even about Plato's views; and even with Aristotle's help we are not always much the wiser. We know, furthermore, little about how (if at all) Aristotle's own thinking evolved in relation to Plato and others in the Academy. What *is* certain is that the ideas of Plato are continuously present, if rarely manifest, in these books, like family ghosts which are hardly mentioned but which it is important to exorcize if possible.

This book, which aims to introduce the reader to *Physics* III and IV, provides a new English translation which tries to avoid introducing anything not present in the Greek. It is necessarily rather literal and does not always read naturally. This translation, together with the notes and this Introduction, try to offer help with obstacles of types (1) to (4) above; the historical background mentioned in (5) has been relatively neglected. The notes owe much to the commentaries of Simplicius, Philoponus, Aquinas, Pacius, Zabarella (unfortunately incomplete) and Ross, even though these scholars are rarely mentioned by name in them. In the rest of this Introduction some general remarks are made on each of the essays in turn.

2. CHANGE (III.1–3)

(a) Summary

III.1: (200^b12–25): A general introduction to books III and IV, motivating the treatment of the topics *change*, the *infinite, place*, the *void*, and *time* as necessary to physics.

(200^b26–201^a9): Discussion of change begins. Classification of changes in terms of the Aristotelian categories.

(201^a9–19): Definition of change.

(201^a19–27): Remarks about mutual acting-upon and being-acted upon.

(201^a27–$^b5$): The definition of change restated; explanation of 'actuality *qua* . . .'.

(201^b5–15): The definition justified by working out an example.

III.2: (201^b16–202^a3): Indirect confirmation of the definition—the defects of other proposed definitions. Why change is thought to be indefinite, and is hard to define.

(202^a3–12): More on acting-upon and being-acted-upon. The need for contact in action. Change as transmission of a 'form'.

III.3: (202^a13–21): The change is in that which is changed. The operations of the agent of change, and of that which is changed, are the same, but 'different in definition'.

(202^a21–$^b5$): A dilemma: objections both to identifying the operations and to distinguishing them.

(202^b5–22): Resolution of the dilemma: the objections to identification are not compelling.

(202^b23–29): Conclusion.

(b) *The definition of change* (201^{a}9–19, 201^{a}27–202^{a}3)

Aristotle's definition of change has been much criticized, but not justly. Some have called it a piece of mere verbal juggling, empty of real content. But, on any plausible interpretation, it is empty only if the whole Aristotelian metaphysics of potentiality and actuality is empty. The definition relates changes to that metaphysical background. A better kind of criticism is contained in the claim that knowledge of changing things, or at least scientific knowledge and explanation of change, does not need, or is even hampered by, a metaphysics of 'powers' or potentialities. Even this claim is controversial, and, even if true, it would not impugn the importance and interest of Aristotle's definition within his own system.[1]

Another possible objection is that there is a vicious circle when change is defined in terms of potentiality and actuality, since these in turn can be understood only in terms of a world in which change occurs. Once again the objection misconceives what the definition aims to do: it does not derive all our understanding of change from our understanding of potentiality and actuality, but exhibits the relationship of change to what Aristotle takes to be metaphysically more basic features of the universe.

What once caused the definition, along with the whole apparatus of powers and actualities, to fall into undeserved disrepute was its association with the pseudo-explanations and bad theories, in physics and other branches of science, offered by some Aristotelians in medieval and early modern times. The deficiencies of Aristotelian science in those times are indeed partly due to Aristotle himself, and perhaps, even, to Aristotle's general theory of change (see section (*f*) below), but at least the definition and the metaphysics of powers and actualities cannot be held responsible. For they are neutral as between particular scientific theories. The same point may be made (more controversially) on the question whether Aristotle was right to take agency rather than event-causation as fundamental to scientific explanation.[2] The definition of change does not in itself

---

[1] On Aristotelian powers, see Mourelatos.

[2] For modern discussion on 'powers' and dispositions see e.g. Mackie (1), ch. 4, Mellor; on agency vs. event-causation, von Wright, Mackie (3).

require either type of explanation, but Aristotle integrates it with his theory of agency (see sections (*e*) and (*f*) below).

(c) The classification of changes (200^{b}26–201^{a}9)

Aristotle's classification of changes is sketched hastily in this section. The classification is structurally important to Aristotle in a number of ways. He needs a determinate notion of 'species of change' in order to be able to deal with questions about the individuation of changes and the giving of identity conditions for them: see, especially, *Physics* V.4, 227^{b}20–228^{a}3; *Physics* VII.4, 249^{a}3–29, ^{b}11–14; *Nic.Eth.* X.4.1174^{a}19–^{b}5 (see also section (*d*) below).[1]

(d) The incompleteness of change (201^{b}16–202^{a}3)

This too is an important component in Aristotle's general account of change, but this too surfaces only briefly in the present discussion. What seems to underlie the doctrine of 'the incompleteness of change' is the thought that the classification of changes, the individuation of changes, and the giving of identity-conditions for changes, all involve an essential reference to the end-states of those changes—as well as to other things: see on 202^{a}3ff. In a different way, the definition of change brings this out as well: it exhibits a change as a potentiality, and for Aristotle a potentiality can be understood only by way of the corresponding actuality, on which it depends ontologically. So the incompleteness of change is due to the fact, reflected in the definition of change, that the key potentiality involved is that of which the actuality is the end-state. So there is an essential asymmetry: a change 'points forward' to its completion in a way in which it does not 'point backward' to its inception.

This 'pointing forward' may still seem rather mysterious. After all, any ordinary change may be arrested at any point: it cannot then have pointed forward, all along, to the end-state it turned out to have. But Aristotle is primarily concerned, not with such cases, which involve disruption of the natural action of the agent, but with the cases in which the action runs to its full natural extent. The 'pointing forward' and the asymmetry it involves, are thus connected

---

[1] In general see Charles, ch. 1, Penner.

with the doctrines that there is always an agent of change, and that change is assimilation to the agent (on which see (*e*) (*iii*) below).[1] But this in turn must rest on the definition of change.

(*e*) *The structure of agency* (201ᵃ19–27, 202ᵃ3–12)

These two paragraphs, though compressed and not integrated with the main discussion, contain important remarks about the relation of 'acting-upon'. Four principles appear which must have been intended as cornerstones of an Aristotelian physics, and are in fact much used by Aristotle.

(*i*) *The necessity of contact* between agent and what is acted upon. The first statement of the principle of 'no action at a distance'.[2]

(*ii*) *The sufficiency of contact.* When a suitable agent and a suitable candidate for being acted upon are in contact, action necessarily occurs—unless there is some further specifiable impeding factor present.[3] The principle is essential if explanations in terms of agents are to be satisfactory.

(*iii*) *Action as transmission of a form* from agent to what is acted upon. There are two parts to this. First, the principle already stated at 200ᵇ32–201ᵃ9, that starting-states and end-states of changes fall into types, the classification of which is logically prior to that of types of change (cf. (*c*) above). The second part is that, in any change with end-state of a particular type, the proximate agent of change must have started acting in a state of that type. What heats, must itself be hot to start with, and so on.

Clearly this is a kind of primitive version of the conservation principles of modern physics (or of the wave or diffusion equations from which those principles may be derived). Taken by

---

[1] There is no incompatibility with the 'backward looking' asymmetry in time and change mentioned at 221ᵃ30–ᵇ3, 222ᵇ16–27: see on 221ᵃ26 ff. Both are connected with the asymmetry of causation, i.e. that a cause precedes (mostly, at least) its effect: on which see e.g. Mackie (2), ch. 7.

[2] For other Aristotelian passages see on 202ᵃ3 ff. For the later history of the principle see Hesse, chs. IV–XI.

[3] For the qualifications see on 202ᵃ3 ff.

itself it does not imply the conservation of any quantity, or even that change can be treated quantitatively at all. But there are scattered indications that Aristotle did, in fact, intend a quantitative treatment of at least some types of change, those involving the ambivalent forms 'hot-cold', 'wet-dry' (for ambivalence see (*iv*) below), as well as of locomotion.[1]

(*iv*) *Ambivalence of forms*. In most cases the 'forms' involved, i.e. the types of starting-states and end-states, fall into pairs of opposites such as hot-cold, dry-moist, up-down. The principle of ambivalence states that whenever A-B are such paired opposites, whatever is in state A is not only a suitable agent for making other things A from B, but is itself liable to be transformed into state B by something else that is B. This principle is above all of importance in the mutual transformations of the four elements, worked out in detail in *Gen. et Corr.* II.1—5.

It is noteworthy that Aristotle's prime case of change, natural locomotion, does not fit easily, if at all, into the kind of structure defined by these four principles; and their applicability to other important cases, e.g. biological and psychological changes, is often far from clear.

(*f*) *Acting-upon and being-acted-upon* (III.3)

This chapter deals with the question whether the acting-upon and the being-acted-upon are the same thing—the same change. The notes on the chapter aim to disentangle the course of the argumentation. Here it is perhaps worth noting that the same problem has recently been discussed by philosophers in connection with the logical analysis of human action. One may ask, for example, whether my raising my arm is the same thing (event, process) as my arm's rising when I raise it. There are only two or three plausible types of answer available: (*i*) that my raising my arm is a whole series of events, of which my arm's rising is the last; (*ii*) that my raising my arm is the cause of my arm's rising (and is therefore not identical with it); (*iii*) that there is only one event, which is both the raising and the rising of the arm. When, as in the simple non-human cases, there is

---

[1] See Additional Note B.

no question of a series of events, only (*ii*) and (*iii*) are available, and (*ii*) is never available to Aristotle because he does not recognize anything like 'bare' causation of events by events, while to postulate an indirect causal connection would involve him in an endless regress. It is, therefore, in the nature of Aristotle's ways of thinking that he should identify the acting-upon and the being-acted-upon.[1]

The upshot of the chapter, then, is that Aristotle identifies the agent's action on the patient with the change of the patient. The grounds of the identification are, roughly, that the action must be taking place 'in' the patient (the changing thing is 'where the action is') and the only thing that *is* manifestly occurring in the patient is the change. To make the action different from the change would be to introduce an unobservable entity, and to do so uneconomically— Aristotle would gain nothing by the action's being different from the change, and would lose the simplicity of his down-to-earth approach to the counting of processes etc.

Unfortunately, such an approach is not conducive to the advancement of science. For there are important cases in which it is necessary to abandon the assumption that the agent is acting only so long as the patient is changing. (For Aristotle, this is of course true by definition: that is the point of saying that the agent's operation is '*on* something, and not cut off' (202^b7–8).) Take the case of a body subjected to two equal and opposite forces. If a rational system of physics is to be possible, it is necessary to say that both forces are acting on the body, though the body remains stationary. Aristotle's schematism cannot accommodate such cases. He can deal with cases of frustration, where an external cause simply prevents action from taking place, e.g. when a teacher tries to teach a pupil whose attention is distracted; in such a case there is no action of the agent

---

[1] These brief remarks are in no way a summary of the complex and subtle discussions of Davidson and others on these questions. See especially Davidson; on human action, Hornsby; on the relation of Aristotle's thinking to such issues—a question needing elaborate discussion, which I have not attempted—Charles. I have received valuable help on these questions from talks on this topic with David Charles and from the friendly advice of Jennifer Hornsby and Gavin Lawrence.

at all, even though the teacher 'does exactly the same things' as he would have done when successfully teaching. But to deal with the case of the stationary body as a case of mutual frustration is inadequate, unless rules are given for the determination of the extent of mutual frustration of forces. And these rules can be formulated only in terms of virtual actions or virtual changes. Moreover, the rules will form an essential part of any scientific explanation. It follows that virtual actions, or virtual changes, will figure in any explanation.

Aristotle in practice allows the existence of virtual actions and virtual changes. (See Additional Note B, sec. 2, for a list of relevant passages.) But that destroys the simplicity of his position in III.3, and makes it possible to identify actions with virtual actions. The consequence would be that actions were not, after all, in any sense the same as changes. To say that actions are identical with virtual actions, and different from changes, only when the actions are prevented from taking effect, looks arbitrary. It would certainly be unhelpful to the progress of physics.

Once it is granted that the action of the agent must somehow be identical with some actual process or change, Aristotle's solution is the only possible one. The only doubt is whether the identity involved is ordinary identity or something weaker. The notes on III.3 assume that only the ordinary notion of identity is in play, and that this is what is indicated by the terms 'same', 'one', and 'same/one in number'. This assumption is controversial; another view takes Aristotle to be operating, here and elswhere, with other notions in addition.[1]

3. THE INFINITE (III.4–8)

(a) Summary

III.4: (202^b30–203^a4) The study of the infinite is closely related to natural philosophy.

---

[1] On these controversies see White, Hartman, and Charles; on the other side, Miller (1) and Nussbaum (2).

(203^a4–16) Opinions about the infinite: (A) some posit a self-subsistent Infinite.

(203^a16–^{b}2) Opinions about the infinite: (B) the natural philosophers.

(203^b3–15) It is reasonable to consider the infinite as a principle.

(203^b15–30) The prima facie case for the existence of something infinite.

(203^b30–204^a7) The different senses of 'infinite' and the different ways in which there might be an infinite.

III.5: (204^a8–34) There cannot be a self-subsistent infinite.

(204^a34–^{b}10) There cannot be an infinitely extended body: (*i*) 'formal' arguments.

(204^b10–205^a7) There cannot be an infinitely extended body: (*ii*) first physical argument.

(205^a8–205^b1) (*iii*) second physical argument.

(205^b1–24) Digression on Anaxagoras.

(205^b24–206^a8) (*iv*) further physical arguments.

III.6: (206^a9–206^b3) The sense in which there is a potential infinite.

(206^b3–12) Infinites 'by addition' and 'by division': their correspondence.

(206^b12–33) More on the potential infinite.

(206^b33–207^a15) Difference between *whole* and *infinite*; the infinite as that of which there is always more outside.

(207^a15–32) Further consequences; the infinite as matter.

III.7: (207^a33–^{b}1–21) The account given explains some puzzles.

(207^b21–27) In some applications, 'infinite' has a derivative sense.

(207^b27–34) The account given is compatible with the actual practice of the mathematicians.

(207^b34–208^a4) The infinite as a material cause.

III.8: (208^a5–23) The arguments of 203^b3–15 disposed of.

(*b*) *The physical arguments against the existence of an infinitely extended body* (204^b10–205^b1, 205^b24–206^a8)

These are best discussed in connection with the arguments against the existence of a void. See section 5(*b*) below.

(*c*) *Aristotle's finitism and the potential infinite* (III.6 and 7)

1. Aristotle's discussion of the 'potential infinite' is by no means as clear and systematic as it might be. What follows is an attempt to reconstruct Aristotle's finitism, with help from some other texts besides these chapters.[1]

Exposition is hampered and understanding made harder by the fact that it is not advisable to use any notion corresponding to that of *set* in modern set-theory. The reason is not just that Aristotle himself does not make explicit use of any such notion; rather it is that it would be necessary to talk about sets which have a career in time, in the sense that at some times some members of the set have yet to exist or have ceased to exist. It is precisely part of Aristotle's finitism that he would refuse to treat, as something existent, a collection of which not all the members were existent at the time of speaking.

It is necessary then to fall back on talk of predicates, and this way of approach will certainly be truer to Aristotle's intentions. (Further complications will arise about sentences which assert something about the future.) Let us say that a predicate 'F' is *co-realized* at any time at which it is true that the things that ever have been, are, or will be F, all are F. And say that a predicate is *completed* at any time at which it is true that all the things that ever have been, are, or will be F, already are F or have already been F. (It is assumed throughout that time is linearly ordered, dense, and without beginning or end.) Obviously, at any time, if a predicate is co-realized it is also completed and will be completed; it will stay completed.

(1) The first point of Aristotle's finitism is that every co-realized predicate has finite extension; or to put it more in conformity with Aristotle's way of thinking, at any time at which a predicate 'F' is co-realized, there exists a finite number of things which are F. In

---

[1] The compressed and difficult passage *Metaphysics* IX.6, 1048^{b}6–17 is not used or discussed.

particular, since we can take at any time 'existent now' as a case of 'F', and since 'existent now' is co-realized now, it follows that there are just finitely many things existent now. (Aristotle's rules for counting things cannot be discussed here; basically one counts substances and other things that can be said to exist via substances.) This finitism about what there is at any time is the basis for Aristotle's philosophy of mathematics. Apparent counter-examples are to be rejected. In particular, the question of the number of actually existing points on an actually existing line, are dealt with by a restrictive account of what it is for a point or a line to actually exist (roughly, they actually exist only if they are physically realized limits of actually existing physical bodies).[1] It is this restrictive account which underlies Aristotle's resolution of Zeno's 'Stadium' and 'Achilles' paradoxes in *Physics* VIII, though the passage is a difficult one.[2]

(2) Suppose that at some time some 'F' is not co-realized. If it is nevertheless completed, that will be because it has a past history and (if we add the past history to the present) all the F things that ever will be, have already been, and been F. Among such 'F' distinguish those that have had a beginning, in the sense that there has been a time before which nothing was ever F. Then the next point of Aristotle's finitism is that whenever any 'F' that has had a beginning is completed, there is only a finite total of things that are or have been F. (Here the total is *not* meant to be restricted to things that now exist: Aristotle does not show signs of being unwilling in general to count and quantify over past existents.) The evidence that Aristotle held such a view is not straightforward; it derives from a particular interpretation of the *Physics* VIII passage discussing Zeno's paradoxes. There is perhaps some support for it in the certainly easier passage at 204^a3-6 which says that the infinite is 'what cannot be traversed'. This may well have the implication that infinitely many things cannot happen or start to exist within a finite length of time (see note on 203^b30ff).

---

[1] On points on a line see note on 220^a4ff.
[2] On the answer to Zeno in *Physics* VIII see esp. Schoedel and Bostock (1).

(3) Next suppose that 'F' is at some time completed but has never had a beginning, i.e. at every past time it has been true that something had already been F. Then it might be true that if we tried to make a list of all the things that had ever been F, starting from the present and working back into the past, we never stopped adding items. In such cases we might say that F was *reverse-incomplete*, i.e. that at every past time it had been true that something had already been F which thereafter was not going to be F (at least down to the present). Obvious examples of reverse-incomplete predicates are: 'is or was a revolution of the celestial sphere', or 'is or was a human being'. Aristotle nowhere considers such cases, but would presumably class them among the kind of infinites he accepted. But, if so, this would be so only derivatively; the infinity is shown and derived from the forward-incomplete infinity of the list that is compiled.

(4) If some 'F' is not completed, at some time, it follows that it is not true that whatever will be F is or has already been F. At this point complications arise about the truth-values of statements in the future tense. I shall follow a particular view of the difficult chapter *de Interpretatione* 9, according to which Aristotle holds that there are statements about the future which are neither true nor false in the present.[1] This means that, at any time, there are two possibilities for a non-completed F. It may be *incomplete*, i.e. it may be definitely *false* that whatever will be F is or has already been F. In that case it will be true that there will in future be something F which has never yet been F. Or it may be *provisionally incomplete*, i.e. it may be neither true nor false that there will in future be something F which has never yet been F. Then Aristotle's central notion of the infinite, as that which is *never* completed, may (it seems) take one of four forms:

(a) it is true that at every future time F will be incomplete.
(b) it is true that at every future time F will be provisionally incomplete.
(c) it is neither true nor false that at every future time F will be incomplete.

[1] On this problem see particularly Frede, Ackrill (1), 132–42, Anscombe (1), Hintikka, ch. 8.

(*d*) it is neither true nor false that at every future time F will be provisionally incomplete.

Of these, however, (*c*) and (*d*) can be eliminated, since for Aristotle a generalization such as 'at every future time F will be G' is not the kind of statement that can fail to be either true or false (it cannot be a contingent matter). This leaves two varieties of incompletability: F is *strongly incompletable* at any time when it is true that at every future time F will be incomplete; and *weakly incompletable* at any time when it is true that at every future time F will be provisionally incomplete.

It is the incompletable predicates which furnish Aristotle's examples of the potential infinite: every potential infinite, in the primary sense, arises from a predicate that is incompletable, whether strongly or weakly, and every such predicate corresponds to a potential infinite. The notion of *potentiality* comes in in two distinct ways. Whenever some 'F' is incomplete, then the series of F things is going to continue: it has a potentiality which is not yet realized, but will be. But in the case of provisional incompleteness, the realization of the potentiality is itself 'potential' in the sense that it is not yet determined whether it will occur or not.

2. So far the discussion has been in terms of what could be infinite in *number*. But what about the infinite in *quantity*? Here the situation, for Aristotle, is greatly simplified by three points: First, measurable quantities must exist all simultaneously. (Of course we can *construct* pseudo-quantities such as 'the total volume of water flowing over Niagara in a century'.) Secondly, the universe is necessarily finite in size. Thirdly, the universe cannot possibly vary in size. It follows that there is no way in which there could be even potentially infinite quantities. What is of interest here is how Aristotle thinks the second and third points are to be proved. The finitude of the universe at any one time follows from the theses, argued for at length in these books, that there is no void and that the sum total of body is finite in extent. But that the universe cannot vary in size, and in particular cannot expand indefinitely, is nowhere actually argued for.

3. If we ask, in general, for the grounds, rational or not, of Aristotelian finitism, the answer is perhaps partly given at 204^b5–10,

which supplies a general argument against infinite quantities and infinite numbers. A number can be counted and a quantity can be measured; but *ex hypothesi* what is infinite cannot be counted or measured as the case may be. This, however, gives no arguments against the existence of collections of things too great to have any number or quantity. The fundamental reason for not supposing these to exist, if it is not just an economical attitude or some cosmological motive, may be found at 207^a21-32: the infinite is as such something formless and *pro tanto* unknowable. If the universe were formless and, as such, unknowable it would offend Aristotelian teleology, being less perfect than it might have been; and the same applies to anything within the universe.[1] In the background are also the paradoxes of Zeno, which draw out the strange consequences of admitting the kinds of infinite which common sense is inclined to admit. In particular, the argument of the 'Stadium' and of its stablemate the 'Achilles' is taken very seriously by Aristotle, being discussed at length both in *Physics* VI (233^a21-28, 239^b11-29) and in *Physics* VIII ($263^a4-{}^b9$). Two arguments preserved in Zeno's own words are also important, though not mentioned in the *Physics*: (*a*) The argument that a definite number must be a finite number (B3 Diels-Kranz); (*b*) The argument that since we can divide any extended thing *ad infinitum*, it is infinite in size (B1 Diels-Kranz).

Aristotle states, and claims to answer, some of the more serious objections to finitism (203^b15-30, 206^a10-12, 207^b27-34, 208^a5-22). His answer to the objection from mathematics—namely, that arithmetic or geometry need infinitely many numbers or points, etc.—is incomplete as it stands. (In Additional Note A I offer a brief sketch of Aristotelian finitism in mathematics.) A related type of objection, raising deep questions, is that of the objections from conceivability. It seems that we can conceive of there being e.g. a completed infinite totality, or a progressive expansion *ad infinitum*

---

[1] Cf. *Gen. Anim.* I.1, 715^b14-16: 'Nature is averse to the infinite because what is infinite is incomplete, and nature always pursues an end (completion).' The converse principle, that what is formed (i.e. has a definite nature) is complete and therefore finite in every way, goes back to Parmenides at least, cf. 207^a15-17.

of the universe; so these things must be possible. Aristotle says a little about this, and has a general psychological theory in reserve (see on 203^b15 ff., 207^b1 ff., 208^a5 ff.). Another kind of objection (of which Aristotle takes little notice) is that a spatially bounded universe is physically implausible, or even impossible (there would have to be something beyond, even if only a void).

It must be pointed out that, if this reconstruction of Aristotle's position is correct, it leads to a startling conclusion about the past. Straightforward realism about the past is no longer possible, since Aristotle holds that there was no beginning of time. He wishes therefore to say e.g., that there have been infinitely many yearly cycles of the sun before the present. But this cannot refer to a completed infinity. On his own account of infinity, it has to be true that, for some number n, there have been n previous yearly cycles and there have not been, but could have been $n + 1$ previous cycles. It is difficult to give any sense to this unless the past is in some sense a creation of the present. On such a view, the past is some thing created by memory and historical records in a lawlike fashion, just as the number series is something created by mathematical operations in a lawlike fashion. In favour of ascribing some such position to Aristotle it can at least be said that a related and equally startling suggestion is made explicitly by Aristotle at 223^a21-29 (see on that passage). In the 'soulless' world there envisaged, there is no time or measurement, so that the problems about infinities of past events cannot arise. So the *measurable* past, at least, is a creation of the present, according to this passage, and that is enough.[1]

Aristotle's finitism has much in common with that of modern intuitionists and constructivists, but it is clearly less liberal than intuitionism in important ways.[2] 'To grasp an infinite structure is to grasp the process which generates it' is a statement unacceptable to the Aristotelian finitist, since for him there is no such thing as an

---

[1] A similar conclusion is reached by Lear, 204−7. See further sec. 6 (*g*) below.

[2] Here I rely on Dummett (2), 55−65, from whom the statement of intuitionistic doctrine is taken. On the relation to intuitionism see Lear, 188−9, 196−8.

actually infinite structure, and if the structure is merely potentially infinite it can be grasped directly. The corresponding Aristotelian statement would be: 'To grasp how a finite but potentially infinite structure is potentially infinite, is to grasp the process which possibly will continue to generate it.'

4. PLACE (IV.1–5)

(a) Summary

IV.1: ($208^a27-{}^b1$) The study of place is necessary for the natural philosopher; its difficulties.

(208^b1-8) The prima facie case for the existence of place: (*i*) the argument from replacement.

(208^b8-25) (*ii*) the argument from natural movements.

(208^b25-27) (*iii*) the argument from void.

($208^b27-209^a2$) Place as pre-existing space: an idea as old as Hesiod.

(209^a2-30) Difficulties about the existence and nature of place.

IV.2: ($209^a31-{}^b6$) Place as the form of the located body.

(209^b6-17) Place as the matter of the located body. Plato's theory.

($209^b17-210^a13$) Arguments to show that place is neither matter nor form.

IV.3: (210^a14-24) The senses of 'in' distinguished.

($210^a25-{}^b21$) Nothing can be in itself in the primary sense.

(210^b21-27) Solution of Zeno's puzzle about place.

(210^b27-31) Again we see that place is neither matter nor form.

IV.4: ($210^b32-211^a11$) Summary of data about place; the aims of the inquiry.

(211^a12-23) Basic facts about change in respect of place.

($211^a23-{}^b5$) What a body is 'in' in the primary sense.

(211^b5-10) The four candidates for being place.

(211^b10-14) Place is not the form of the located body.

($211^{b}14-29$) Place is not an interval in between the limits of the surrounding body.

($211^{b}29-212^{a}2$) Place is not the matter of the located body.

($212^{a}2-14$) Place is the limit of the surrounding body.

($212^{a}14-21$) Place as 'unchangeable'.

($212^{a}21-30$) This solution fits some important data.

IV.5: ($212^{a}31-^{b}22$) Problems about being in place.

($212^{b}22-29$) This account of place solves the difficulties.

($212^{b}29-213^{a}11$) Natural motion and rest understandable in this light.

(b) Places, locations, and space

1. The primary purpose of Aristotle's discussion of place is to make locations respectable, i.e. to give an account, compatible with Aristotelian physics and metaphysics, of how there can be such things as locations which persist at least for a time and are for that time in existence independently of any body which may happen to be located in them.

'Where' is a label for one of the categories; one way of being is to be somewhere. But the located-ness involved in 'being somewhere' might not entail the existence of semi-permanent locations or places. It might be that being somewhere consisted in just in having a certain spatial relationship to some relatively fixed landmark, e.g. being 100 miles west of Athens. Such relationships would not be independent of the bodies between which they held.[1] In arguing for the existence of places Aristotle mentions the common-sense notion that everything is 'somewhere' and so 'in a place', but the two more substantial arguments he has go beyond mere located-ness. The argument from 'replacement' ($208^{b}1-8$) does so only in a fumbling way, appealing once again to ordinary intuitions. The argument from natural motions ($208^{b}8-25$) brings us into contact with Aristotle's own particular motivation, which is to give a satisfactory basis to the theory of locomotion (cf. $211^{a}12-14$). The general theory of change requires that such an end-state of change as a place ought to

---

[1] Compare Aristotle's treatment of time.

exist in a form-like way, not independently of all bodies but enjoying a more or less continuous career in transmission from one body to the next. Particularly ought this to be true of the 'natural places' of the elemental bodies, which must be permanent features of the universe. Places have a role in scientific explanation.

Thus Aristotle's inquiry into place is, from the outset, not quite a free investigation into the ways we locate things. There is a half-declared metaphysical interest. He is inquiring how we can plausibly turn locations into features of the world that are 'semi-permanent' and 'semi-independent' in the ways described. For the time being he considers only relative locations, i.e. locations relatively to the immediate environs of the body (on relative and absolute locations see below). For locomotion has to be observed and explained as locomotion relative to the environs. (For example, in Aristotle's case of the boat rowed upstream, the boat's behaviour must be explained as motion relative to the stream, and the stream's as motion relative to the banks.) So for most of the discussion Aristotle quite reasonably assumes that the environs may be considered fixed.

2. Aristotle's discussion of place will seem strange, even primitive, at first sight to many modern readers, because of the almost total absence of any concept of *space*. It is important to realize that this absence is a matter of deliberate policy on Aristotle's part, and one for which he has good reasons.

Pre-philosophical notions of 'space', in the sense of something occupied by all bodies but existing quite independently of them, appear in the introductory chapter ($208^b29-209^a2$), and are there attributed by interpretation to Hesiod. It cannot, then, be claimed that the notion of space simply had not occurred to Aristotle. In any case, the same features reappear in Plato's 'receptacle' theory in the *Timaeus*, on which Aristotle duly reports at 209^b11-17. It needs explanation, then, why Aristotle never gives any serious consideration to *any* space-based theory of places. It is not correct to say that Aristotle is concerned only with what actually goes on when we locate things, and that we do not involve 'space' in so doing.[1] For it might still be that space was indispensable to our

[1] That Aristotle is *refining* ordinary common-sense notions of location has been rightly remarked by Owen (7), 252–3.

being able to locate things. In other analogous cases Aristotle is usually eager to refute theories of self-subsistent non-bodily entities; he has argued in III.5 against self-subsistent infinites, and does so for example in *Metaphysics* X, XIII, and XIV against self-subsistent numbers. His dialectical method, indeed, *requires* him to consider generally held theories or those of eminent thinkers such as Plato.

An attack on theories of self-subsistent space does indeed appear in this book, but in chapter 8, under the guise of arguments against void. (On this attack, see Introduction 5(c).) If this fact partly solves one of the puzzles, the other may be treated as follows. For the purpose of providing locations for particular objects, Aristotle could have argued, self-subsistent space will be useless. For either (1) we have to suppose that all locations that bodies ever actually have, or could have, pre-exist in space; but there are infinitely many possible locations, so that space would comprise a completed infinite—it would be internally differentiated to an infinite degree. This is, for Aristotle, clearly impossible. Or (2) the locations exist only potentially in space, until a body actualizes them. But in this case the space is superfluous; everything it does can be accounted for just as well by the sum of matter formed by the body and its environs. (Space might still be needed as a metaphysical guarantee that spatially extended bodies, locomotion, and spatial relationships will continue to be possible—but, in so far as it is needed in this role, Aristotle does have a 'space' (see below) which he does not need to introduce here.)

3. In the light of the reductive argument to short-circuit space theories, it can be seen that places have to be accounted for in terms of the located body itself and its immediately environing bodies, which may be thought of as one homogeneous surrounding mass. In this light, Aristotle's list of 'four things, some one of which place must be' (211^b6-7) becomes intelligible. The place must be either something that just surrounds the body and coincides with its outer boundary, or something that is spatially coextensive with the body. In the first case, it can be taken as the outer boundary of the located body or the inner boundary of the surrounding body; in the second case, it can be taken either as the extension of the located body or as a gap or bubble in the surrounding body.

It is an objection to the 'short-circuit' argument that it fails if there is void. And in fact it is clear that at various points in the discussion of place Aristotle is assuming the impossibility of void. When Aristotle comes to discuss void, the whole question of space naturally is, or ought to be, reopened, and in fact Aristotle does then attack theories of space as well (see Introduction, sec. 5).

4. Within the framework of the presuppositions described above, Aristotle's discussion of place is reasonably straightforward in outline, though in places obscure in detail and (it seems) occasionally interpolated. As was to be expected, 'being somewhere' (i.e. having a location) turns out to be a necessary but not a sufficient condition for being in a place (see on 212^a31 ff.).

Even on its own terms, however, Aristotle's account of place seems inadequate. One way of introducing the difficulties is to consider (say) a fish swimming across a tank full of water. The fish moves, relative to the water, so its place must be different at different times. The place of the fish at any moment is the inner boundary of the water in contact with the fish at that moment. But Aristotle gives no account of what it is for this boundary at one moment to be the same as, or other than, the boundary at another moment. If its difference lies in the fact that different portions of the water are adjacent to it, then the place might change even though the fish remained stationary relative to the mass of water as a whole; perhaps Aristotle would not object to this conclusion. If the difference is made to depend on difference of *location* relative to the water as a whole, the theory will be more in accord with common sense and not circular. Possibly this is the correct interpretation of 'unchangeable' at 212^a14-21, the only place at which Aristotle (suddenly) insists that places 'ought' to be somehow fixed. That they should be fixed *relative to the whole universe* would be at odds with both the common-sense and the metaphysical motivations of Aristotle's theory. But fixed relative to the surrounding body they ought to be. (For difficulties in this solution see on 212^a14 ff.) At the very least Aristotle does not give this point the careful treatment it deserves. Further inadequacies appear in the difficulties about the outermost sphere of the world system and its rotation, where once more the link between locomotion and place is menaced, and Aristotle crawls quickly through a narrow loophole in order to appear, at least, to preserve it. The discussion at $212^a31-{}^b22$ is saved from disaster only by the dubious expedient of claiming that rotation of a body is primarily motions of the parts of that body, rather than one of the whole. Even this defence fails if the body is internally homogeneous, for then the parts are properly speaking not in a place at all and cannot therefore move in their own right.

Another point at which the theory fails to meet its obligations: it gives no full understanding of the absolute directions in the cosmos, which Aristotle calls 'the kinds and varieties of place' (205^b31-32) or 'parts and kinds of place' (208^b12-13). Aristotle does indeed provide a partial metaphysics, based on the theory of place, of the 'above-below' directions, but not for the others (on this obscure topic see on 208^b8 ff., 212^b29 ff.).

5. Though Aristotle would have rejected any theory of self-subsistent space, he does have a substitute for space in some of its roles—namely the notion of *matter*. As a reservoir of potentially existing shapes, it is an Aristotelianized version of Plato's 'receptacle', but unlike that it has no sort of independent existence, unless as an abstraction in geometry.

The separation Aristotle makes between matter as a reservoir of physical possibilities and the framework of locations and places (the components of the world and the places they give rise to) has been repeated in the development of physics. Newton's space has both roles; but Minkowski space-time (in Special Relativity), the space-times of General Relativity, and the 'inner spaces' of particle theories, are reservoirs of possibilities which are more and more divorced from the business of providing a framework of locations.

6. Plato's 'receptacle' theory in the *Timaeus* is the prototype of the reservoir theories and it has (unlike Aristotle's) another 'modern' feature: it seeks to represent the contents of space, physical objects and events, as mere epiphenomena of the 'field'—as Einstein sought to do, and, in the General Theory of Relativity, partially did.

Aristotle's treatment of Plato's theory is interesting as a pointer to his own presuppositions and preoccupations. Aristotle represents Plato's 'receptacle' as a kind of matter. That is correct in the sense that it fills the role, to some extent, of ordinary Aristotelian matter. Aristotle's criticism of Plato is that there is in fact (i.e. within the Aristotelian system) no kind of matter which can persist independently of the body it serves as the matter of. This is yet another case of Aristotle's criticisms of previous thinkers being made in Aristotelian terms and using Aristotelian assumptions. Plato is not so much misrepresented as automatically excluded from serious consideration because his ontology is different. Apart from that fact Aristotle is quite sympathetic to Plato's theory: it is praised as constructive at 209^b16-17, and 211^b29-36 looks like an attempt to provide a common-sense motivation for it. For a more thorough criticism see *Gen.et Corr.* II.1, 329^a8-24, and on this Joachim, 194–8. On Aristotle's criticisms of Plato's theory see in general Taylor, A.E., 401–3, 407–8; Cherniss (2), 112–23, 165–73, and Appendix I, 479–87.

5. THE VOID (IV.6–9)

(a) Summary

IV.6: (213^a12-22) The study of the void: introduction.

(213^a22-^b2) The usual case against void mistaken.

(213^b2-29) The prima facie case in favour of the existence of void.

IV.7: ($213^b30-214^a16$) The senses of 'void'.

(214^a16-^b11) Beginning of the demonstration that there is no void: answer to the prima facie case in favour.

IV.8: (214^b12-28) Arguments against the existence of void: (a) general arguments.

($214^b28-215^a24$) (b) physical arguments that there can be no motion in a void.

($215^a24-216^a23$) (c) argument from 'laws of motion' that there can be no motion in a void.

(216^a23-^b21) (d) general argument; paradoxes about occupancy of void.

IV.9: (216^b22-30) The argument for the existence of void from 'dense and rare': (a) the argument stated.

(216^b30–217^a10) (*b*) impossibility of 'internal void'.

(217^a10–20) (*c*) the argument restated.

(217^a20–$^b11$) (*d*) the argument answered.

(217^b11–20) (*e*) footnote on density and rarity.

(217^b20–28) Conclusion.

(*b*) *Aristotle versus Ionian cosmology: the arguments against infinite body (III.5) and against void (IV.8)*

1. Aristotle's universe comprises a single cosmos of finite extent, outside which is nothing having spatial extension, not even a void. A satisfying construction, but radically at variance with the main Ionian cosmological tradition, to which in details Aristotle owed so much. The standard Ionian picture was of an infinitely extended universe containing at any time infinitely many world-systems with the interspaces filled either by void (the Atomists) or by some one homogeneous stuff. The amount of space Aristotle devotes to arguing in favour of his own type of cosmology must be partly explained by the presence in the background of an influential rival type.

To the Ionian cosmology it is evident that Aristotle had objections of a general, metaphysical kind. Thus, it involved infinites of unacceptable kinds: an actual infinity of world-systems and an actually infinite quantity of body. Again, Aristotle seems to have held that the universe can be intelligible as a whole only if it is itself a single individual, having a form and a completedness which would exclude its being infinite (*de Caelo* I.1, 268^b8–10). But Aristotle does not officially put much weight on such considerations. His distinction between 'formal' (*logikos*) and 'physical' arguments (see on 202^a21 ff.), on topics belonging to physics, seems always to be made to the detriment of the 'formal' arguments (see esp. *Gen. et Corr.* I.2, 316^a5–14: only physical arguments are really appropriate to a physical topic).

In holding to physical arguments and distrusting 'formal' ones, Aristotle may seem like a saviour rescuing physics from the undesirable embraces of metaphysics and giving it the necessary autonomy. So Aristotle did, perhaps, indeed see his role; the reality, unfortunately, is rather different. On examination it turns out that even the physical arguments are loaded with assumptions, purportedly drawn from ordinary experience, but in fact going far beyond. The arguments rest mainly upon the concepts of 'nature' and 'natural motion'. These, in themselves, are harmless. For Aristotle 'nature' is not a universal Nature of a teleological or vitalist kind (he sometimes speaks as if it were, but this is only a way of speaking). Aristotle recognizes only 'natures' of individual things, a thing's nature, roughly, being the way it behaves of necessity and because of its essence, if left to itself. Such a conception can be accommodated in any physics (unless there is something radically wrong with essentialism). But Aristotle seems to think that, since it is the concept of *nature* that defines physics as a subject, it must ultimately be possible to deduce the whole of physics, at least in broad outline, from certain general principles about natures and natural motions. At any rate Aristotle makes great play with general principles of this sort in arguing against pre-Socratic cosmology. The assumptions on which they rest are never submitted to a detached criticism.[1]

2. Examples of the kind of argument described are found in the passages where Aristotle encounters Ionian cosmology, particularly in arguing against infinite body (*Physics* III.5 and *de Caelo* I.5–7), against plurality of worlds (*de Caelo* I.8–9), and against void (*Physics* IV.8). The notes on III.5 and IV.8 aim to help the reader to understand them.

At certain places Aristotle appeals directly to observed facts. This happens most notoriously, in *Physics* IV.8, at 215^a25 ff., and 216^a13 ff., where he claims that certain rules of proportionality hold for falling bodies (perhaps only in wholly natural motions, though he does not say so). These 'laws of motion' have figured largely in the history of Aristotelian physics: they were attacked in antiquity, as we know from the criticisms of Philoponus, and again by Galileo and others in the beginnings of modern dynamics. At present, some scholarly opinion inclines to deny them any great significance: 'It was . . . no part of the dialectic of his argument to give these proportionalities the rigour of scientific laws or present them as the

---

[1] On all this see e.g. Mourelatos, Mansion (2), Wieland (2).

record of exact observation'.[1] This would be a more credible story if the proportionalities, as usually interpreted, were approximately correct, but in fact they are, as usually interpreted, so obviously at variance with experience that very short and easy experiments would refute them decisively.

It is not the place here to defend an alternative interpretation. I believe such an interpretation can be given, which will restore to Aristotle the credit he deserves as a pioneer of theoretical physics.[2]

(c) *Theories of void and theories of space*

What is a void? It must be something (*i*) three-dimensionally extended; (*ii*) incorporeal; (*iii*) not containing any body within itself. These requirements leave open a number of further questions which Aristotle is inclined to regard as decided. In particular, he consistently assumes that a theory of void must be a theory of *space*, i.e. of pure 'unsupported' extension, which when invaded by a body remains to be occupied by that body (rather than retreating before it or being extinguished by it). It is for this reason that Aristotle repeatedly assimilates theories of void to theories of *place* (see on 213^a12 ff., 213^b30 ff.).

Aristotle is here probably misinterpreting at least the Atomist theory of void, which there is no reason to suppose to have been a 'space' theory in this sense. (At $216^a27-{}^b2$ he does at least argue that every void must be 'receptive' of an occupying body, though the argument is quite inadequate.) There may, of course, have been other theories of void or space current (for instance in the Academy) which fitted Aristotle's discussion better. Plato's 'receptacle' theory in the *Timaeus* comes close to being a theory of space.

Aristotle's criticisms of the theories of void fall into two groups: (*a*) those that are essentially criticisms of theories of space; (*b*) those that apply to any theory of void. Only the physical arguments of $214^b28-216^a21$, probably derived from a polemical discussion of Atomism, fall under (*b*). The rest of chapter 8 contains a searching attack applicable to *all* theories of space, even those which do not

---

[1] Owen (7), 254. Cf. Solmsen, 137–8, Carteron (2).
[2] See Additional Note B for the outline of such an interpretation.

actually imply the existence of any void space. There is therefore an unexpected reappearance here of the topic, space, which seemed to be puzzlingly avoided in the discussion of place.

The criticism of theories of pure unsupported extension, generally, would belong for Aristotle to metaphysics rather than physics. *Metaphysics* XIII and XIV contain a prolonged attack on Platonizing theories of Forms and mathematical objects, mostly numbers, but occasionally geometrical objects as well. The discussion of theories of void looks like a not very well-integrated sum of two residues: arguments left over from a criticism of space theories, and arguments left over from a discussion of Atomism.

6. TIME (IV.10–14)

(a) Summary

IV.10: (217^b29–32) Introduction.

(217^b32–218^a30) Problems about time.

(218^a30–$^b9$) Previous opinions about time.

(218^b9–20) Transition to substantive discussion: time is not change.

IV.11: (218^b21–219^a10) Interrelation of time and change.

(219^a10–14) Dependence of time on change.

(219^a14–21) The 'before and after'.

(219^a22–$^b1$) How we become aware of time.

(219^b1–9) Time as a number of change.

(219^b9–33) The 'now'.

(219^b33–220^a4) Interrelation of time and the 'now'.

(220^a4–24) Time and the 'now' dependent on change and the changing thing.

(220^a24–26) Summary of the discussion so far.

IV.12: (220^a27–32) Note on least numbers and magnitudes.

(220^a32–$^b5$) Note on 'quick' and 'slow'.

(220^b5–14) Note on sameness and difference of times.

(220^b14–32) On measuring time.

(220^b32–221^a26) On being in time: (*i*) what it is to be in time;

(221^a26-^b7) (*ii*) the action of time;

(221^b7-23) (*iii*) time measures rest as well as change;

$(221^b23-222^a9)$ (*iv*) what is and what is not in time.

IV.13: (222^a10-24) Definitions of temporal words: (*i*) 'now' and 'the now';

(222^a24-^b7) (*ii*) 'at some time'. Will time give out?

(222^b7-16) (*iii*) 'just', 'recently', 'long ago', 'suddenly'.

(222^b16-27) The effects of time.

(222^b27-29) Summary of the discussion so far.

IV.14: $(222^b30-223^a15)$ On being in time (another version).

(223^a16-29) Time and the soul.

(223^a29-^b12) On sameness and difference of times.

$(223^b12-224^a2)$ On measuring time.

(224^a2-15) Note on sameness and difference of numbers.

(224^a15-17) Conclusion.

(*b*) *Note on contents and arrangement*

The treatment of time is elaborate and involved, but not altogether well arranged. It is clear that, as they stand, these chapters contain portions of successive drafts which have not been worked into a unity; and treatments of the same and related topics are not always found together. The following table shows the approximate relationships of the different sections:

A. *Introduction*

$(10, 217^b29-218^a9)$: introduction, problems about time; previous opinions about time.

B. *Time as a number of change*

(1) $(10, 218^b9-11, 219^a14; 11, 219^b1-9)$ *the main discussion:* time is not change; interrelation of time and change; dependence of time on change; time a number of change.

(2) $(12, 220^b 14-32; 14, 223^b12-224^a2)$ *corollary to the main discussion*—on measuring time.

(3) *notes appended to the main discussion*

(*a*) $(12, 220^a27-32)$ Note on least numbers.

(*b*) (12, 220^{a}32–^{b}5) Note on 'quick' and 'slow'.

(*c*) (12, 220^{b}5–14; 14, 223^{a}29–^{b}12; 14, 224^{a}2–15): notes on the sameness and difference of numbers and times.

C. *The 'before and after' and the 'now'*

(1) (11, 219^{a}14–^{b}1) the 'before and after' and our awareness of time;

(2) (11, 219^{b}9–220^{a}24) the 'now' and its relation to time;

(3) (13, 222^{a}10–^{b}7) the 'now' (earlier version?) and the infinity of time.

D. *Being in time, and the effects of time*

(1) (12, 220^{b}32–222^{a}9) main discussion;

(2) (13, 222^{b}16–27) the effects of time (?earlier version).

(3) (14, 222^{b}30–223^{a}15) on being in time (?earlier version).

E. *Time and the soul*

(14, 223^{a}16–29)

Thus the present arrangement and division into chapters does roughly correspond to some important distinctions. Chapter 10 contains the introductory matter; Chapters 11 and 12 the main discussions; Chapters 13 and 14 are rag-bags containing bits and pieces never worked into the main discussions (some parts of super-seded versions, some notes containing second thoughts). (Other such rag-bags are found at *de Anima* III.7, *Metaphysics* XIII.8–9, 1083^{b}23–1086^{a}21.)

(*c*) *Time as a number of change*

1. Aristotle describes time as 'a number of change in respect of the before and after'. The qualification 'in respect of the before and after' is of course important—see section (*e*) below. But the basic idea can be understood independently of an understanding of this qualification. Aristotle's thought is that (roughly) there is nothing more to time than that it is a measurable quantity which attaches to changes in just the same sort of way as e.g. length and heaviness attach to material bodies. There is, in particular, no unified, all-embracing, self-subsistent 'Time': there are just changes having greater or lesser quantities of time-length.

Simple and fruitful as the thought is, Aristotle's expression of it is in places involved, and perhaps confused. Various sources of difficulty may be distinguished. One, which will be considered in section (*d*) below, is Aristotle's grand programme of reduction, by which all properties (or at least all metrical and topological properties) of time and change are somehow to be derived from, and shown dependent upon, corresponding properties of spatial magnitudes. But even apart from this grand design, which Aristotle at some stage superimposed upon his original account of time as a quantity, there are other complications. In what follows I shall briefly consider: Aristotle's general theory of number, measurement, and measurable quantities; the problem of the time-unit; the problem of simultaneity, and the introduction of 'abstract time'.

2. *Number, measurement, quantity.* About quantities and their measurement Aristotle says a good deal in various places.[1] Except, possibly, for the abstract realm of mathematics, (on which see Additional note A), Aristotle does not think in terms of disembodied quantities, numbers or measures. Suppose, then, that some body is three feet long. First, Aristotle would resist the suggestion that 'three feet long' is not predicated directly of the body but of its 'length' or 'extension'. Rather, these are abstractions made possible by the very existence of such predicates. Nor, of course, does 'three-feet-longness' exist in abstraction from all actual bodies. But 'three feet long' is a complex which needs to be analysed. The meaning is given (obviously) by reference to the unit of measurement, the foot. But what is 'a unit' or 'a foot' here? Again, it cannot for Aristotle be an abstract, Platonic entity existing in independence from actual bodies. It may of course be convenient to speak as if it were. But there must always be a translation into perfectly definite terms. 'Three feet long' can only be understood as 'three times as long as F', where F denotes a body one foot long: at worst, F might be a body not actually existing but constructible, according to definite specifications, in such a way that its length could not have been other than it was.

---

[1] Esp. *Metaphysics* X.1, 1052^b14–1053^b9; *Metaphysics* V.13; *Categories* 6; *Metaphysics* X.6; in our text, *Physics* IV.12, 220^b14–32, and 14, 223^b12–224^a2; on the application to time see Annas (2).

The only remaining loophole at which an abstract entity might insert itself is now the number 'three'. But to 'three times as long as F', we can give an operational meaning: B is three times as long as F just in the case in which three copies of F 'exhaust' B when laid alongside it. And here, in 'three copies', the 'three' is not an abstract number but a *predicate* of numerousness. We have to distinguish, in Aristotle's terminology, the 'number by which we count' (the 'abstract' number, e.g. '3') and the 'number counted', the 'three' which is a predicate of a particular collection of actual things, or as Aristotle would say, of particular actual things. (On this distinction see further Additional Note A.)

Whatever difficulties there may be with the anti-Platonist programme in general, the application to time is fairly straightforward. The place of actual physical bodies is taken by actual changes; it is these of which quantities of time, e.g. 'two hours long' are predicated. Once more, we may analyse such predicates in terms of unit time-lengths, which again are not abstractions, but actual changes, or specifiable in terms of such changes. A peculiar problem emerges in the process of measurement: there is nothing that quite corresponds to the 'laying off' of the unit length along the length to be measured. In general, different changes at different times cannot be directly compared in respect of time-length; whereas different bodies can always, in principle, be directly compared by laying them alongside one another. How, then, can there be any known unit of time?

3. *Time-measurement and the time-unit.* Aristotle's answer to these problems is to use, as a cosmic universal clock, the sphere of the fixed stars. The revolution of this sphere is taken to be uniform. So all other changes may be measured by the amount of its revolution or revolutions that they take up, and the measurement in principle an easy one to make. As a time-unit it is natural to use a single revolution, i.e. a sidereal day, though of course others might be used. What is measured, in time-measurement, is ultimately the amount of this particular change, i.e. an angular distance.

The sphere of the fixed stars is also, for Aristotle, in a genuinely *causal* sense the pacemaker for all other natural changes, so that it is understandable that measuring natural changes in terms of sidereal revolutions should give consistent results, i.e. that changes of the same natural kind, in similar circumstances, should take the same time. So to define time-length in terms of this movement is to adopt a definition which makes good sense at least for natural changes, and is therefore not arbitrary.

In other places (*de Caelo* II.6, *Physics* VIII.10, 267^{a}21–^{b}9) Aristotle provides arguments to show that the motion of the celestial sphere must be uniform. By 'uniform' he seems to mean 'proceeding at the same rate' (*Physics* V.4, 228^{b}15–30 discusses possible senses of 'uniform change'). But if time-length is *defined* in terms of this motion, then the motion must by definition be uniform in this sense. Is there an inconsistency here? Perhaps not. For, in raising the question whether the celestial rotation is uniform Aristotle is asking whether there is any reason to think that it could ever be non-uniform in terms of some other, higher time-measurement not accessible to us, and what his arguments aim to prove is that there is no reason to think so.

4. *Abstract time.* Aristotle has some difficulty in handling the notion of simultaneity, because this is a temporal relation (and, obviously, essential to the business of time-measurement), but is not explicable in any obvious way in terms of 'time as the number of 'change'. In his remarks on sameness and difference, as applied to numbers and times (12, 220^{b}5–14; 14, 223^{a}29–^{b}12 and 224^{a}2–15) we find him being driven to introduce the notion of an abstract time-stretch. The same thing happens in the remarks on time-measurement (220^{b}14–32). Moreover, as will be seen, the notion of an abstract time-stretch is required by the programme of derivation (see (*d*) below).

The means for introducing abstraction is given by Aristotle's general theory of number (on which see more fully Additional Note A). Aristotle's position seems to be that, in order to be able to count, one must have already mentally abstracted a series of abstract numbers: 1, 2, 3, 4, . . . from the instances of oneness, twoness, etc., in experience. Since time is the 'number of change', it follows that one can abstract time from particular changes, just as one can abstract numbers from particular totalities of things, or lengths from particular space-occupiers. So abstract time-lengths such as 'a year' (not being any particular year) may be formed, and used in measuring particular changes. In this sense 'we measure the change by the time' and 'the time' figures in the role of 'the number by which we count'—a derivative and yet indispensable role.

There is, however, yet a further complication. Intermediate between time as a number attached to a particular change, and time as an abstract time-length, there is the further notion of time as a 'semi-abstract' time-length, i.e. as abstracted from particular changes but still tied to a particular date or temporal location in the ordered sequence of changes. Thus the years 1981 and 1982 are both the same time-length, viz. a year, but they are not the same year, and not the same stretch of time if a 'stretch of time' is understood as carrying a particular location in history. Aristotle uses 'time' in this sense too, and it cannot be said that he ever explains clearly the differences between the three senses of 'time' or the rationale behind their derivation, or even signals clearly which sense he is using in each context.

(d) The derivation of temporal from spatial structure

Aristotle does not attempt to reduce time itself, in any of the senses of 'time', to something non-temporal. But as far as possible he seeks to exhibit it as something which is derivative, in the sense that all talk of it can be understood only by reference to the properties of something else, in this case of spatially extended magnitudes and their changes. The attempt to implement this programme takes up a good deal of chapter 11: 219^a10-21, 219^b9-220^a24 are largely concerned with it, and not only time and its properties but other temporal phenomena, in particular 'the before and after' and 'the now' (on which see (e) below) are brought within the scope of the attempt. On the details of this attempted derivation, see especially the notes on 219^a10 ff., 219^a14 ff., 219^b9 ff.

Behind the notion of derivative senses of a word lies Aristotle's conception of 'focal meaning' (to use Owen's term). This conception appears in these books of the *Physics*, not only in the treatment of time, but also at 207^b21-25 (meanings of 'infinite') and in the enumeration of senses of 'in' at 210^a14-24.[1] It is important not

[1] On it see esp. the classic discussion of Owen (2).

to misconstrue the intent behind the programme of derivation. In saying that e.g. time (a time-stretch) is continuous only in a derivative sense, Aristotle is not asserting that there are no really continuous time-stretches or that time-stretches are not really continuous. He is, rather, claiming that their continuity is not something that they have in their own right and of their own nature. Rather, their continuity is a kind of shadow thrown on to them by other entities which are full-bloodedly continuous, in their own right. In trying to show this, Aristotle is *inter alia* trying to show that there is nothing intrinsically mysterious about time-stretches: all their inner structure is, as it were, borrowed from other, quite unmysterious things like spatially extended bodies, and they in themselves are straightforward, unstructured abstractions. The de-mystification of time is one of Aristotle's aims, and that perhaps is the reason why he spends relatively so much time on the description of (e.g.) time-measurement, and on the derivability of its properties.

(*e*) 'The before and after' *and* 'the now'

1. Aristotle's discussion of what he calls the 'before and after' and 'the now' is difficult. Some of the difficulty, though, is due simply to the fact that (as too often) Aristotle explains inadequately, or not at all, the machinery which he sets to work. Aristotle gives no set explanation of what he understands by 'the now', by the 'before and after', or by a *ho pote on*. The interpretation which is given in the notes is, I believe, the only one to make satisfactory sense of Aristotle's text, and I have tried to do something in the notes to demonstrate its adequacy. In this part of the Introduction I take the interpretation for granted and offer a connected survey of Aristotle's position.

2. 'The now' *and the present*. We have seen that Aristotle's account of time as 'the number of change' does not bring with it any account of the temporal relation of simultaneity. One way of arriving at the notion of an indivisible instant of time is by reflection on the notion of simultaneity, and how it should be defined; conversely, given the notion of an instant, 'simultaneous' can be defined as 'at the same instant' (cf. the definition of '(spatially) together' at *Physics* V.3, 226^{b}21–22 as 'in one first place'). Again, the analogy

of the point and its relation to length (the point is itself indivisible, of no length, but is the limit of a length, etc.) suggests the possibility and perhaps the need for a corresponding concept in the case of time. Certainly the thoroughgoing exploration of the analogy, and in particular of the topology of change and time, in *Physics* VI, would be impossible without the notion of a 'now' in the sense of 'an instant'.

But besides that of the instant, there is another notion for which Aristotle wishes to make room: that of the *present*. The notion of the present had had a prehistory in Parmenides, Zeno, and Plato's *Parmenides*.[1] The most important text is Plato's *Parmenides* 151^e3-152^d4. Aristotle, therefore, naturally takes over a notion of 'the now' which involves the now's being present as well as being an instant. In chapter 10, among the puzzles arising out of our intuitions, is the puzzle of whether the now is always different from time to time, or always the same (218^a8-25). At chapter 11, 219^b9-33, Aristotle gives his solution, which in outline is that while we must distinguish between the fixed, unrepeatable instant and anything that persists in time, still there *is* something that persists in time, and, in some sense, *is* each instant successively: something that is persistently 'in the present' and divides past from future.

Aristotle justifies this notion of a persistent present by reference to his analogy with spatial magnitudes and change. But the analogy does not require the existence of any such thing (on the details see notes on 219^b9 ff.). And in accepting the existence of a persistent present Aristotle complicates his theory considerably. The fact must be that Aristotle thinks he has to accept the notion of a permanent present as given in the phenomenology of the subject.[2] The notion does no further work within Aristotle's system.

3. *The before and after.* In explaining what the persistent present is, Aristotle identifies it with 'the before and after in change' (219^b26-28). 'The before and after' is another inadequately explained term. It is argued in the note on 219^a14 ff. that 'the before and after' in a particular change must be conceived of as a

---

[1] On these roots of 'the now' see particularly Owen (5), (6); Schofield (2).
[2] This is suggested by 219^b28-31.

temporal boundary to that change, marking off what has occurred of it from whatever is yet to come, and continuously moving out into the future. Abstracting from particular changes, the notion of a persistent present is given Aristotle as that of a temporal boundary which is constantly shifting its temporal location.

But it must be more than merely a boundary. After all, the horizon of a traveller is a boundary which 'moves', but few would claim (Aristotle certainly not) that the horizon is a genuinely persisting thing which keeps an identity through change. A spatial boundary, in order itself to be a genuinely persisting thing, must for Aristotle be defined as the boundary of some persisting space-occupying body. Presumably 'the before and after' in a change gets its identity, analogously, from being the boundary of a particular actual change; and 'the before and after' in change generally from being the boundary of the whole history of the universe, the whole past. So 'the past' seems to be thought of here as a persisting, developing thing.

4. If this account of Aristotle's theory of the persistent present is correct, it appears that the theory, of itself, commits Aristotle to a belief in the reality of becoming. For if becoming is an illusion, and the true view of persisting things or changes is that they have (timelessly) extension in the temporal dimension, then they do indeed have temporal boundaries, but *only* at their beginnings and ends. Any intermediate temporal boundaries are merely illusions of temporal perspective, like the traveller's horizon.

The conclusion is acceptable, since it is obvious in any case that Aristotle held that becoming was real (see (g) below). But it is perhaps worth pointing out further that the converse entailment does not hold. Aristotle could have held (as many philosophers since) to the reality of becoming, without being thereby committed to a theory of a persistent present.

Not only that, but if we were to take the talk of the present as the 'boundary dividing past and future' literally, it would follow that the existence of the present entailed the existence of the future *in* the present, and Aristotle would have made a self-contradictory concession to the opposed view. But, as Aristotle claims in another connection (208^{a}11), there is a conceptual difference between being limited and being in contact with something beyond the limit. The past may be limited by the present even if nothing exists beyond the present. Here Aristotle's spatial analogy limps, on Aristotle's own view.

(f) *The effects of time*

Aristotle's remarks on this subject (221^a30–$^b7$, 222^b16–27) are discussed in the note on 221^a26 ff. Here a brief summary may be useful.

Aristotle does not hold that time itself literally acts as an agent on things—this would be difficult to reconcile with the view of time explained in (*c*) above. But he is willing to speak metaphorically of 'time's action' in cases where there is a long-run natural degeneration in a closed natural system (e.g. the ageing of an animal). Such a process is to be explained in terms of the natural interactions of the components of the system. The fact that closed systems degenerate in this way is, however, of metaphysical significance for Aristotle. First, it shows, like modern statistical mechanics, an asymmetry in physical processes with regard to the direction of time. Such asymmetry would be possible to reconcile with the thesis of the unreality of becoming, but it does at least give a particular point to the claim that this kind of change is in a remote sense due to 'the long run' as such, i.e. to the sum total of a long series of events in the sublunary world. Secondly, there is a fairly well worked out theory of the over-all structure of events in the sublunary world, which underwrites everything so far stated. This sees the pattern of short-term fluctuation and long-term stability in the sublunary world as due to a balance between an input of form-giving forces from outside (the celestial world) and an inherent tendency of matter or en-mattered form to degenerate if left to itself.

The whole of this elaborate structure of thought neither implies, nor is implied by, the thesis of the reality of becoming; nor does Aristotle make any explicit connection between the two. Nevertheless, the asymmetry of physical explanation involved certainly sits more happily with a metaphysical theory, such as that of the reality of becoming, that offers a deep-seated metaphysical asymmetry.

(g) *General metaphysics of time: summary*

Time, in the senses Aristotle is prepared to give to 'time', is for him an ontologically secondary and dependent thing. In particular it is not something self-subsistent. But while this is so, the temporal processes from which talk about time gets its meaning are eminently real. Not merely do they occur, but their apparently serial occurrence is no illusion. For Aristotle, temporal becoming is a fact. That this is so is not argued by Aristotle anywhere in these chapters, but it is implied by the doctrine of the persistent present (see (*e*) above). Further confirmation that Aristotle held the reality of temporal becoming is given by his doctrine of the indeterminacy of the future (see below).

Aristotle's conception of temporal becoming seems to be that of a past that 'grows out' continuously in the direction of the future, with the persistent present as a genuinely persisting and travelling boundary of the past. Within the history of the universe, the relation of simultaneity between changes (or limits of changes) is taken as real and absolute, though Aristotle seeks to ground it in the existence of spatial relationships. With simultaneity goes the notion of the instant (the unrepeatable 'now'). Instants enjoy some sort of derivative existence, as limits of time-stretches, or equivalently as abstractions from stages of changes.

As to the future, Aristotle's position has to be gathered from *de Interpretatione*, chapter 9 and other passages. While it is necessary that there *will be* a future, in the sense that change will continue to occur (see e.g. 222^b6-7), the future while it is future is quite indeterminate in its details, and can be said to exist (if at all) only perhaps in some potential sense. There are no such things as future objects (any more than there are possible objects) and the future career of an existing object exists in the present in a potential sense only.

About the past, Aristotle is more nearly an unqualified realist. The preliminary problem ($217^b33-218^a3$, cf. 218^a5-6) shows him entertaining scepticism about the past, and this problem is not explicitly answered. But the only obvious source of doubt as to Aristotle's realism about the past is the fact that the past seems to involve various undesirable infinities. Not only is it infinitely long in temporal extension, but there have been in it infinitely many changes of various kinds—infinitely many celestial revolutions, in particular, and infinitely many generations of animals. The difficulty this makes has already been pointed out (above, Introduction, 3 (c) 3). If Aristotle is to be a consistent finitist, it may seem that he must deny any but *potential* existence to the infinitely long series of past time. He must say 'however far back anyone may explore, it will alway be possible for there to have been a past before that'. The assurances that 'there always has been change' (e.g. *Physics* VIII.1) would then be read in the same potential sense. But this is straining the natural sense, and in any case may not be necessary to secure consistency. The solution suggested briefly (at p. xxv above) is to use the remarkable passage 223^a21-29. Here it is claimed that if there were no mind, there would be no time, since time depends on things being countable, and nothing is countable except by a mind, and therefore nothing is countable if there is no mind. By a slight extension of the doctrine it follows that nothing is countable unless it can be simultaneously present to a mind. And that, perhaps, is just what the past cannot be—if, *per impossibile*, it were, then a completed simultaneous infinite would be present to a mind, which is absurd. If that is right, then it will be consistent for Aristotle to assert, *both* that before any change there was a previous change *and* yet that the total number of past changes is not infinite, because there is no such number. Past changes will not form a numbered totality at all. Likewise, past time-lengths will not be in sum a measurable quantity. Only so much of the past will be countable and measurable as is comprehensible by a single mind at a single moment. Such a position does not affect realism about individual past events (or processes or objects); but only about the numbers or measures that they have collectively. And the past, or past time, could still be said to be 'infinite' (*apeiros*) but *only* in the non-quantitative sense of 'not having a limit'.

(h) Eternity

Aristotle in these chapters has little to say about timelessness and eternity though the discussion of 'being in time' does touch on these topics (esp. 221^b3-7, $221^b23-222^a9$). Physics is by definition concerned only with the changeable part of the universe, so that the opposition between what is and is not in time, though important for Aristotle's metaphysics, would not be expected to emerge here.

BOOK III

CHAPTER 1

200ᵇ12. Since nature is a principle of change and alteration, and 200ᵇ
our inquiry is about nature, it must not escape us what CHANGE is:
for if it is not known, it must be that nature is not known either.
And after making an analysis of change, we must try to inquire in 15
the same way about the subjects next in order. Change is thought to
be something continuous, and the INFINITE is the first thing that
presents itself to view in the continuous (which is why those who try
to define the continuous often find themselves making use of the
definition of the infinite as an auxiliary, the supposition being that
what is divisible *ad infinitum* is continuous). Further, [it is thought] 20
that there cannot be change without PLACE and VOID and TIME.
So it is clear that, both for these reasons, and because they are
common to everything and universal, we must give a treatment of
each of these subjects, as a preliminary to further inquiry (for the
consideration of specialities is subsequent to that of things that are
common)—beginning, as we said, with change. 25

200ᵇ26. Things are—some only actually, some potentially and
actually—either (*a*) a 'this'; or (*b*) so much; or (*c*) of such a kind, and
likewise they are in the other categories of that-which-is. (Of the
relative, one kind is said in respect of excess and of deficiency,
another in respect of the active and the passive, and, in general, in 30
respect of that which is productive of change and that which is
changeable. For that which is productive of change, is so *in* that
which is changeable, and that which is changeable is so *by the
agency* of that which is productive of change.) There is no change
apart from actual things; for whatever alters always does so in
respect either of substance, or of quantity, or of qualification, or of
place, and there is, as we assert, nothing to be found as a common 35
item superior to these, which is neither a 'this' nor a quantity nor a 201ᵃ
qualification nor any of the other occupants of categories; and so

1

there is no change or alteration either of anything apart from the
things mentioned, because nothing *is*, apart from the things mentioned. But each [occupant of a category] is present in everything in
two ways, e.g. the 'this' (one case of it is the form, the other is the
5 privation); and in respect of qualification (one case is *white* and the
other *black*); and in respect of quantity (one case is *complete* and
the other *incomplete*). So too in respect of locomotion, one case is
above, the other is *below*, or one case is *light*, the other is *heavy*. So
that there are just as many species of change and alteration as of
that-which-is.

201ª9. There being a distinction, in respect of each kind [of being],
10 between [being] actually and [being] potentially, the actuality of
that which potentially is, *qua* such, is change. For example: the
actuality of what admits of qualitative change, *qua* admitting of
qualitative change, is qualitative change; of what admits of increase
and decrease (there is no common term to cover both), it is increase
and decrease; of what admits of coming-to-be and ceasing-to-be, it is
15 coming-to-be and ceasing-to-be; of what admits of locomotion, it is
locomotion. That this is change is clear from the following: when
that which is buildable is in actuality, in the respect in which we call
it such, it is being built, and this is the process of building; and
similarly with learning and healing and rolling and jumping and
maturing and growing old.

201ª19. (Since some things are the same things both actually and
20 potentially, not at the same time or not in the same part, but, e.g.,
hot in actuality, cold in potentiality—from this it already follows
that many things will act and be acted upon mutually. For everything [of this kind] will be at the same time both active and passive.
So too, then, that which produces change naturally will itself be
changeable; for everything of that kind is itself changed when it
25 produces change. Some even think that everything that produces
change is itself changed; however, the truth about that will become
clear from other considerations—in fact, there is something that produces change and is not changeable.)

201ª27. The actuality, then, of what is potentially—when being in
actuality it is operating, not *qua* itself but *qua* changeable—is change.
30 I mean '*qua*' thus: the bronze is potentially a statue, but yet it is not

the actuality of bronze *qua* bronze that is change. For it is not the same thing to be bronze and to be potentially something: if indeed it were, without qualification and by definition, the same thing, then the actuality of the bronze, *qua* bronze, would be change, but, as has been said, it is not the same thing. The case is clear with opposites: to be capable of being healthy and to be capable of being sick are 35 different—otherwise being sick and being healthy would be the same 201^b thing—but the underlying subject, that which is healthy and that which is diseased, be it moisture or blood, is one and the same. Since then it is not the same thing, just as *colour* is not the same as *visible thing*, it is manifest that the actuality of the potential, *qua* potential, is change.

201^{b}5. That change is this, and that change occurs just when the 5 actuality is this actuality, and neither before nor after, is clear; for it is possible for each thing to operate at one time and not at another, e.g. the buildable, and the operation of the buildable, *qua* buildable, is the process of building. For the operation is either the process of 10 building or the house; but when the house is, the buildable no longer is; but to get built is what the buildable does, so that the process of building must be the operation. And the process of building is a kind of change. But now the same argument will apply in the case of the other changes as well. 15

CHAPTER 2

201^{b}16. That this is a good account is clear also from what others say about change, and from the fact that it is not easy to define it in any other way. In the first place, one would not be able to put change and alteration into another genus; and, again, it is clear when we consider how some people treat it, asserting that change is differ- 20 ence and inequality and that which is not—it is not necessary for any of these things to change, either different things or unequal things or things which are not; nor, even, does alteration take place into or from these things more than it does [into or] from their opposites. The reason why they assign change to these things is that change is thought to be something indefinite, and the principles in the second 25 column [of correlated opposites] are indefinite because they are

3

privative; none of them is a 'this' or is of such a kind, nor belongs to
one of the other categories. And the reason why change is thought
to be indefinite is that it is not possible to assign it either to
potentiality of things that are, nor yet to [their] operation: for
30 neither that which it is possible may be a quantity, nor that which is
a quantity in operation, necessarily changes, and besides change does
seem to be a kind of operation, but an incomplete one—the reason
being that the potential, of which it is the operation, is incomplete.
This, then, is why it is difficult to grasp what it is; for it is necessary
to assign it either to privation or to potentiality or to simple
35 operation, but none of these is obviously admissible. There remains,
202^a then, the way that has been stated, that it *is* a kind of operation, but
an operation such as we said, which is difficult to spot but of which
the existence is possible.

202^{a}3. As was said, everything that produces change is also
changed, if it is potentially changeable and its not being changed is
5 rest (the not being changed of that which admits of change is rest).
For to operate on this, *qua* such, is just what it is to produce change,
and this it does by contact, so that it will at the same time also be
acted upon. That which produces change will always carry some
form, either 'this' or 'of such a kind' or 'so much', which will be the
10 principle of, and responsible for, the change, when it produces
change—e.g. what is actually a human being makes, out of that
which is potentially a human being, a human being.

CHAPTER 3

202^{a}13. Again—a point which makes difficulty—it is manifest that
the change is in that which is changeable. For it is the actuality of
this, brought about by that which is productive of change. Yet the
15 operation of that which is productive of change, also, is not other—
there must in fact be an actuality of both—for it is productive of
change by its being capable of so doing, and it produces change by
its operation, but it is such as to operate on what is changeable;
so that the operation of both is one in the same way as it is the same
interval from 1 to 2 as from 2 to 1, and as the uphill and the down-
20 hill—these are one, yet their definition is not one, and similarly with
that which produces and undergoes change.

4

202^a21. This presents a difficulty of a formal kind.* (1) It is perhaps necessary that there should be some operation of that which is active and of that which is passive: the one is an acting-upon, the other is a being-acted-upon, and the product and end of the one is a product of action, and of the other a modification. (2) Since then both [of the operations] are changes, (3) if they are different, what 25 are they in? Either (b) they are both in that which is acted upon and changes; or (a) the acting-upon is in that which acts, the being-acted-upon in that which is acted upon (if one has to call this too an acting-upon, it is so by homonymy). But if this [(a)] is the case, the change will be in that which produces change, since the same argument applies to that which produces and that which undergoes change: so that either everything that produces change will change; 30 or having change it will not change. But if [(b)] both are in that which changes and is acted upon, the acting-upon *and* the being-acted-upon, and the teaching and the learning are, being two, in the learner, then in the first place it will not be true that the operation of each thing is present in each thing; and again, it is absurd that it should change by *two* changes at the same time: what two qualitative changes will there be of one thing to one form? This is impossible. 35 (4) Suppose then that the operation will be one. But it is unreasonable that there should be one and the same operation of two things 202^b different in form. And if teaching and learning are the same thing, and acting-upon and being-acted-upon, then to teach will be the same thing as to learn, and to act upon as to be acted upon, so that it will be necessary that every teacher learns and everyone that acts upon is acted upon.

202^b5. Or can it be that: (a) it is *not* absurd that the operation of 5 one thing should be in another (for teaching is the operation of that which is disposed to teach, but it is *on* something, and not cut off, but is of this on this); and (b) there is, also, nothing to prevent the operation of two things being one and the same, not as the same in being, but in the way that what potentially is is related to what is operating, and (c) it is also not necessary that the teacher learns, 10

---

* Reference numbers and letters in this section correspond to those used in the notes.

even if to act upon and to be acted upon are the same thing, provided they are not the same in the sense that the definition that gives the 'what it was to be' is one (as with 'raiment' and 'clothing'), but in the sense in which the road from Thebes to Athens is the same as the road from Athens to Thebes, as was said earlier? For it is not the case that all the same things are present in things that are the same in
15 any sense whatever, but only of those of which the being is the same. And, in any case, even if teaching is the same thing as learning, to learn is not [therefore] the same thing as to teach, just as, even if two things separated by an interval have one interval between them, to be distant in the direction from A to B is not one and the same thing as to be distant in the direction from B to A. But speaking generally, the teaching is not the same, in the primary sense, as the
20 learning, nor the acting-upon as the being-acted-upon, but that in which these things are present, namely the change, [is the same as the being acted upon]; for to be the operation of A in B, and to be the operation of B by the agency of A, are different in definition. 202^b23. It has been said, then, what change is, both generally and in particular, for it is not unclear how each of the kinds of it will be defined: qualitative change, for example, is the actuality of that
25 which admits of qualitative change, *qua* admitting of qualitative change. And an account will be given in the same way about each of the other kinds of change.

CHAPTER 4

30 202^b30. Since the science of nature is concerned with magnitudes, change, and time, each of which must be either infinite or finite (even if it is true that not everything is either infinite or finite, e.g. a property or a point—for perhaps none of such things need be
35 either), it will be fitting for the student of nature to consider the infinite, [and ask] whether it is or not, and if it is, *what* it is. That the inquiry about the infinite is germane to this science is indicated
203^a by the fact that all who have a reputation for important work in this branch of philosophy have given an account of the infinite, and all of them posit it as some kind of principle of things that are. 203^a4. (A) On the one hand, some, such as the Pythagoreans and

Plato, make the infinite in itself a principle, not as an accident of
some other thing, but as a substance, being the Infinite pure and 5
simple. The difference is that (*a*) the Pythagoreans count it among
objects of sense-perception (as they do not make number separable)
and think that what is outside the heavens is infinite; while (*b*) Plato
holds that there is no material body outside, nor are the Forms
outside—since they are not *anywhere*—but that the infinite is present
both in the objects of sense-perception and in the Forms. Again, the 10
Pythagoreans say the infinite is the even (because, they say, it is the
even, entrapped and becoming limited by the odd, that gives things
their infinity; this they hold to be confirmed by what happens with
numbers—when 'gnomons' are arranged round the one and otherwise,
the form is always different in one case, and the same in the other);
while Plato says that the infinites are two, namely the great and the 15
small.

203ª16. (B) On the other hand, the natural philosophers all posit,
as subject for the infinite, some other kind of thing, one of the
things said to be elements, e.g. water or air, or what is intermediate
between these. But (*a*) none of those who make the elements [more
than one but] finite [in number] makes them infinite [in extent];
(*b*) all those who make the elements infinite [in number], as do 20
Anaxagoras (from the 'homoeomeries') and Democritus (from the
hodge-podge of shapes), say that the infinite is continuous by
contact. (*i*) Anaxagoras says that any portion whatever [of matter] is
a mixture in the same way as the whole sum is, because he sees anything whatever coming to be out of anything whatever. (This seems
also to be the reason why he says that all things were once together; 25
for example, this flesh and this bone, and thus anything whatever,
and therefore everything. And hence simultaneously. For there is a
starting-point of separation, not merely one in each thing, but one
for all things. For since what comes to be, does so from body of
such a kind, and there is coming-to-be of everything but not simultaneously, there must also be some principle of the coming-to-be, 30
and this is a single principle such as what Anaxagoras calls Mind, and
Mind takes thought and sets to work from some starting-point; so
that it must be that all things are at some time together and at some
time begin to change.) (*ii*) Democritus denies that any of his primary

bodies comes to be the one from the other. Even so, the body
203ᵇ common to them all is his principle, which is differentiated by size
and shape in the different portions.

203ᵇ3. It is clear from these facts that this inquiry is appropriate to
students of nature. It is with good reason, too, that they all make
5 the infinite a principle, since neither can it exist to no end, nor can it
have any power except as being a principle. For everything is either a
principle or derived from a principle, but there is no principle from
which the infinite is derived, for [if so] it would have a limit. Besides,
it does not admit of coming-to-be or ceasing-to-be, which suggests
that it is a kind of principle; for what come to be must come to an
end, and there is an end of every ceasing-to-be. And so, as I say, the
10 infinite is thought not to have a principle [to which it is subject] but
itself to be a principle of other things, and to 'surround everything'
and 'steer everything' as is said by all those [natural philosophers]
who do not provide other explanatory factors besides the infinite
(such as Mind or Love); and it is thought to be the divine, for it is
'immortal and imperishable' as Anaximander says, and most of the
natural philosophers.

15 **203ᵇ15.** The more plausible arguments for the existence of something infinite are five: the arguments (*i*) from time, since this is
infinite; (*ii*) from the division of magnitudes (for mathematicians too
make use of the infinite); (*iii*) that only so will coming-to-be and
ceasing-to-be not give out, i.e. only if there is an infinite from which
20 that which comes to be is subtracted; (*iv*) that what is limited always
reaches a limit in relation to something, so that there can be no
[ultimate] limits, since one thing must always reach a limit in
relation to another; (*v*) above all, and most decisively, the argument
which makes a common difficulty for all thinkers: because they do
not give out in thought, number and mathematical magnitudes and
25 what is outside the heavens all are thought to be infinite. (And if
what is outside is infinite, then it is thought that there is infinite
body and infinitely many world-systems, for why should these be
here rather than *there* in the void? Hence [it is thought that] body
with bulk is everywhere, since it is in one place. And again, even if
there is void, and place is infinite, there must be infinite body, since
30 in everlasting things there is no difference between being possible
and being.)

8

203^{b}30. Inquiry into the infinite presents difficulties: if one supposes it not to exist, many impossible things result, and equally if one supposes it to exist. Besides, in which of two ways does it exist: as a substance, or as an accident in itself of some kind of thing? Or does it exist in neither of these two ways, and yet none the less there is an infinite, or things infinite in number? The question most appropriate for a student of nature to consider is whether there is a 204^a magnitude, perceptible by sense, which is infinite. The first thing then, is to determine in how many ways the infinite is [so] called. (1) In one way [we call infinite] that which it is impossible to traverse, because it is not the kind of thing to be traversed—just as a voice is invisible; (2) in another, that which has a traverse but one 5 which is unending; (3) or [which has a traverse but] with difficulty; (4) or that which is the kind of thing to have a traverse but does not have one. Again, everything infinite is [so] either (*i*) with respect to addition or (*ii*) with respect to division or (*iii*) in both ways.

CHAPTER 5

204^{a}8. First, then, that the infinite should be separable from the objects of sense-perception, being something that is 'just-infinite', is not possible. (1) If the Infinite is neither a magnitude nor a multitude, but substance and not accident, it will be indivisible, 10 since what is divisible is either a magnitude or a multitude. But if indivisible it will not be infinite, except in the way in which a voice is invisible. But it is not [the infinite] in *this* sense which is said to be by those who affirm the existence of the infinite, or which we are inquiring into, but [the infinite] in the sense of 'untraversable'. (But if the infinite is accidentally, it can never be an elementary 15 constituent of things, *qua* infinite, just as what is invisible is not such a constituent of speech, though a voice is invisible.) (2) Again, how is it possible for there to be something 'just-infinite', unless there is also 'just-number' and 'just-magnitude', since the infinite is a property in itself of number and magnitude? There is even less necessity [for the infinite to exist in separation] than for number or magnitude [to do so]. (3) Besides, it is manifest that it is not possible 20 for the infinite to exist as something in actual operation *and* as a

9

substance and principle. For any part whatever of it that may be
taken will be infinite, if it is resoluble into parts (for if the finite is
substance and not predicated of an underlying subject, the being
infinite is the same as the infinite) so that either it is indivisible or
25 divisible into infinites. But it is impossible that the same thing
should be many infinites (yet, just as a part of air is air, so a part of
infinite is infinite, if it *is* substance and a principle). So it is irresoluble into parts and indivisible. But it is impossible that an actual
infinite should be so, since it must be a quantity. Therefore the
30 infinite is present in things accidentally. But if so, it has been said
above that it is not possible to call it a principle, but what it is an
accident of (air, or the even) [should be called a principle]. So that
those who say what the Pythagoreans say have an absurd position:
they both make the infinite a substance and resolve it into parts.

204^a34. But perhaps this question is a general one—whether it is
35 possible for there to be an infinite among mathematical entities also
204^b and in things which are objects of thought and have no magnitude—
while our investigation concerns objects of sense-perception and the
other objects of our course of inquiry, whether there is or is not
among *them* a body infinite in extent. If we argue formally, it would
5 appear that there is not, as follows: If the definition of 'body' is
'that which is bounded by a surface', then there cannot be an infinite
body, either as an object of thought or of sense-perception. (Nor, for
that matter, can there be a separated infinite number: for number,
or what has number, is countable, and so, if it is possible to count
what is countable, it would then be possible to traverse the infinite.)
10 **204^b10.** If we look at it more from the standpoint of physical
science, [the same conclusion follows] from the following. [An
infinite material body] can neither be composite nor simple. (A) It
will not be composite, if the number of elements is finite. For there
must be more than one element, and the opposite ones must always
be equal, and (1) one of them cannot be infinite. For let the power
15 in one body be less than the other by never so much—e.g. fire is
finite, air is infinite, and an equal amount of fire is any multiple you
please in power of an equal amount of air, only let it bear some
proportion—still, it is manifest that the infinite body will exceed and
destroy the finite one. But (2) that each of them should be infinite

is impossible; for material body is that which is extended in all
dimensions, and what is infinite is what has infinite extension, so   20
that infinite material body will be extended to infinity in all
dimensions. (B) Yet it is not possible either that an infinite body
should be one and simple, whether (1) it is (as some say it is) the
body that exists additionally to the elements, and out of which they
make the elements come into being, or whether (2) it is taken
without qualification. (1) There are some who make this [additional
body] the infinite, not air or water, in order that the other bodies   25
may not be destroyed by the infinite they posit, since the elements
have an opposition to one another: e.g. air is cold, and water moist,
and fire hot; if one of these were infinite, the others would by now
have been destroyed. But as it is, they say, there is another thing
from which these [elements come to be]. But it is impossible that
there should be such a thing, not because it is infinite (on *that*   30
point there is something to be said which applies in common to
every case alike, whether to air or water or what you like), but
because there is no such perceptible body over and above those
called the elements. All things are dissolved into that out of which
they come to be, so that it would have to be here in the world alongside of air and fire and earth and water, but no such thing is   35
observed. (2) Neither can fire, or any other of the elements, be   205^a
infinite. And in general, even apart from one of them's being infinite,
it is impossible that the sum of things, even if it is finite, should be
or come to be any one of the elements—as Heraclitus says that at
some time everything becomes fire—and the same argument applies
to the one thing, such as the natural philosophers posit in addition   5
to the elements. For everything alters from opposite to opposite, for
example from hot to cold.

205^a8[7]. That, in general it is impossible for there to be an infinite
body, perceptible by sense, is clear from the following. Every thing
perceptible by sense is such as to be naturally somewhere, and each   10
such thing has a certain place, and the same place for a portion of it
as for the whole of it: e.g. for the whole of the earth and a single
clod, and for fire and a spark. Hence, (A) if it [the infinite body]
is homogeneous, it will be immobile or it will always be in motion.
Yet this is impossible. For what will be down rather than up, or

anywhere whatever? I mean, for example: if there were a lump
15 [of the infinite body], where will that be in motion or where
will it be at rest, since the place of the body of the same kind is
infinite? Will it then occupy the whole of the place? How could it?
So what sort of being at rest or what motion will it have, and where?
Or will it be in motion everywhere? In that case it will not come to
20 a halt. But (B) if the whole is not homogeneous, the places too will
be different. And in the first place the body of the whole will not
be one, except by being in contact. Next, these [components]
will in form either be finite, or infinite in number. But they cannot
be finite, for if the whole is infinite some will be infinite and some
not (e.g. fire or water [will be infinite]); but such a thing destroys
25 the opposites. But if they are infinite in number and simple, the
30 places will be infinite [in number] too and the elements will be
infinite [in number]. So if. this is impossible, and the places are
finite, the whole is too. (For it is impossible that the place and the
body should not fit, since neither is the place as a whole larger than
the possible size of the body (at the same time, the body will not
35 even be infinite any more), nor is the body larger than the place;
205ᵇ1, ᵃ25 for [otherwise] there will either be void or a body with no natural
whereabouts. It was for this reason that none of the natural philosophers made fire or earth the one infinite body, but either water or
air or that which is intermediate between them, because each [of fire
and earth] has clearly a determinate place, but these [others] are
ambiguous between up and down.)
205ᵇ1. Anaxagoras talks oddly about the infinite's being at rest; he
says that the infinite keeps itself still, and that this is because it is in
itself, since no other thing surrounds it; as if a thing's nature were to
5 be there, wherever it is. But this is not true: a thing may be somewhere because forced to be there, and not where it is naturally.
So, however true it may be that the whole is not in motion (what is
kept still by itself and is in itself must be immobile), it is still
necessary to say why it is not in its nature to be moved. It is not
sufficient to leave the matter with this statement; for it might be
10 that it had, not moving, nowhere else to move to, yet there was
nothing to prevent its being by nature such [as to move]. After all
the earth does not move either, nor, if it were infinite, but held

back by the centre, [would it do so]; but it would stay still at the
centre, not because there is nowhere where it will be moved to, but
because it is by nature such [as to do so]. Yet one might say that it
kept itself still. If, then, this is not the reason even in the case of the
earth, if that were infinite, but the reason is that it has weight, and 15
what has weight stays still at the centre, and the earth is at the
centre; in the same way, the infinite would stay still in itself for
some other reason and not because it is infinite and keeps itself still.
At the same time it is clear that any part whatever [of the infinite]
would have to stay still; for, just as the infinite stays still in itself,
keeping [itself] still, so too if any part whatever is taken, that will 20
stay still in itself. For the places of the whole and of the part are of
the same form—e.g. of the whole of the earth and a clod, below, and
of the whole of fire and a spark, above. So that, if the place of the
infinite is that which is in itself, the place of a part is the same;
hence it will stay still in itself.

205^{b}24. (1) In general, it is manifest that it is impossible to say at
the same time that there is an infinite body and that there is some 25
[natural] place for bodies, if every body perceptible by sense has
either heaviness or lightness and, if it is heavy, has a natural motion
to the centre, and if it is light, upwards. For this must be so of the
infinite too: but it is impossible, both for all of it to have either
[heavy or light] as properties and for half of it to have each of the
two. How will you divide it? And how, of what is infinite, can there 30
be an above and a below, or an extreme and a centre? (2) Again,
every body perceptible by sense is in place, and the kinds and
varieties of place are: above, below, forward, backward, right and
left. These are not determined only relatively to us, and conven-
tionally; they are so in the universe itself. But they cannot exist in 35
the infinite. (3) And in general, if there cannot be an infinite place, 206^a
and every body is in a place, there cannot be an infinite body. Yet
what is somewhere is in a place, and what is in a place is somewhere.
If then, the infinite cannot even be any quantity—for then it will be
some particular quantity, e.g. of two or three cubits; that is what
'quantity' means—so too that which is in place [is so] because it is 5
somewhere, and that is either above or below or in some other of the
six dimensions, and of each of these there is some limit. It is

13

manifest, then, from these considerations that there is in actual operation no infinite body.

CHAPTER 6

206ᵃ9. But if there is, unqualifiedly, no infinite, it is clear that
10 many impossible things result. For there will be a beginning and end of time, and magnitudes will not be divisible into magnitudes, and number will not be infinite. Now when the alternatives have been distinguished thus and it seems that neither is possible, an arbitrator is needed and it is clear that in a sense [the infinite] is and in a sense it is not. 'To be', then, may mean 'to be potentially' or 'to be
15 actually'; and the infinite is either in addition or in division. It has been stated that magnitude is not in actual operation infinite; but it *is* infinite in division—it is not hard to refute indivisible lines—so that it remains for the infinite to be potentially. (We must not take 'potentially' here in the same way as that in which, if it is possible
20 for this to be a statue, it actually will be a statue, and suppose that there is an infinite which will be in actual operation.) Since 'to be' has many senses, just as the day is, and the contest is, by the constant occurring of one thing after another, so too with the infinite. (In these cases too there is 'potentially' and 'in actual operation': the Olympic games *are*, both in the sense of the contest's being able to occur and in the sense of its occurring.) But [the
25 infinite's being] is shown in one way in the case of time and the human race, and in another in the case of division of magnitudes. In general, the infinite is in virtue of one thing's constantly being taken after another—each thing taken is finite, but it is always one
206ᵇ followed by another; but in magnitudes what was taken persists, in the case of time and the race of men the things taken cease to be, yet so that [the series] does not give out.
206ᵇ3. The infinite by addition is in a sense the same as the infinite by division. For in that which is finite by addition there is an
5 inversely corresponding process: to see it as being divided *ad infinitum* will be at the same time to see it as being added to a definite amount. For if, in a finite magnitude, one takes a definite

amount and takes in addition [always] in the same proportion, (but
not taking a magnitude which is the same particular one) one will
not traverse the finite magnitude; but if one increases the proportion
so that one always takes in the same particular magnitude, one will 10
traverse it, because every finite quantity is exhausted by any definite
quantity whatever.

206^{b}12. The infinite, then, is in no other way, but is in this way,
potentially and by way of reduction (and actually too, in the sense
in which we say that the day and the games are). It is potentially, in
the way in which matter is, and not in itself, as the finite is. The 15
infinite by addition, too, is potentially in this way; this infinite, we
say, is in a way the same thing as the infinite by division. For it will
always be possible to take something which is outside—though it will
not exceed every magnitude in the way in which, in division, it
exceeds every definite quantity and will always be smaller. To be 20
[infinite] so as to exceed every [definite quantity] by addition is not
possible even potentially unless there is something which is actually
infinite, accidentally, as the natural philosophers say that the body
outside the world-system, of which the substance is air or some
other such thing, is infinite. But if it is not possible for there to be a
perceptible body which is actually infinite in this sense, it is manifest 25
that there cannot be one even potentially infinite by addition,
except in the way that has been stated, in inverse correspondence to
the division-process. (Even Plato, for this reason, made two infinites,
because there seems to be an excess and a going-to-infinity both in
extent and in reduction; but, having made two, he does not make
use of them, for in [Plato's] numbers neither the infinite by 30
reduction is present, the unit being a minimum, nor the infinite in
extent, because he makes number end with the number ten.)

206^{b}33. It turns out that the infinite is the opposite of what people
say it is: it is not that of which no part is outside, but that of which
some part is always outside. (An indication is this: people call rings 207^a
infinite too if they have no hoop, because it is always possible to
take something outside, and they talk so because of a certain
similarity, though not using the primary sense—for *that*, this
property must be present and also one must never take the same 5
thing [as before] and this is not so in the case of the circle, where

only the next thing is always different [from its predecessor].) So, that is infinite, of which it is always possible to take some part outside, when we take according to quantity. But that of which no part is outside, is complete and whole: that is how we define 'whole', as meaning that of which no part is absent—e.g. a whole man or a
10 whole box. And as what is whole in a particular case, so is that which is whole in the primary sense: [it is that] of which no part is outside. (That outside which absence is, is not all, whatever may be absent.) ('Whole' and 'complete' are either exactly the same or very close in their nature. Nothing is complete unless it has an end, and an end is a limit.)

15 **207ª15.** So one must judge Parmenides to have spoken better than Melissus: the latter says that the infinite is whole, the former that the whole is finite, 'evenly balanced from the middle'. For the *infinite* is a different kettle of fish from the *universe* or *whole*—yet it is from this that people derive the dignity attributed to the
20 infinite, that it surrounds everything and contains everything in itself, because it has some similarity to the whole. In fact, the infinite is the material of the completeness of magnitude, and is that which is potentially but not actually whole, being divisible by a process of reduction and by the inversely corresponding addition, but being whole and finite not in itself but in respect of something
25 else. Nor does it surround, *qua* infinite, but is surrounded, and for this reason is unknowable, *qua* infinite; for the material cause has no form. Hence it is manifest that the infinite is to be reckoned rather as a portion than as a whole; for the material cause is a portion of the whole, as the bronze is of the bronze statue. (If it surrounds in the perceptible world, in the intelligible world too the
30 large and the small ought to surround the intelligibles.) It is absurd and impossible that the unknowable and indefinite should surround and define.

CHAPTER 7

207ª33. That there seems to be no infinite by addition such as to exceed any magnitude, while there is [an infinite] in division [of that

kind]—this too is a reasonable result. For it is matter, and [so] the 35
infinite, that is surrounded [and] inside, and it is the form that
surrounds.

207^{b}1. Reasonable, too, it is that while in number there is a limit at 207^b
the minimum, but in the direction of 'more' [number] always
exceeds any multitude, yet in the case of magnitudes, on the
contrary, they exceed any magnitude in the direction of 'less', but in
that of 'more' there is no infinite magnitude. The reason for this is 5
that the one is indivisible, whatever may be one (e.g. a man is *one*
man and *not* many), but number is plurality of ones, a certain
'many' of them. So there must be a halt at the indivisible. ('Three'
and 'two' are derivative names, and similarly each of the other numbers.) But in the direction of more it is always possible to conceive 10
of [more]—since the halvings of magnitude are infinite. Hence [the
infinite in number] is potentially, but not in actual operation,
though what is taken always exceeds any definite multitude. But this
number is not separable, and the infinity does not stay still but
comes to be, in the same way as time and the number of time. In the 15
case of magnitudes the contrary is true: the continuous is divided
into infinitely many parts, but there is no infinite in the direction of
'greater'. For a magnitude in actual operation may exist of any size,
of which a magnitude may potentially exist. Since therefore no
perceptible magnitude is infinite, there may not be an exceeding of
every definite magnitude—for then there would be something greater 20
than the world.

207^{b}21. The infinite is not the same in magnitude and in change
and in time, as some one kind of thing, but the [kind of infinite
which is] posterior is said [to be] in respect of [that which is]
prior—e.g. change [is called infinite] because the magnitude is, along
which something is changed (or changes qualitatively or increases in
size), and time is because the change is. For the present let us use 25
these statements, but later we shall also say what each [of the
infinites] is and why every magnitude is divisible into magnitudes.

207^{b}27. This reasoning does not deprive the mathematicians of
their study, either, in refuting the existence in actual operation of an
untraversable infinite in extent. Even as it is they do not need the
infinite, for they make no use of it; they need only that there should 30

be a finite line of any size they wish. But another magnitude of any size whatever can be divided in the same proportion as the greatest magnitude; so that, at least for the purpose of proof, it will make no difference to them that [a magnitude] is among the magnitudes that exist.

207^{b}34. There being a fourfold division of explanations, it is
35 manifest that the infinite is an explanation as matter is; and that its
208^a being is privation, and what in itself underlies it is the continuous and perceptible by sense. All other thinkers, too, obviously use the infinite as a material cause; so it is absurd to make it what surrounds, and not what is surrounded.

CHAPTER 8

5 208^{a}5. It remains to review those arguments which seem to show that the infinite is not only potentially but as something distinct. Some points in them are not compelling, and others may be met in other ways without falsehood. (*iii*)* In order that coming-to-be should not give out, it is not necessary that there should be in actual operation an infinite perceptible body, for it is possible that, the
10 universe being finite, the ceasing-to-be of one thing should be the coming-to-be of another. (*iv*) Again, to be in contact and to be finite are different. The former is relative; it is [to be in contact] *with* something—everything [in contact] is in contact with something. It is an accident of some finite things. But what is finite is not relatively so. Nor is it possible for anything you please to come into contact with anything you please. (*v*) It is absurd to rely on thought:
15 the excess and deficiency are not in the actual thing but in thought. Thus, one might think of each of us as being many times as large as himself, increasing each of us *ad infinitum*; but it is not for *this* reason, because someone thinks it is so, that anyone exceeds this particular size that we have, but because it is the case; and *that* [(someone's thinking it)] just happens to be true [(when it is true)].
20 (*i*) Time, change, and thought are infinite things of the kind in which

* The numbering corresponds to that given at 203^{b}15 ff.

what is taken does not persist throughout. (*ii*) Magnitude is not infinite either by the reduction process or by the increase in thought. This ends our discussion of the infinite, in what senses it is and is not, and what it is.

BOOK IV

CHAPTER 1

208ª27. A student of nature must have knowledge about *place* too, just as he must about the infinite: whether it is or not, and in what way it is, and what it is. For everyone supposes that things that are
30 are somewhere, because what is not is nowhere—where for instance is a goat-stag or a sphinx? And of change, the most general and basic kind is change in respect of place, which we call locomotion. But there are many difficulties [in asking] what place is: the same conclusion does not seem to result as we consider the matter from all the facts. Moreover, we have inherited no preliminary discussions
35 or stock of good ideas about it from others.

208ᵇ **208ᵇ1.** That place is, seems to be clear from replacement: where there is now water, there air in turn is, when the water goes out as if from a vessel, and at some other time some other body occupies this same place. This then, seems to be something different from all the
5 things that come to be in it, which move about—for water was formerly in that in which air now is—so that it is clear that place, and the space into which and out of which they moved in moving about, must be something other than either.

208ᵇ8. Again, the locomotions of the natural simple bodies (such as
10 fire and earth and the like) not only show that place is something but also that it has some power, since each body, if not impeded, moves to its own place, some above and some below. These are the parts and kinds of place: above, below, and the rest of the six dimensions. These are not just relative to us. Relatively to us, they—
15 above, below, right, left—are not always the same, but come to be in relation to our position, according as we turn ourselves about, which is why, often, right and left are the same, and above and below, and ahead and behind. But in nature each is distinct and separate. 'Above' is not anything you like, but where fire, and what is light,
20 move [to]. Likewise, 'below' is not anything you like, but where

20

heavy and earth-like things move [to]. So they differ not by position
alone but in power too. (Mathematical objects, too, make this clear:
they are not in place, but still have right and left according to their
position relatively to us, with 'right' and 'left' in a sense merely
relative to position, since they do not have either of these by nature.) 25
208^b25. Again, those who assert that there is void say that there is
place; for the void would be place deprived of body.
208^b27. These are the reasons, then, for which one might suppose
that place is something over and above bodies, and that every body
perceptible by sense is in place. Hesiod, too, might seem to be
speaking correctly in making Chaos first; he says   30

> Foremost of all things Chaos came to be
> And then broad-breasted Earth

suggesting that it was necessary that there should first be a space
available to the things that are, because he thinks as most people do
that everything is somewhere and in place. If such a thing is true,
then the power of place will be a remarkable one, and prior to all
things, since that, without which no other thing is, but which itself   35
is without the others, must be first. (For place does not perish when 209^a
the things in it cease to be.)
209^a2. For all that, it is a problem, if place is, *what* it is: whether it
is some kind of bulk of body or some other kind of thing—for we
must first inquire what its genus is. (1) It has three dimensions,
length, breadth, and depth, by which every body is bounded. But it   5
is impossible that place should be a body, for then there would be
two bodies in the same thing. (2) Again, since a body has a place and
a space, it is clear that a surface does too, and the other limits, for
the same argument will apply: where previously the surfaces of the
water were, there there will be in turn those of the air. Yet we have 10
no distinction between a point and the place of a point; so that if
not even a point's place is different [from itself], then neither will
the place of any of the others be, nor will place be something other
than each of these. (3) Besides, whatever *could* one assert place to
be? It is not possible for it, being the sort of thing it is, to be either
an element or composed of elements, whether of corporeal or of   15
incorporeal: it has magnitude, but it has no body; but the elements
of things perceptible by sense are bodies, and from intelligible things

21

no magnitude comes to be. (4) Again, for what [effect] on things
that are could one make place responsible? No one of the four kinds
20 of explanation is present in it: it is not an explanation as material of
things that are, for nothing is composed of it; nor as a form and
definition of things; nor as an end; nor does it change things that are.
(5) Again, if place itself is one of the things that are, it will be somewhere; Zeno's puzzle needs to be given some account of: if everything that is, is in a place, clearly there will be a place of place too,
25 and so *ad infinitum.* (6) Again, just as every body is in a place, so in
every place there is a body; so what shall we say about things that
increase in size? From what has been said, it must be that their place
increases together with them, if each thing's place is neither smaller
nor larger than it. For these reasons, then, it must be doubted not
30 only what it is, but even whether it is.

CHAPTER 2

209ª31. Since some things are said in respect of themselves, some
in respect of another thing, and place may be either (*a*) the
'common' place, in which all bodies are; or (*b*) the special place
which is the first in which a body is (I mean, for example, that you
are now in the heavens because you are in the air and that is in the
heavens, and you are in the air because you are in the earth and
35 similarly in that because you are in this place which surrounds
209ᵇ nothing more than you), then, if place is the first thing surrounding
each body, it will be a kind of limit. So place would appear to be the
form and the shape of each thing, by which the magnitude, and the
matter of the magnitude, are bounded; for that is what the limit of
5 each thing is. If one considers it in this way, then, place is the form
of each thing.
209ᵇ6. But [if one considers it] in the way in which place is thought
to be the extension of the magnitude, [place is] the matter. For this
[extension of the magnitude] is different from the magnitude;
this is that which is surrounded and bounded by the form, as by a
surface and a limit; and it is this kind of thing that matter and the
10 indefinite are. For when the limit and the properties of the sphere

are removed, nothing is left but the matter. That is why Plato, too, says in the *Timaeus* that matter and space are the same thing (for 'the participative' and space are one and the same thing. Though he gave a different use to 'the participative' in what are called his 'unwritten doctrines' from that in the *Timaeus*, he still declared that place and space were the same thing. While everyone says that place is something, he alone tried to say *what* it is.)

209ᵇ17. It is reasonable that when we consider the question on this basis it should appear difficult to recognize what place is, if it is one or other of these two, whether the matter or the form. For not only does the question require, in any case, the keenest examination, but it is not easy to recognize [matter and form] in separation from one another. And yet it is not difficult to see that it is impossible that place can be either of the two. (1) The form and the matter are not separated from the object, but the place may be: in that in which air was, water in turn comes to be, as we said, when the water and the air replace one another, and likewise when other bodies do, so that the place of anything is not a portion or a state of it but is separable from it. And in fact place is thought to be some such thing as a vessel (for the vessel is a moveable place), and a vessel is not anything pertaining to the object [contained]. Hence, inasmuch as it is separable from the object, place is not the form; and (2) inasmuch as it surrounds, it is different from the matter. That which is somewhere is always thought both itself to be something and to have some other thing outside it. (3) (If a parenthetic remark may be allowed, we should ask Plato why the Forms and numbers are not in place, if place is 'the participative', whether 'the participative' is the great and the small or whether it is matter, as he writes in the 210ᵃ *Timaeus*.) (4) Again, how could a thing move to its own place, if the place is the matter or the form? It is impossible that that of which there is no change and no above and below should be place. So place must be looked for among the things of this kind. And (5) if place is in the object (it must be, if it is either form or matter) place will be in place. (For both the form and the indefinite move about and change together with the object, not always in the same [spot], but just where the object itself is.) So there will be a place of the place. (6) Again, when water comes to be from air, the place has perished, 10

23

for the body that comes to be is not in the same place. What then is the ceasing-to-be [of place]? These then are the arguments that show that place must be something and then again that give cause for doubt about what it really is.

CHAPTER 3

210ᵃ14. Next we must find in how many ways one thing is said to
15 be *in* another. (1) In one way, as the finger is in the hand, and, generally, the part in the whole. (2) In another, as the whole is in the parts—the whole does not exist apart from the parts. (3) In another, as man is in animal and, generally, form in genus. (4) In another, as the genus is in the form, and, generally, the part of the form in the
20 definition. (5) In another, as health is in hot and cold things, and, generally, as the form is in the matter. (6) In another, as the affairs of Greece are in [the hands of] the king [of Persia], and, generally, as [things are] in the first thing productive of change. (7) In another, as [a thing is] in its good, and, generally, in its end, (that is, the that-for-the-sake-of-which). (8) And (the most basic way of all) as [a thing is] in a vessel and, generally, in a place.
25 **210ᵃ25.** It is a problem whether something can be in itself, or nothing can, and everything is either nowhere or in something else. This ['in itself'] is in two ways: either in respect of itself or in respect of something else. For when that which something is and that which is in it are portions of the whole, the whole will be said to be in itself, for ['in'] is said in respect of the parts too; e.g. [a man
30 is] white because the surface is white, and knowledgeable because the reasoning part is so. So the jar will not be in itself, nor the wine; but the jar of wine will be, for that which is in, and that in which it is, are both portions of the same thing. In this way it is possible for something to be in itself, but in the primary way it is not possible. For example, white is in the body, for the surface is in the body, and
210ᵇ knowledge is in the soul. The descriptions are in respect of these things, which, at least when considered as being in the man, are parts. (The jar and the wine are parts, not when separate, but when they are together, and so when they are parts, the thing will be in

itself.) For example, white is in the man because it is in the body, and in that because it is in the surface; but it is in this no longer in 5 respect of anything else. And these things, the surface and the white, are different in form, and each has a different nature and power. So both (a) investigating inductively we do not see anything in itself, on any of the definitions; and (b) it is clear by reasoning that this is impossible. For it would require that either of two things should be 10 present as both—e.g. that the jar should be both the vessel and the wine, and the wine both the wine and the jar—if it is possible for a thing to be in itself. So, however much they may be in one another, the jar will still contain the wine, not *qua* itself being wine but *qua* a jar; and the wine will be in the jar, not *qua* itself being a jar but 15 *qua* wine. So it is clear that in being they are different, since the definition of 'that in which' is different from that of 'that which is in' it. Neither, in fact, is it possible even accidentally. For then two things will be in the same thing at once: the jar will be in itself, if that of which the nature is receptive can be in itself; and so will 20 that of which it is receptive, e.g. the wine, if it is receptive of wine.

210^{b}21. It is clear, then, that it is impossible for something to be in itself in the primary sense. As for Zeno's problem (if place is something, it will be in something), it is not difficult to solve. There is nothing to prevent the primary place's being in another, though not in the way in which the thing is in the primary place, but in the way 25 in which health is in hot things as a state, and the hot is in the body as a property. So it is not necessary to go on *ad infinitum*.

210^{b}27. One thing, though, is manifest: that since the vessel is nothing pertaining to that which is in it (the primary 'what' and 'in which' are different) place will not be either the matter or the form, but something else. For these, both matter and form, are something 30 pertaining to that which is in [the place]. Let this, then, be our treatment of these problems.

CHAPTER 4

210^{b}32. What place is, should become manifest in the following way. Let us assume about it all the things that are thought truly to

belong to it in respect of itself. We require, then, (1) that place
should be the first thing surrounding that of which it is the place;
211ᵃ and (2) not anything pertaining to the object; (3) that the primary
[place] should be neither less nor greater (than the object); (4) that
it should be left behind by each object [when the object moves] and
be separable [from it]; further, (5) that every place should have
'above' and 'below'; and (6) that each body should naturally move
5 to and remain in its proper places, and this it must do either above
or below. It is from these, that we take to be true, that the rest of
the inquiry must proceed. We must try to make inquiry in such a
way that the 'what-is-it' is provided; and so that (*a*) the problems are
solved; (*b*) the things that are thought to be present in place are in
10 fact present; (*c*) finally, the reason for the difficulty and for the
problems about it is manifest; this is the best way of demonstrating
anything.

211ᵃ12. First it should be noticed that place would not be a subject
for inquiry if there were not change in respect of place. This too is
chiefly why we think that the heavens are in place, because they are
always in change. This change divides into (*a*) locomotion,
15 (*b*) increase and decrease; for in increase and decrease too something
moves, and what formerly was there changes position in turn into a
smaller or a larger. What is changed is so in actual operation (*a*) in
itself; or (*b*) accidentally; and what are changed accidentally are
either (*i*) what can in themselves be changed: e.g. the parts of the
20 body and the nail in the boat; or (*ii*) things that cannot be changed
in themselves but are always changed accidentally—e.g. whiteness
and knowledge; these alter their place in the sense that that in which
they are present does so.

211ᵃ23. Now we say we are in the heavens as in a place, because we
25 are in the air and it is in the heavens; and in the air—not the *whole*
air, but it is because of the limit of it that surrounds us that we say
we are in the air (if the *whole* air were our place, a thing would not
in every case be equal to its place, but it *is* thought to be equal; this
kind of place is the primary place in which it is). So (*a*) when that
which surrounds is not divided from, but continuous with, [the thing
30 surrounded], the latter is said to be in the former not as in a place
but as the part is in the whole; but (*b*) when that which surrounds is

divided from and in contact with [the thing surrounded], the latter is in the extreme of the surrounding thing first; and this extreme is neither a part of that which is in it, nor is it greater than the extension [of the thing surrounded] but equal to it, since the extremes of things which are in contact are in the same [spot]. And (*a*) if [the thing surrounded] is continuous it is moved not *in* [the 35 surrounding thing] but with it; (*b*) if it is divided, it is moved *in* the latter—just as much, whether or not the surrounding thing is itself 211^b moved.

211^{b}5. Now it is already manifest from these points what place is. 5 Roughly, there are four things, some one of which place must be: form, or matter, or some extension (that which is between the extremes), or the extremes, if there is no extension apart from the magnitude of the body which comes to be in [the place]. But that it is not possible for it to be three of these, is manifest. 10

211^{b}10. It is because it surrounds that form is thought to be place, for the extremes of what surrounds and of what is surrounded are in the same [spot]. They are both limits, but not of the same thing: the form is a limit of the object, and the place of the surrounding body.

211^{b}14. And because the thing surrounded and divided off often moves about while the surrounding thing remains (e.g. water leaves a 15 vessel), what is in between is thought to be something, on the supposition that there is some extension over and above the body which changes position. (But that is not so: what happens is that whatever body it may chance to be, of those that change position and are such as to be in contact, comes in). If there were some extension which was what was naturally [there] and static, then 20 there would be infinitely many places in the same spot. For, when the water and the air change position, all the parts will do the same thing in the whole as all the water does in the vessel, and at the same time the place will be moving about; so that the place will have another place and there will be many places together. (But the place of the part, in which it moves when the whole vessel changes 25 position, is not different but the same: for the air and the water (or the parts of the water) replace each other in the place in which they are, not in the place which they are coming to be in; *that* [latter]

place is a part of the place which is the place of the whole world.)
211ᵇ29. Matter, too, might be thought to be place, if one considered
30 the case of something at rest and not separated but continuous. For
just as, if it changes qualitatively, there is something which now is
white but once was black, and now is hard but once was soft (this is
why we say there is matter), so too place is thought to be because of
this kind of phenomenon, except that *that* [(matter's being thought
35 to be)] is because what was air is now water, while place [is thought
to be] because where there was air, there now is water. But, as was
212ᵃ said earlier, matter is neither separable from the object, nor does it
surround it, while place has both properties.

212ᵃ2. If, then, place is none of the three, neither the form nor the
matter nor some extension which is always present and different
from the extension of the object that changes position, it must be
5 that place is the remaining one of the four, the limit of the surrounding body, at which it is in contact with that which is surrounded.
(By 'that which is surrounded' I mean that *body*, that which is
changeable by locomotion.) Place is thought to be something
profound and difficult to grasp, both because the matter and the
form, in addition, appear involved in it, and because of the fact
10 that change of position of a moving body occurs within a surrounding body which is at rest; for [from this] it appears to be possible
that there is an extension in between which is something other than
the magnitudes which move. Air, too, helps to some extent [to give
this impression] by appearing to be incorporeal; place seems to be
not only the limits of the vessel but also that which is in between,
which is considered as being void.

212ᵃ14. Just as the vessel is a place which can be carried around, so
15 place is a vessel which cannot be moved around. So when something
moves inside something which is moving and the thing inside moves
about (e.g. a boat in a river), the surrounding thing functions for it
as a vessel rather than as a place; place is meant to be unchangeable,
so that it is the whole river, rather, that is the place, because as a
20 whole it is unchangeable. (So that is what place is: the first unchangeable limit of that which surrounds.)

212ᵃ21. And it is for this reason that the centre of the world and
the extreme limit (with respect to us) of the circular motion [of the

heavens] are thought by everyone to be 'above' and 'below' in the primary way more than anything else, because one of them is always at rest, and the limit of the circular motion remains in the same state. So since the light is that which naturally moves upwards, and the heavy that which naturally moves downwards, the surround- 25 ing limit which is towards the middle is below, and so is the middle itself, and the limit which is towards the extreme is above, and so is the extreme itself. And it is for this reason that place is thought to be some surface and like a vessel and surrounder. Moreover, place is together with the object, because the limits are together with what is 30 limited.

CHAPTER 5

212^{a}31. Hence, a body is in place if, and only if, there is a body outside it which surrounds it. So, even if such a thing [(a body with no surrounding body outside)] were to come to be water, its parts will be moved, since they are surrounded by one another, but the whole will in a sense move and in a sense not. For considered as a whole, it does not alter its place all together, but it moves in a circle. 35 *That* is the place of the parts. ([Of the parts] some move upward, 212^b and [some] downward, (but not in a circle), and others (all those that admit of condensation and rarefaction) move both upward and downward.) As was said, some things are potentially in place, others in actual operation. Thus, when a thing with like parts is continuous, the parts are potentially in place, but when they are separate but in 5 contact, as in a heap, they are actually so. Again, some things are [in place] in respect of themselves: for example, every body which is changeable in respect of locomotion or increase is somewhere in respect of itself (but the heavens, as has been said, are not, as a whole, somewhere or in some place, since no body surrounds them. But on the path they move along, in this way they are a place for 10 their parts—for the parts are in contact one with another). Other things are accidentally [in place]: for example, the soul, and the heavens, since their parts are all in a sense in place, as one thing contains another on the circle. Hence, the upper part moves in a circle, but the whole is not anywhere. What is somewhere is both

15 itself something, and, in addition, there must be something else
    besides that, in which the thing is, and which surrounds. But there is
    nothing besides the universe and the sum of things, nothing which is
    outside the universe; and this is why everything is in the world. (For
    the world is (perhaps) the universe. The place [of changeable body]
    is not the world but a part of the world, which is an extreme and in
20 contact with changeable body. Hence the earth is in the water, the
    water in the air, the air in the ether, and the ether in the world, but
    the world is no longer in anything else.)
    212^b22. It is manifest from these considerations that all the prob-
    lems, too, will be solved by this account of place. It is not necessary
    either (*i*) that the place should increase together with the object, or
    (*ii*) that there should be a place of a point, or (*iii*) that two bodies
25 should be in the same place, or (*iv*) that there should be a corporeal
    extension (what is in between a place is whatever body it may be,
    not the extension of a body). And (*v*) place will even be somewhere,
    though not in the sense of 'in a place', but as the limit is in what is
    limited. For not everything that is, is in a place, but [only] change-
    able body.
    212^b29. What is more, each thing moves to its own place, and this
30 is reasonable; for what is next to something and in contact (not
    forced) with it, is of the same kind—if they are fused, they are not
    capable of being acted on, but if in contact, they are reciprocally
    active and passive. Again, everything remains naturally in its proper
    place, and this is not unreasonable; for so does the part, and what is
35 in place is like a detached part in relation to the whole—as when one
213^a produces change in a portion of water or of air. (And it is in this way
    that air is related to water: it [(water)] is as it were the matter, and
    the other is the form, the water being the matter of the air, and the
    air as it were some operation of the other. For water is potentially
    air, but air is potentially water in another way. These questions must
5   be determined later; while it is necessary because occasion arises to
    say this, what is at present obscurely expressed will then be clearer.
    If, then, the same thing is matter and actuality (water is both, but
    one potentially and one actually), it will be related somehow as a
    part to the whole—which is why these things have contact, and
10 fusion when they both become actually one.) Such is our account of
    place, that it is, and what it is.

CHAPTER 6

213^{a}12. We must likewise suppose that it is the business of a student of nature to consider concerning the void as well, whether it is or not, in what sense it is, and what it is, just as in the case of place. The void, in fact, because of what people assume, attracts roughly the same kinds of disbelief and of belief [as place does]. For 15 those who say there is void suppose it to be a kind of place and a vessel; it is thought to be a plenum when it contains the extended body it is capable of receiving, and void when deprived [of that body], the supposition being that void and plenum and place are the same thing, though their being is not the same. We must begin the inquiry by grasping (*a*) what is said by those who assert that it is; 20 (*b*) what is said by those who deny that it is; and (*c*) the common opinions on these matters.

213^{a}22. Those, then, who try to show that there is no void in fact refute, not what people mean by void, but what they mistakenly call void; as Anaxagoras does, and those who try to refute it in that way. 25 They prove, in fact, that air is something, by twisting wineskins and showing how strong the air is, and by trapping it in pipettes. But people mean by 'void' an extension in which there is no body perceptible by sense. However, because they think that all that is is body, they say that that in which there is nothing at all is void, so 30 what is full of air is void. But it is not *this* (that air is something) that needs to be shown, but that there is no extension, whether separable or in actual operation, distinct from bodies, which (*a*) separates the sum of body so that it is not continuous—as Democritus and Leucippus and many others of the natural philos- 213^b ophers say—or possibly (*b*) is outside the sum of body, the latter being continuous.

213^{b}2. These people, then, do not attack the question head-on; those who assert that there is void more nearly do so. (1) They say, first, that there would be no change in respect of place (that is, locomotion and increase), if there were no void. For what is a 5 plenum cannot receive anything [into itself]; if it were to do so, and there were two things in the same [spot], it would be possible for any number whatever of bodies to be together, since one cannot

say what is the difference which would explain why the thing stated could not be. But if *this* is possible, then the smallest thing will
10 receive the largest thing [into itself], since the large is many smalls; so that, if it is possible that many equal things should be in the same spot, it is possible also that many unequal things should be. (Melissus even uses this argument to show that the sum of things is unchangeable: if it is to change, he says, there must be void, but void is not one of the things that are). One way, then, in which they try to
15 show that there is a void is by these points. (2) Another is from the fact that some things manifestly contract and are compressed (for example, they even say that wine-jars will contain the wine *and* the wineskins), because (as they think) the body that is condensed contracts into the voids within [itself]. (3) Again, everyone thinks that increase of size occurs through the void; for the nourishment
20 is body, and there cannot be two bodies together. (4) They also invoke as evidence the business of the ashes which admit as much water as the empty vessel does. (The Pythagoreans, too, said that there was void, and that it was imported into the world, which they thought of as breathing in the void, which distinguishes things, from
25 the unbounded breath, void being thought to be a kind of separation and distinguishing of things which are adjacent; they said it was what was primary in numbers, for the void distinguished their nature.) The arguments, then, for and against there being a void are roughly such and so many.

CHAPTER 7

30 **213**^b**30.** To deal with the question of which of these alternatives is right, we must grasp the meaning of the word. Now the void is thought to be place in which there is nothing. (The reason for this is that people think that what is, is body , and that every body is in a place, and that void is a place in which there is no body; so that, if anywhere there is no body, then there is nothing there. Further,
214^a they think that every body is tangible, and that of such a kind is whatever has heaviness or lightness. Hence it results by syllogism that that is void, in which there is nothing heavy or light.) These consequences then, as we said earlier, follow by syllogism. But it is absurd,

if a point is to be void; for [void] must be [place] in which there is 5
an extension between tangible body. Still, it seems that in one sense
'the void' is used to mean 'that which is not full of body perceptible
by touch', and what is perceptible by touch is whatever has weight
or lightness (so that one might also raise the puzzle: what would
they say if the extension contained a colour or a noise; would it be 10
void, or not? But perhaps it is clear that, if it would admit a tangible
body, it is void, and if not, not). Another sense is 'that in which
there is no 'this' or corporeal substance'. This is why some say that
the void is the matter of body (and they say that place too is this
same thing), but this is a bad account of it, because matter is not
separable from objects, whereas they are inquiring into void as some- 15
thing which is separable.

214^a16. Since an analysis of *place* has been made, and void, if it is,
must be place deprived of body, and it has been stated in what sense
there is and is not place, it is manifest that in this sense there is no
void, whether separated or inseparable. (For void is not meant as
body but as an extension between body, and this is why the void is 20
thought to be something, because place too is, and for the same
reasons.) It is change in respect of place that comes to the aid, both
of those who assert that place is something apart from the bodies
that come to occupy it, and of those who assert the same of void.
They think that the void is responsible for change in the sense of
being that in which change occurs—this would be the sort of thing 25
that some people say place is. But there is no necessity that there
should be void if there is change: (*a*) in general, with regard to all
kinds of change, this is quite false, for the reason (which Melissus
overlooked) that it is possible for a plenum to change qualitatively;
and (*b*) it is not even true for change in respect of place, since it is
possible for things simultaneously to make way for one another,
even though there is no separable extension apart from the moving 30
bodies—this is shown by the rotations of continuous [solid] bodies,
as well as by those of liquids. And it is possible for a thing to be
condensed, not into [internal] void, but through the squeezing out
of what is inside it (e.g. the air inside, when water is compressed), 214^b
and for it to increase in size not only by the entry of something but
also by qualitative change (e.g. when air comes to be from water).

In general, the arguments about increase in size and about the water
5 poured on to ashes are self-obstructing. For either (*a*) nothing whatever increases in size; or (*b*) it does not increase by [the addition of]
body; or (*c*) it is possible for two bodies to be in the same spot; or
(*d*) it is necessary for the *whole* body to be void, if it increases at
every point and increases through the void. (So they are requiring us
to resolve a difficulty shared by both sides, not demonstrating that
10 there is void.) The same argument applies to the ashes as well. It is
manifest, then, that it is easy to dissolve the arguments by which
they seek to show that there is void.

CHAPTER 8

214^b12. Let us go back to saying that there is no such separated
void as some people maintain. (1) If each of the simple bodies has by
nature a certain motion (e.g. fire upwards, earth downwards and
15 towards the centre), it is clear that the void cannot be responsible for
the motion. For what then *will* the void be responsible? It is thought
to be responsible for change in respect of place, but for this it is not.
(2) Again, if when it is void, it is something like place deprived of
body, where will a body, placed in this, move to? It cannot be that it
20 moves into the whole [of the void]. The same argument applies to
those who think that place is something separate into which a body
moves: how will a body placed in it move? (Or will it stay at rest?)
The same argument fits both in the case of upward and downward
and in that of the void, with good reason; for those who assert that
there is void make it place. (3) And in what way will [a body] be *in*
25 either place or the void? It does not work out, when some body is
placed as a whole in a separate place, which persists; for the part, if
not placed separately, will not be in place but in the whole.
(4) Again, if place is not [separated], then neither will void be.
214^b28. Though some say that there is void because it is necessary
if there is to be change, in fact, if one considers carefully, it is rather
30 the opposite that results: that if there is void it is not possible for
anything to move. (1) Just as some say that the earth is at rest
because of symmetry, so in the void too [a body] must be at rest,

there being nowhere for it to move to more or less [than anywhere else], since the void, as such, admits no differences. (2) Again, every change is either forced or natural, and if there is forced change there   215^a must also be natural, since forced change is change contrary to nature, and change contrary to nature is secondary to change according to nature. Hence, unless each of the natural bodies has a 5 natural change, they will not have any of the other changes either. But how can there be a natural [change], if there is no differentiation throughout the void and the infinite? In as much as it is infinite, there will be no above or below or centre; in as much as it is void, the above will be no different from the below, for just as there is no differentiation of what is nothing, so neither is there of void, since 10 void is thought to be something that is not, and privation. But the natural motion *is* different [for different things] so that [above and below] will be naturally different. Either, then, there is no natural motion anywhere for anything, or, if there is, there is no void. (3) Again, in actual fact things that are thrown move when that which propelled them is not in contact with them—whether this is through 'cyclical replacement', as some say, or because the air 15 displaced propels with a motion quicker than the motion of the thing propelled by which it moves to its proper place. In the void none of this is available, and it will be impossible to move except as that which is carried moves. (4) Again, no one could say why something moved will come to rest somewhere; why should it do so here rather than there? Hence it will either remain at rest or must move 20 on to infinity unless something stronger hinders it. (5) Again, as things are it is thought a body moves into a void because the void yields to it; but in the void this property is everywhere alike, so that it will move in every way.

215^a24. What is being said is manifest from the following also. (1) We see that the same weight and body moves faster for two 25 reasons: either (*a*) because the medium through which it moves is different (e.g. through water or earth, or through water or air), or (*b*) because the moving thing, other things being the same, is different in respect of excess of weight or lightness. (2) Now the medium through which it moves is responsible because it resists the thing, especially when it itself is moving in the opposite direction, but even 30

when it is stationary. What is not easily divisible resists more, i.e.
what is of thicker texture. So [body] A will move through [medium]
215^b B in time C, and through D, which is of finer texture, in time E, in
proportion to the resisting body, (assuming that the length of B is
equal to that of D). For example, let B be water and D be air. A will
move faster through D than through B by the amount by which air is
5 of finer texture and less corporeal than water. So let the speeds have
the same proportion one to another as that in which air differs from
water, so that, if air is twice as fine in texture, it will traverse B in
twice as much time as it takes to traverse D, and the time C will be
double the time E. And so it will always be that the body will move
10 faster by the amount by which the medium through which it moves
is less corporeal and less resistant and more easily divisible. (3) But
the void has no proportion in which it is exceeded by body, any
more than nothing has to number. (For while four exceeds three by
one, and two by more than one, and one by even more than that by
15 which it exceeds two, yet with nothing there is no longer any proportion by which four exceeds it, since that which exceeds must be
divided into the excess and that which is exceeded, so that four will
be the amount of the excess plus nothing.) For this reason, too, it is
that a line does not exceed a point, unless the line is composed of
points. In the same way, the void cannot bear any proportion to
20 what is a plenum. (4) So neither can the change, and if a thing moves
a given length through the finest medium in such-and-such a time,
then through the void it exceeds all proportion. Thus, let F be
a void, equal to B and to D. If then A traverses it and moves
25 during a certain time, G, less than E, that proportion of G to
E] will the void bear to the plenum. (But in a time equal in length
to G, A will traverse an amount H of D.) And yet, if F is something
superior to air in fineness of texture in the same proportion as time
30 E has to time G, [body A] will also traverse [F in the same time];
for if body F is finer in texture than D by the amount by which E
exceeds G, the body A, if it moves, will traverse F, with a speed
216^a which is inversely proportionate, in the same amount of time as G.
If, then, there is no body in F, it will traverse it even faster. But it
was assumed to do so in G. Hence it will traverse F in an equal time
if it is a plenum, as it will if it is a void. But this is impossible. So it

is manifest that, if there is a time in which it moves through any
amount whatever of the void, then this impossible consequence will 5
result; it will be found to traverse in an equal time a plenum and a
void, since there will be some body which bears to another the same
proportion as time does to time. To speak in a summary way, the
reason for this result is clear. Every change bears a proportion to a
change, since it is in time, and every time bears a proportion to a 10
time, both being finite; but there is no proportion that the void
bears to a plenum. These then are the consequences in respect of the
differences of media. (5) In respect of the excess of the moving
bodies, they are as follows. We see that the things which have a
greater preponderance of weight or of lightness, other things being
equal, move through equal distances faster, following the proportion 15
which the magnitudes bear to one another. So they do so through
the void as well. But this is impossible: for what reason could there
be for its moving faster? In plena, of course, this occurs of necessity,
for what is greater divides [the medium] more quickly by its
strength—the moving or projected body divides it either by means of
its shape, or by the preponderance which it has. So all bodies will
move with equal speed; but this is impossible. It is manifest, then, 20
from what has been said that, if there is void, the result is the
opposite of the reason for which a void is manufactured by those
who assert that there is a void.

216ª23. Some people, then, think that if there is to be change in
respect of place, there is a void which is in itself distinct. This is the
same thing as to say that place is something separated, and that this 25
is impossible has been said before. But even if we consider it in itself,
that which is called void will appear void indeed. Just as, if one
places a cube in water, water equal in amount to the cube will be
displaced, so it is with air too, though this is not obvious to sense-
perception, and so too it must always be with every body that
admits of change of position: that if it is not compressed it changes 30
position, to the extent that its nature allows, (either always downwards, if its motion, like that of earth, is downwards, or upwards, if
it is fire, or either way), of whatever kind the inserted object may
be. But in the void this is impossible, for it is not any body, and [it
must be that] the extension equal [to the cube], which was there 35

37

216^b previously in the void, has permeated the cube, just as if the water or
the air were not to be made to change position by the wooden cube,
but were to permeate it at every point. And yet the cube, too, has a
magnitude equal in amount to the void it occupies, and even if this—
I mean the extended body of the wooden cube—is hot or cold or
5 heavy or light, yet none the less it is different in being from all the
qualities even if not separable [from them]. Hence (even if it were
separated from all the other things and were neither heavy nor light),
it will occupy an equal amount of void and will be in the same spot
as the part of place and the part of void equal to itself. How then
10 will the body of the cube differ from the equal amount of void and
place? And if there are two such things, why should there not be any
number of things in the same spot? This then is one absurd and
impossible consequence. Again, it is manifest that the cube when it
changes position will still have this [volume], which all other bodies
have. So if it is in no way different from place, what need is there to
construct a place for bodies other than the volume of each one, if
15 the volume is impassive? No contribution is made by any *other* equal
extension of this kind there may be apart from it. It is clear, then,
20 from these arguments that there is no separate void.

CHAPTER 9

216^b22. There are some who think that from the rare and the dense
it is manifest that there is void. If there is no rare and dense, then it
is impossible to contract and be compressed; but if that is impossible,
25 either there will be no change at all, or the universe will bulge (as
Xuthus said), or there must always be alteration into an equal
amount (I mean, for example, that if from a pint of water air comes
to be, then simultaneously there comes to be that amount of water
from an equal amount of air); or there is (they say) of necessity
void, because otherwise it is not possible for things to be compressed
and expanded.
30 216^b30. Now if they say that 'rare' is 'that which has many separate
voids', it is manifest that if it is not possible for there to be a
separable void, any more than it is possible for there to be a place

having an extension within itself, then neither can there be what is
rare in this sense. But if [they say that] there is still some void,
though not separable, within it, this is less impossible, but the consequences are (1) that the void is responsible not for every movement, but for movement upwards (what is rare is light, which is why 35
they say fire is rare); (2) that the void will be responsible for move- 217^a
ment not in the sense in which the medium is, but, just as wineskins,
by moving upwards themselves, carry with them what is continuous
with them, so void carries things upwards. Yet how can there be a
motion of void or a place for void? That into which void moves
comes to be void of void. Again, in the case of what is heavy, how 5
will they account for its moving downwards? It is clear, too, that if
it is to be carried upwards [the more] by the amount by which it is
rarer and more void, it would move fastest if it were completely
void. But perhaps even this [supposed void] cannot move; the argument to show that the void is immobile is the same as that to show
that in the void all things are immobile: the speeds are not com- 10
parable.

217^{a}10.* [[Since, though we deny that there is void, the rest of the
problem is rightly stated—that either there will be no change, if there
is no condensation and rarefaction, or the world will bulge, or it will
always be that equal amounts of water come from air and of air
from water (it is clear that a greater amount of air comes to be from
water)—it must be, then, if there is no compression, either that 15
[each] neighbouring thing [in turn] is pushed out, and makes the
extreme limit bulge, or that somewhere else an equal amount of
water alters from air, so that the whole volume of the universe may
be the same, or that nothing changes, since whenever there is change
of position this happens (unless there is a change of position round a
circle; but locomotion is not always in a circle, but also in a straight
line).]]

217^{a}20. Some, then, would say for these reasons that there is void, 20
but we assert, on the basis of what we take as true, that the matter
of opposites (hot and cold and the other natural oppositions) is one,

_____

* There is reason to think that most of this paragraph is a later intrusion—
see notes.

and, from that which is potentially, that which is in actual operation
comes to be; and the matter is not separable, but its being is
25 different; and it is one in number—the matter, it may be, of a colour
and of hot and cold. Further, the matter of a body is the same when
it is large and when it is small. This is clear, for when air comes to be
from water, the same matter without acquiring anything in addition
becomes another thing: what it was potentially it becomes actually,
and so again with water coming to be from air; [the change is] now
30 from smallness to largeness, now from largeness to smallness. So
too then, when the air being of a large quantity comes to be in a
smaller volume, or when it becomes larger from a smaller one, the
matter, which potentially is, comes to be each of the two. For, just
as the same matter comes to be hot from cold and cold from hot,
because it was so potentially, so too from hot it comes to be hotter,
217^b though nothing in the matter comes to be hot which was not hot
when [the matter] was less hot—just as, if the circumference and
convexity of a larger circle came to be that of a smaller circle
(whether or not it is the same circumference), the convex has not
come to be in anything which was previously not convex but
5 straight, because the greater or the less is not constituted by there
being gaps. Nor can one find any magnitude of flame in which heat
and whiteness are not present. In this way, then, the former heat
also is, in comparison with the later one. So too the largeness and
smallness of the perceptible volume are extended, not because the
matter acquires anything extra, but because it is potentially the
10 matter of either. So the same thing is dense and rare, and the matter
of them is one.

[15] **217^b11.** The dense is heavy, the rare light; for two things are
associated with either of the dense and the rare: the heavy and the
hard are thought to be dense, and the opposites, the light and the
soft, to be rare. (But the heavy and the rare do not go together in
the cases of lead and iron.)

20 **217^b20.** From what has been said, then, it is manifest that there is
neither a distinct void, whether without qualification or in the rare,
nor potentially a void, unless one insists on calling 'void' that which
is responsible for motion. In this sense, the matter of the heavy and
the light, *qua* such, would be the void: for the dense and the rare are

productive of motion, in respect of this opposition, and in respect of
the hard and soft they are productive of being acted upon and not 25
being acted upon, and so not of motion but rather of qualitative
change. Let this then be our determination about void and of the
ways in which it does and does not exist.

CHAPTER 10

217^b29. After what has been said, the next thing is to inquire into
time. First, it is well to go through the problems about it, using 30
the untechnical arguments as well [as technical ones]: whether it is
among things that are or things that are not, and then what its
nature is.

217^b32. That it either is not at all or [only] scarcely and dimly is,
might be suspected from the following considerations. (1) Some of it
has been and is not, some of it is to be and is not yet. From these
both infinite time and any arbitrary time are composed. But it 218^a
would seem to be impossible that what is composed of things that
are not should participate in being. (2) Further, it is necessary that,
of everything that is resoluble into parts, if it is, either all the parts
or some of them should be when it is. But of time, while it is
resoluble into parts, some [parts] have been, some are to be, and 5
none is. The now is not a part, for a part measures [the whole], and
the whole must be composed of the parts, but time is not thought to
be composed of nows. (3) Again, it is not easy to see whether the
now, which appears to be the boundary between past and future,
remains always one and the same or is different from time to time. 10
(*a*) If it is always different, and if no two distinct parts of things that
are in time are simultaneous—except those of which one includes the
other, as the greater time includes the smaller—and if the now which
is not but which previously was must have ceased to be at some
time, then the nows too will not be simultaneous, and it must always 15
be the case that the previous now has ceased-to-be. Now, that it has
ceased-to-be in itself is not possible, because then it is; but it cannot
be that the former now has ceased to be in another now, either. For
we take it that it is impossible for the nows to be adjoining one

41

another, as it is for a point to be adjoining a point; so, since the now
has not ceased to be in the next now but in some other one, it will
20 be simultaneously in the nows in between, which are infinitely
many; but this is impossible. (*b*) Yet it is not possible either that the
same now should always persist. For (*i*) nothing that is divisible and
finite has [only] one limit, whether it is continuous in one direction
or in more than one. But the now is a limit, and it is possible to take
25 a finite time. Again (*ii*) if to be together in time and neither before
or after, is to be in the one and the same now, and if both previous
and subsequent [nows] are in this present now, then events of a
thousand years ago will be simultaneous with those of today and
none will be either previous or subsequent to any other.

30 **218ª30.** Let this much, then, be our examination of difficulties
about the properties of time. As to what time is and what its nature
is, this is left equally unclear by the recorded opinions [of earlier
thinkers] and by our own previous discussions. Some say it is the
218ᵇ change of the universe, some the [celestial] sphere itself. Yet of the
[celestial] revolution even a part is a time, though it is not a
revolution. (The part considered is a part of a revolution, but not a
revolution.) Again, if there were more than one world, time would
equally be the change of any one whatever of them, so that there
5 would be many times simultaneously. The sphere of the universe
was thought to be time, by those who said it was, because everything
is both in time and in the sphere of the universe; but this assertion is
too simple-minded for us to consider the impossibilities it contains.
218ᵇ9. Since time is above all thought to be change, and a kind of
10 alteration, this is what must be examined. Now the alteration and
change of anything is only in the thing that is altering, or wherever
the thing that is being changed and altering may chance to be; but
time is equally everywhere and with everything. Again, alteration
may be faster or slower, but not time; what is slow and what is fast
15 is defined by time, fast being that which changes much in a short
[time], slow that which changes little in a long [time]. But time is
not defined by time, whether by its being so much or by its being of
such a kind. It is manifest, then, that time is not change (let it make
20 no difference to us, at present, whether we say 'change' or 'alteration').

CHAPTER 11

218^{b}21. And yet [time is] not apart from alteration, either. When
we ourselves do not alter in our mind or do not notice that we alter,
then it does not seem to us that any time has passed, just as it does
not seem so to the fabled sleepers in [the sanctuary of] the heroes in
Sardinia, when they wake up; they join up the latter now to the   25
former, and make it one, omitting what is in between because of
failure to perceive it. So, just as, if the now were not different but
one and the same, there would be no time, in the same way, even
when the now *is* different but is not noticed to be different, what is
in between does not seem to be any time. If, then, when we do not
mark off any alteration, but the soul seems to remain in one   30
indivisible, it happens as a consequence that we do not think there
was any time, and if when we do perceive and mark off [an alter-
ation], then we do say that some time has passed, then it is manifest
that there is no time apart from change and alteration. It is manifest,
then, that time neither is change nor is apart from change, and since   **219^a**
we are looking for what time is we must start from this fact, and
find what aspect of change it is. We perceive change and time
together: even if it is dark and we are not acted upon through the
body, but there is some change in the soul, it immediately seems to   5
us that some time has passed together with the change. Moreover,
whenever some time seems to have passed, some change seems to
have occurred together with it. So that time is either change or some
aspect of change; and since it is not change, it must be some aspect
of change.
219^{a}10. Now since what changes changes from something to some-   10
thing, and every magnitude is continuous, the change follows the
magnitude: it is because the magnitude is continuous that the change
is too. And it is because the change is that the time is. (For the time
always seems to have been of the same amount as the change.)
219^{a}14. Now the before and after is in place primarily; there, it is   15
by convention. But since the before and after is in magnitude, it
must also be in change, by analogy with what there is there. But in
time, too, the before and after is present, because the one always
follows the other of them. The before and after in change is, in   20

respect of what makes it what it is, change; but its being is different
and is not change.

219^a22. But time, too, we become acquainted with when we mark
off change, marking it off by the before and after, and we say that
25 time has passed when we get a perception of the before and after in
change. We mark off change by taking them to be different things,
and some other thing between them; for whenever we conceive of
the limits as other than the middle, and the soul says that the nows
are two, one before and one after, then it is and this it is that we say
time is. (What is marked off by the now is thought to be time: let
30 this be taken as true.) So whenever we perceive the now as one, and
not either as before and after in the change, or as the same but pertaining to something which is before and after, no time seems to
have passed, because no change [seems to have occurred] either. But
whenever [we do perceive] the before and after, then we speak of
time.

219^b **219^b1.** For that is what time is: a number of change in respect of
the before and after. So time is not change but in the way in which
change has a number. An indication: we discern the greater and
5 the less by number, and greater and less change by time; hence time
is a kind of number. But number is [so called] in two ways: we call
number both (*a*) that which is counted and countable, and (*b*) that
by which we count. Time is that which is counted and not that by
which we count. (That by which we count is different from that
which is counted.)

219^b9. Just as the change is always other and other, so the time is
10 too, though the whole time in sum is the same. For the now is the
same X, whatever X it may be which makes it what it is; but its
being is not the same. It is the now that measures time, considered as
before and after. The now is in a way the same, and in a way not
the same: considered as being at different stages, it is different—that
is what it is for it to be a now—but whatever it is that makes it a now
15 is the same. For change follows magnitude, as was said, and time, we
assert, follows change. As it is with the point, then, so it is with the
moving thing, by which we become acquainted with change and the
before and after in it. The moving thing is, in respect of what makes
it what it is, the same (as the point is, so is a stone or something else

of that sort); but in definition it is different, in the way in which
the sophists assume that being Coriscus-in-the-Lyceum is different 20
from being Coriscus-in-the-marketplace. That, then, is different by
being in different places, and the now follows the moving thing as
time does change. For it is by the moving thing that we become
acquainted with the before and after in change, and the before and 25
after, considered as countable, is the now. Here too, then, whatever
it is that makes it the now is the same—it is the before and after in
change. But its being is different: the now is the before and after,
considered as countable. Moreover, it is this that is most familiar;
for the change too is known by that which changes, and the motion
by the moving thing, because the moving thing is a 'this', but the 30
change is not. So the now is in a way the same always, and in a
way not the same, since the moving thing too [is so].

219^b33. It is manifest too that, if time were not, the now would
not be either, and if the now were not, time would not be. For just 220^a
as the moving thing and the motion go together, so too do the number of the moving thing and the number of the motion. Time is the
number of the motion, and the now is, as the moving thing is, like a
unit of number.

220^a4. Moreover, time is both continuous, by virtue of the now,
and divided at the now—this too follows the motion and the moving 5
thing. For the change and the motion too are one by virtue of the
moving thing, because that is one (not [one] X, whatever X it may
be that makes it what it is—for then it might leave a gap—but [one]
in definition). And this bounds the change before and after. This too
in a sense follows the point: the point, too, both makes the length 10
continuous and bounds it, being the beginning of one and the end of
another. But when one takes it in this way, treating the one [point]
as two, one must come to a halt, if the same point is to be both
beginning and end. But the now is always different, because the
moving thing changes. Hence time is a number, not as [a number] of
the same point, in that it is beginning and end, but rather in the way 15
in which the extremes [are the number] of the line—and not as the
parts [of the line] are, both because of what has been said (one will
treat the middle point as two, so that there will be rest as a result),
and further [because] it is manifest that the now is no portion of

45

time, nor [is] the division [a portion] of the change, any more than
20 the point is of the line (it is the two lines that are portions of the
one). So, considered as a limit, the now is not time but is accidentally
so, while, considered as counting, it is a number. (For limits are of
that alone of which they are limits, but the number of these horses,
the ten, is elsewhere too.)

220^a24. It is manifest then that time is a number of change in
25 respect of the before and after, and is continuous, for it is [a num-
ber] of what is continuous.

CHAPTER 12

220^a27. The least number, without qualification, is the two; but
[a least] particular number there in a way is and in a way is not, e.g.
of a line, the number least in multiplicity is two lines or one line, but
30 in magnitude there is no least number, for every line always gets
divided. So it is, then, with time too: the least time in respect of
number is one time or two times, but in respect of magnitude there
is none.

220^a32. It is manifest too that it is not said to be fast or slow, but
220^b is said to be much and little, and long and short. It is as being continuous that it is long and short, and as a number that it is much and
little. But it is not fast or slow—nor indeed is any number by which
we count fast or slow.
5 220^b5. It is the same time, too, everywhere together, but before
and after it is not the same [time], since the present alteration is one,
but the past alteration and the future one are different, and time is
not the number by which we count but the number which is
counted, and this number turns out to be always different before
10 and after, because the nows are different. (The number of a hundred
horses and that of a hundred men is one and the same, but the things
of which it is the number are different—the horses are different from
the men.) Again, in the sense in which it is possible for one and the
same change to occur again and again, so too with time: e.g. a year,
or spring or autumn.
15 220^b14. Not only do we measure change by time, but time by

change also, because they are defined by one another. The time defines the change, being its number, and the change the time. We speak of 'much time' and 'little time', measuring it by change, just as we measure the number by what is countable: e.g. by the one horse we measure the number of the horses, for it is by number that 20 we become acquainted with the multiplicity of the horses and, conversely, by the one horse that we become acquainted with the number of horses itself. Similarly, in the case of time and change, we measure the change by the time and the time by the change. It is reasonable that this should turn out so, because change follows 25 magnitude, and time follows change, in being a quantity and continuous and divisible: for it is because the magnitude is of this kind that the change has these properties and because change is that time does. And we measure both magnitude by change and change by magnitude: we say the road is long, if the journey is long, and we 30 say the journey is long, if the road is; and the time, if the change is, and the change, if the time is.

220^{b}32. Since time is a measure of change and of being-in-change, and since it measures change by defining some change which will 221^a measure out the whole change (just as the cubit measures length by defining some magnitude which will measure off the whole magnitude), and since for a change the being in time is the being measured by time both of the change itself and of its being (time measures at 5 once the change and the being of the change, and this is what it is, for the change, to be in time, viz. its being's being measured), it is clear, then, that for other things too this is what it is to be in time: their being's being measured by time. For to be in time is one or other of two things: *either*, to be when time is; *or*, [to be in it] in 10 the way in which we say that some things are 'in number', which means that [something is in number] *either* as a part or property of number, and, in general, that it is some aspect of number, *or* that there is a number of it. And since time is a number, the now and the before and everything of that kind are in time in the way in which the limit and the odd and the even are in number (they are aspects 15 of number as the others are of time). But objects are [in time] as they are in number. If so, they are surrounded by time just as the things in number are by number and the things in place by place.

It is manifest, too, that to be in time is not to be when time is, any
20 more than to be in change or in place is to be when change is or
place is. If this is what 'in something' is to mean, then all objects will
be in anything whatever, and the world will be in the grain of millet,
since when the grain is, the whole is too. This is accidentally so, but
the other is a necessary consequence: for what is in time there must
25 be some time when that too is, and for what is in change there must
then be change.

221ᵃ26. Since what is in time is so as in a number, there will be
found a time greater than anything that is in time, so that of
necessity all things that are in time are surrounded by time, just like
all other things that are in something: e.g. the things that are in place
30 [are surrounded] by place. Moreover, they are acted upon in some
respect by time, just as we are in the habit of saying 'time wears
things away' and 'everything grows old through time' and 'forgets
because of time'—but not 'learns because of time' or 'becomes
221ᵇ young' or 'becomes beautiful'. For time, in itself, is responsible for
ceasing-to-be rather [than for coming-to-be]; for it is the number of
change, and change removes what is present. So it is manifest that
the things that always are, considered as such, are not in time, for
5 they are not surrounded by time, nor is their being measured by
time, and an indication of this is that they are not acted on at all by
time either, which shows that they are not in time.

221ᵇ7. And since time is the measure of change, it will be the
measure of rest also. For all rest is in time; it is not the case that, as
10 what is in change must change, so what is in time must, since time is
not change but the number of change, and in the number of change
there can also be that which is at rest. For it is not everything that is
unchanging that is at rest, but that which, while deprived of change,
has it in its nature to change, as was said earlier. For a thing to be in
15 number is for there to be some number of the object, and for its
being to be measured by the number in which it is, and so, if it is in
time, by time. Time will measure what is changing and what is at
rest, the one *qua* changing and the other *qua* at rest; for it will
measure their change and their rest, [measuring] how great each is.
Hence, what is changing is not measurable by time simply inasmuch
20 as it is of some quantity, but inasmuch as its change is of some

quantity. And so all that neither changes nor is at rest is not in time; for to be in time is to be measured by time, and time is a measure of change and rest.

221^{b}23. It is manifest, therefore, that not everything that is not will be in time either; for example, all the things that cannot be otherwise [than not being], like the diagonal's being commensurate with 25 the side. For in general, if time is a measure in itself of change and of other things accidentally, it is clear that all things of which it measures the being must have their being in being at rest or changing. Now all things that admit of ceasing-to-be and coming-to-be and, generally, that at some time are and at some time are not, must be in time—there will be some greater time which will exceed both their 30 being and that [time] which measures their being. But, of things that are not, all that time surrounds either were (e.g. Homer once was) or will be (e.g. something future), on whichever side [of the present] 222^a it may surround them; and if on both sides, both. But all the things that it nowhere surrounds neither were nor are nor will be; and, among things that are not, such are all those that are such that their contraries always are: e.g. the diagonal's being incommensurable 5 always is, and this will not be in time. So its being commensurable will not be [in time] either; so *that* always is not being opposite to what always is. But everything of which the opposite not always is, is capable of being and of not being, and there is coming-to-be of it and ceasing-to-be.

CHAPTER 13

222^{a}10. The now is a link of time, as has been said, for it links 10 together past and future time, and is a limit of time, since it is a beginning of one and an end of another. But this is not manifest, as it is in the case of the point at rest. It divides potentially, and *qua* such, the now is always different, but *qua* binding together it is always the same, just as in the case of mathematical lines: [a point is] not 15 always the same point in thought, for if one divides the line it is different in different cases, but inasmuch as [the line] is one, [the point] is the same everywhere. So too the now is on the one hand a division of time, in potentiality, on the other hand the limit and

union of both [times]; the division and the unification are the same
thing and in respect of the same thing, but their being is not the
20 same. This then is one sense of 'now'; another is when the time of a
thing is close at hand: 'he will come now' because he will come
today, 'he has now come', because he came today. But it is not the
case that the Trojan war has *now* occurred, or the deluge: the time
is continuous [from now] to then, but they are not close at hand.
222^a24. The 'at some time' is a time defined in relation to the now
25 (in the former sense): e.g. 'Troy fell at some time', 'the deluge will
occur at some time'—the time must be finite in relation to the now.
Therefore there will be a certain quantity of time from this to that,
and there was [from this] to the past one. If there is no time which
is not 'at some time', every time will be finite. Will time then give
30 out? Or not, if there always is change? Will it then be different, or
the same many times over? It is clear that, as change is, so will time
too be; if one and the same change comes to be at some time, the
time too will be one and the same, and if not, not. Since the now is
222^b an end and a beginning of time, but not of the same time, being the
end of past time and the beginning of future time, time will be like
the circle—the convex and the concave are in what is in a sense the
same—so too time is always at a beginning and at an end. And for
5 this reason it is thought always different, for the now is not the
beginning and the end of the same thing; otherwise opposites would
hold simultaneously and in respect of the same thing. And so time
will not give out, for it is always at a beginning.
222^b7. The *just* is that which is close to the present indivisible
now, whether it is a part of future time ('when are you taking a
walk?' 'I'm just taking it'—because the time in which he is going to
10 go is near) or of past time, when it is not far from the now ('when
are you taking a walk?' 'I've just taken it'). But to say that Troy has
just fallen—we do not say it, because that is too far from the now.
The *recently* is the portion of the past which is close to the present
now. ('When did you come?' 'Recently', if the time is close to the
actual now.) What is far away [from the now] is *long ago*. The
15 *suddenly* is that which removes out of its previous state in a time
which is so small as to be imperceptible.
222^b16. It is in time that everything comes to be and ceases to be.

For this reason some called it the wisest of things, but the
Pythagorean Paron the most foolish, because people forget in time
too; and he was more correct. It is clear, then, that it is, in itself,
responsible for ceasing-to-be rather than for coming-to-be, as was 20
stated earlier, because alteration, in itself, is productive of removal
from a previous state—but it is, accidentally, responsible for coming-
to-be and for being. A sufficient indication is that nothing comes to
be without its being changed in some way and being acted upon, but
a thing may cease to be even though it is not changed, and this is
above all what we usually call ceasing-to-be by the agency of time. 25
Yet even this is not produced by time, but it happens that this
alteration too occurs in time.

222^b27. It has now been stated that time is, and what it is, and in
how many ways 'now' is said, and what 'at some time' and 'recently'
and 'just' and 'long ago' and 'suddenly' are.

CHAPTER 14

222^b30. Now that we have determined these matters in this way, it 30
is manifest that every alteration and all that changes is in time.
'Faster' and 'slower' apply to every alteration, since in every case
this is obviously true. (I say that changes faster which is earlier to
alter into a given [state], changing over the same extension and with 223^a
a uniform change (e.g., in the case of locomotion, if both things are
changing along the curve or along the straight line, and in other cases
similarly).) But the before is in time, for we use 'before' and 'after' 5
according to the distance from the now, and the now is the boundary
of the past and the future. So, since the nows are in time, the before
and after will also be in time; for the distance from the now will be
in that in which the now is. ('Before' is applied in opposite ways in
relation to past time and to future time: in the past, we call 'before' 10
what is further from the now, and 'after' what is nearer to it, but in
the future we call 'before' what is nearer and 'after' what is further.)
So, since the before is in time, and the before accompanies every
change, it is manifest that every alteration and every change is in 15
time.

223^a16. It is also worth investigating how time is related to the soul, and for what reason it is that time is thought to be in everything—on earth and in the sea and in the heavens. Is it that it is a property or a state of change, being the number [of it], and all these

20 things are changeable, since they are all in place, and time and change are together both in potentiality and in actual operation? One might find it a difficult question, whether if there were no soul there would be time or not. For if it is impossible that there should be something to do the counting, it is also impossible that anything should be countable, so that it is clear that there would be no number either, for number is either that which has been counted or that

25 which can be. But if there is nothing that has it in its nature to count except soul, and of soul [the part which is] intellect, then it is impossible that there should be time if there is no soul, except that there could be that X which time is, whatever X makes it what it is; as for example if it is possible for there to be change without soul. The before and after are in change, and time is these *qua* countable.

223^a29. One might also find it a difficult question: of what kind of

30 change is time a number? Perhaps of any kind whatever? After all, [things] come to be and cease to be and increase in size and change qualitatively and move in time. So it is a number of each change, in as much as there is change. Hence it is, without qualification, a number of continuous change, not of a particular [kind of] change. But

223^b it is possible that now something else as well has been made to change: so it would be the number of either change. Is there then another time, and will there be two equal times together? Perhaps not, for the time which is equal and together is one and the same (and even those which are not together are the same in kind).

5 Suppose there are some dogs and some horses, seven of each; the number is the same. In the same way, the time is the same of changes that reach a limit together, though one perhaps is fast and one not, one is locomotion and one a qualitative change. Still, the time is the same, if it is equal and together, of both the qualitative

10 change and the locomotion. And this is why, while changes are various and in different places, time is everywhere the same, because the number, too, of things equal and together is one and the same everywhere.

223^{b}12. Since there is locomotion, and, as a kind of locomotion, circular motion, and since each thing is counted by some one thing of the same kind (units by a unit, horses by a horse), and therefore time too by some definite time, and since, as we said, time is 15 measured by change and change by time (that is, the quantity of the change and of the time is measured by the change defined by time)— if, then, that which is first is the measure of all things of the same sort, then uniform circular motion is most of all a measure, because the number of this is most easily known. (There is no uniform 20 qualitative change or uniform increase in size or uniform coming-to-be, but there *is* uniform locomotion.) This is why time is thought to be the motion of the [celestial] sphere, because the other changes are measured by this one, and time by this change. And for this reason too, what is commonly said turns out true: people say that human affairs are a cycle, and so is what happens to the other things 25 that have a natural motion and come to be and cease to be. This is so because all these things are discerned by means of time, and make an end and a beginning as if according to some circular course. Indeed, time itself is thought to be a kind of cycle, and this, in turn, is thought because it is the measure of that kind of motion and is itself 30 measured by that kind. So that to say that those things that come to be are a cycle is to say that there is a kind of cycle of time; and this is so, because it is measured by circular motion. For, over and above the measure, nothing else is apparent which is obviously measured, 224^a but the whole is either one measure or more than one.

224^{a}2. It is correct, too, to say that the number of the sheep and of the dogs is the same, if each number is equal, but that the ten is not the same [ten] nor [are there] ten of the same; just as the equilateral and the scalene are not the same triangles, though they are the same 5 figure, in that both are triangles. For a thing is said to be the same X if it does not differ by the difference of an X, but not [the same X] if it does: e.g. a triangle differs from a triangle by the difference of a triangle, and therefore they are different triangles; but it does not [differ by the difference] of a figure, but the two are in one and the same division. For one kind of figure is a circle, another a triangle, 10 and one kind of triangle is equilateral, another is scalene. So they are the same figure, namely a triangle, but not the same triangle. And so

53

too it is the same number, since the number of them does not differ
by the difference of a number, but not the same ten, since the things
15 it is said of are different: dogs in one case, horses in another.

224ª15. An account, then, has been given both of time itself and of
the connected matters proper to our inquiry.

NOTES

BOOK THREE

CHANGE

CHAPTER 1

200^{b}12. Reasons for the choice of topics discussed in III and IV.

(1) The five topics are (or are thought to be) necessary parts of a complete discussion of the concept of *nature*. Here, as often in introductory discussions, Aristotle uses noteworthy opinions which he does not necessarily share to build up a prima facie case (see Introduction, sec. 1). Only a prima facie case for regarding these topics as conceptually basic to physics is needed to put them on the agenda. The argument is in two stages: first, *change*: the notion of change is presupposed by the definition of *nature* worked out in *Physics* II.1 and here quoted; secondly, *the infinite* and *place* and *void* and *time* are thought to be closely bound up with change.

Change. 'Nature is a principle of change and alteration': *Physics* II.1, 192^{b}20−7. The distinction between 'change' (*kinēsis*) and 'alteration' (*metabolē*) is not very important in III and IV, and Aristotle sometimes uses the terms interchangeably. ('Alteration' is, strictly, the more inclusive term, which includes coming-to-be and ceasing-to-be as well as change (*Physics* V.1).)

'Change is thought to be something continuous': or possibly 'change is thought to be (change) of continua', i.e. whatever changes is continuous. Aristotle held both opinions to be true, and grounded the former in the latter (*Physics* VI.4, 235^{a}13−^{b}5). But it is the former that is the more generally held. The point here made suggests that continuity and continua ought to be discussed along with change and the infinite: as it is, they are treated later (V.3, VI).

The Infinite. 'The infinite is the first thing that presents itself . . .': or possibly 'It is in the continuous that the infinite first presents

itself.' The preferred translation is supported both by word-order
and by the movement of thought, as well as by the appeal to a
definition of 'continuous' as 'divisible *ad infinitum*'. (On the other
translation, Aristotle refers to his doctrine that the infinite 'by
division' is prior to any other kind (207^b1-15); but such a reference
is here out of place).

Place, void, time. Change naturally presupposes time; and locomotion presupposes place and was often held to be impossible
without void (213^b4-14). This is a feeble way of showing that these
topics belong specifically to *physics*.

(2) The five topics are 'common to everything and universal'.
There is a tacit restriction here to the realm of nature, since (*a*) we
need a reason for discussing them here; (*b*) outside the natural world
there are or are thought to be things not subject to change and not
in place or time (e.g. Plato's Forms, or in Aristotle's own view
mathematical truths, 221^b3, and whatever lies outside the heavens,
de Caelo I.9, 279^a11-22), and outside physics there are sciences not
concerned with change and time, e.g. arithmetic.

Within the natural world, in what sense are the five topics
'universal'? Possibly just in the sense that every primary component
of that world, i.e. every physical body, is necessarily subject to
change, in place, in time, and continuous (and therefore infinite in a
sense). For the contrast of 'things that are common' and 'specialities'
cf. *Post. An.* I.10, $76^a37-{}^b11$, which suggests Aristotle's point may
be that the existence of change, the infinite, etc. has to be assumed,
and other facts about them used, in every physical explanation.
Here again, void rides on the back of place: if there is a void, it will
be identical with place or closely bound up with it.

(Different motivations for the physicists' study of the infinite,
place and void are found at the beginnings of the respective discussions of those topics.)

200^b26. Aristotle passes abruptly to the substantive discussion of
change, omitting the usual review of previous opinions (which
appears belatedly and briefly at 201^b16 ff.). The *existence* of change
is taken for granted (cf. *Physics* I.2, 185^a12-4; II.1, 193^a3-9).

This section introduces two stock pieces of Aristotelian
machinery—the 'potentially'–'actually' distinction, and the
categories—and indicates rapidly how they yield an exhaustive
classification of changes. It is also *the* classification, determining the
species of change, and therefore of importance in Aristotle's account
of identity and individuation of changes. A similar, more elaborate
treatment, occurs in *Physics* V.1 and 2; cf. *Gen. et Corr.* I.4.

Aristotle has two theses, propounded here as more or less obvious:

(1) For each category there is a corresponding species of change (or alteration)

(2) Every change (or alteration) corresponds in this way to some one category;

yielding as a conclusion a one-one correspondence of categories with species of change (or alteration). (In what follows 'change' includes alterations.)

(1) *For each category there is a species of change.* On categories in general, see Ackrill (1), Moravcsik, Owen (4), Jones. The following simple-minded account suppresses problems about what category-occupants are. In any sentence of form 'X is F' the term 'F' in some sense stands for a category-occupant. Examples of 'F' corresponding to some of the categories are: (*a*) 'Socrates' to the category of *substance* ('a 'this''), (*b*) 'six feet tall' to the category of *quantity* ('so much'); (*c*) 'dark-skinned' to the category of *qualification* ('of such a kind'); (*d*) 'in Athens' to the category of *place* or *where*. But in most cases when a sentence 'X is F' is sometimes true, a sentence 'X is only potentially F' is also sometimes true, and there occur changes in which X changes from being only potentially F to being actually F (or the reverse). This gives a species of change corresponding to each category.

Qualifications must be made: (*i*) in some cases, as Aristotle notes at ^{b}26, what is F is never not F and so never makes any corresponding change; (*ii*) some categories yield changes which Aristotle takes to be necessarily secondary to and dependent on changes in other categories. It is for this reason that at 200^{b}33–4 change in only four categories is recognized, whereas Aristotle here and in general recognizes more than four categories altogether. The restriction of basic or *per se* change to only four categories is repeated and argued for at *Physics* V.2.

(2) *Every change corresponds to some one category.* Again the general idea is straightforward. In any change there is a unique subject of change, say X; and X changes from being not F to being F. (For this general schematic description of change see *Physics* I.7.) At some time it is true that X is F and for this to be capable of being a truth, 'F' must fall unambiguously into some one category. So any change corresponds, in the way already explained, to some one category.

Some points of detail:

(*a*) 'There is no change apart from actual things (^{b}32–3) . . . nothing *is* apart from the things mentioned' (201^{a}2–3). These remarks are meant to support thesis (2). The denial that there is any 'common item' which falls into no category is the foundation of all else, but the line of thought intended is not clear. 'There is no change apart from actual things (*ta pragmata*)' may be intended as a separate point: in every change there is not merely an X that changes, but an X belonging to the actual world (an anti-Platonist point). 'For whatever alters . . . or of place' (^b33–4) may well be an intrusion; it anticipates the results of *Physics* V.2, and if it is removed the passage runs more easily.

(*b*) At ^b28–32 is a parenthesis dealing with 'the relative', which usually figures as a category in its own right. On it see generally *Categories* 7 and Ackrill (1), 98–103. The point of this parenthesis is obscure, though it anticipates 201^a19 ff. and 202^a15–17.

(*c*) 'Each (occupant of a category) is present in everything in two ways' (201^a3–4), i.e. anything (that can be F at all) can be F either actually or potentially, for any F. There follow examples drawn from different categories. In the category of substance ('this'), the opposition of 'form' and 'privation' is explained by the analysis of *Physics* I.7. When some substance (say, an animal) comes-to-be, the underlying subject must be the matter of which it is made. The end-state, in which the matter has become an animal, is the state of 'form'; the starting-state, in which it is still formless, is the state of 'privation'. In the other categories, what is actually white is potentially black, and vice versa; and so on. It is puzzling that 'light' and 'heavy' should be given as end-states or starting-states for changes of place, unless they are meant as names of regions of the cosmos ('light' = the upper regions, 'heavy' = the lower regions).

201^a9. The definition of change is given in this section and further elucidated in the rest of the chapter (apart from the digression at 201^a19–27).

'The actuality of that which potentially is, *qua* such'. First, how is the *qua*-clause attached? It might conceivably qualify either (*a*) 'is'; or (*b*) 'potentially is'; or (*c*) 'actuality'. But we know that '*qua* such', as the following examples show, is to be expanded to '*qua* potentially being'. Hence possibilities (*a*) and (*b*) give no promise of sense. This conclusion is reinforced by the paraphrase at ^a27–9, where the *qua*-clause is clearly attached to the verb 'is operating', corresponding to 'actuality'. So the *qua*-clause here must be attached and rephrased as follows: 'The actuality-*qua*-potentially-being of that which potentially is'.

Next, what is 'the actuality-*qua*-potentially-being?' The gloss at 201^a27–9 is: 'when, being in actuality, it is operating not *qua* itself but *qua* changeable.' The general purpose of the *qua*-clause is of course to pick out a particular kind of actuality corresponding to a particular kind of potentiality. So we need some kind of actuality corresponding to the potentialities expressed by 'potentially-being' and 'changeable'.

The usual correspondence is as follows: If the potentiality is expressed by 'being potentially F' then the actuality consists in just actually being F. This will work in the case of 'changeable', provided this is read as 'potentially in process of change' and not as 'potentially having changed'. But it will not work in the case of 'potentially being', since this can only plausibly be expanded to 'potentially being F' where 'F' gives the end-state. And the fact that this is the only plausible reading casts doubt on the reading of 'changeable' as 'potentially in process of change', since the version of ^{a}27−9 is clearly meant to be a mere rephrasing. So we must, it seems, understand 'changeable' at ^{a}29, and the corresponding potential words at ^{a}12−15 ('what admits of qualitative change' etc.), on the model of 'potentially having changed'.

It follows that sense can be made of the definition only if a different kind of correspondence between potentialities and actualities is found. In the discussion of soul (*psuchē*) at *de Anima* II.1, Aristotle distinguishes two kinds of actuality corresponding to certain potentialities. 'It (actuality) is spoken of in two ways: (1) in the way in which knowledge (is an actuality); (2) in the way in which the exercise of knowledge is' (412^{a}22−3). This suggests the following scheme. Whenever there is a disposition which may be present in something without being always exercised, we may distinguish (*a*) capacity to acquire the disposition; (*b*) having the disposition; (*c*) exercising the disposition. Of these (*b*) and (*c*) may be called actualities; and a further passage (*de Anima* II.5, 417^{a}21−^{b}2) shows that (*a*) and (*b*) may both be called potentialities. Thus there are conceivably three different kinds of correspondences between potentiality and actuality here, given by the pairings (*a*)−(*b*), (*a*)−(*c*), (*b*)−(*c*).

If there is to be any hope of using these passages to elucidate the definition of change, we must next find something which is a disposition (or something like one) in any case of change. The only way to do this is to take something's admitting of a particular kind of change as a disposition to change in that way, which will be exercised in appropriate circumstances. The exercise of the disposition will then be the changing, not the having changed; and change will then appear, as required, as an actuality, corresponding to the potentiality as (*c*) to (*b*) above.

The only objection to this reading is that the disposition involved is specified by Aristotle in such a way as to obscure the issue. Take the example of a breakable piece of glass. There is no difficulty in understanding 'breakable' as ascribing a disposition to the glass, which it exercises only when it actually breaks. The difficulty lies in the fact that Aristotle's phraseology 'actuality of what potentially is' must in this particular case be filled out as 'actuality of what potentially is *broken*', i.e. Aristotle is (misleadingly) specifying the disposition not as 'potentiality to break' but as 'potentiality to be broken'. But this is perhaps not very serious. And it is not necessary to claim that Aristotle would have been willing to speak of a disposition (*hexis*) in all cases of changeability; only that he would have admitted the situation was analogous to that of having a disposition. The explanation at ^{a}27–9 'when being in actuality it is operating . . . *qua* changeable' supports the interpretation in terms of dispositions, since 'operate' (*energein*) is the standard verb to indicate the exercise of a disposition. See, on 'passive' dispositions in Aristotle, Kosman, with whose account of the definition the above interpretation largely coincides.

A different interpretation has sometimes been given, according to which 'actuality' is to be understood as 'process of actualization'. Such a sense of *entelecheia* is, however, unparalleled in Aristotle. On this reading the definition would therefore not only use the technical term in an otherwise unknown sense but would fail to link change in any clear way to the rest of Aristotle's metaphysical scheme. On the definition considered from a wider viewpoint see Introduction, 2(*b*).

A question raised by the ancient commentators is whether in Aristotle's opinion 'change' is a homonymous word, i.e. has a different meaning according to the type of change involved. If it is, it follows that the definition of change is really a definition-schema, to be filled out differently for each type of change.

201^{a}19. Aristotle remarks in parenthesis that many powers are two-faced, combining a disposition to act on other things with a disposition to be acted upon. The subject recurs at 202^{a}3 ff.; see notes on that section. The present section is brief and elliptical, with the sequence of thought apparently as follows:

(1) 'Some things are the same things both potentially and actually': what follows shows that this means that, for some F, there are things that oscillate between being F and being not F but potentially F (with possible intermediate states of being F in one part and not in another).

(2) It follows that any things of this kind will be at once active and passive, since in many cases being F brings with it both a disposition to be changed to being not F and a disposition to act on other things so as to make them F.

(3) It then follows further that many cases of reciprocal action will occur between pairs of bodies in contact. When, for example, a hot body (X) comes into contact with a cold body (Y), there

will be reciprocal action involving both the active and passive potentialities of each: X will warm Y, and Y at the same time will cool X.

(4) At ^{b}23, 'So too then . . .', Aristotle moves to a different point: whatever is producing change naturally is necessarily itself undergoing change at the same time (though the action is not necessarily reciprocal here). It is left unclear here (*a*) what it is to produce change 'naturally', (*b*) how the thesis is to be established. For an elaborate argument to show that, apart from the one prime mover, all agents producing change are themselves under-going it, see *Physics* VIII.4–6 (a primitive version in *Physics* VII.1). At 202^{a}3 ff., however, the thesis is clearly grounded in the necessity for reciprocal action between bodies in contact; see on that section. For the existence of an 'unmoved mover' see *Physics* VIII.5, 6.

201^{a}27. The definition of change is restated, with an explanatory clause, and a footnote on 'actuality-*qua*-F'.

'When being in actuality it is operating . . .' The verb *energein* ('operate') is appropriate to the exercise of a disposition or capacity. For change as an 'operation' see 201^{b}27–202^{a}2 and notes there.

'I mean *qua* thus . . .' The actuality of any X picked out as actuality-*qua*-F is the actuality corresponding to the potentiality indicated by F. As has been seen, there are different kinds of corre-spondence between actuality and potentiality, and different ways in which 'F' may indicate a potentiality: Aristotle's usage is not standardized. The point is borne out by the example here given. Being bronze is not a disposition or a potentiality: so actuality-*qua*-bronze is just being bronze. Being potentially a statue, though, involves a disposition to turn into a statue: so actuality-*qua*-potentially-a-statue is the exercise of that disposition.

Aristotle's further point is that difference between actuality *qua*-F and actuality-*qua*-G rests upon 'difference in definition' between *being F* and *being G*. On sameness and difference in definition see on 202^{b}5 ff. If *what it is to be F* and *what it is to be G* were exactly the same then it would follow that actuality-*qua*-F and actuality-*qua*-G would be the same. When the actualities are differ-ent, there must be a corresponding difference in definition. Aristotle does not stop to explain difference in definition, but throws out a couple of examples, taking the notion for granted.

(1) *Being potentially healthy and being potentially sick.* Any X that can be said to be potentially healthy can necessarily also said to be potentially sick, and vice versa. Nevertheless, *being potentially*

healthy and *being potentially sick* must be different in definition; otherwise the corresponding actualities, being healthy and being sick, would be the same.

(2) *Being a colour and being visible*. Again the predicates 'is a colour' and 'is visible' are necessarily coextensive, according to Aristotle's theory of light, colour, and vision (*de Anima* II.7). But *being a colour* is not the same as *being visible* in this theory, since 'colour' is not defined as 'what is visible'. And the difference is once again demonstrated by the actualities: the actuality of some colour *qua* colour is just its being a colour; the actuality of the same colour *qua* visible is either its being seen or its coming to be seen.

201^{b}5. The aim of this section seems to be to demonstrate that the definition works out correctly in a model case, that of building. To call something 'buildable' is to say that it might be made into a house. A house is not called 'buildable' (unless as a joke, as when we say that a film has the makings of a good film) so that 'when the house is, the buildable no longer is' as such. This shows that 'what potentially is', in the original definition, must be understood in the restricted sense of 'potentially and not actually', as is of course necessary if it is to be read as expressing a disposition.

So there are only very few candidates for the state or process which is 'the operation of the buildable, *qua* buildable'. 'Being a house' is obviously not the right answer, since then there is nothing buildable left. The buildability is there when the buildable is just lying around as an unused heap of bricks and mortar; but during that time it is not 'doing' anything characteristic of it *qua* buildable. The only time at which the buildability of the heap *is* essential to what is happening is when it is getting built into a house: 'to get built is what the buildable does'. So, if the definition makes any sense at all, it gives the right result in the case of building and by analogy in all other cases.

CHAPTER 2

201^{b}16. The formal structure of this section is as follows: After the introductory sentence (^{b}16–18), Aristotle (1) states that change cannot be placed in another genus (than that in which his definition places it) (^{b}18–19); (2) considers some opinions of previous philosophers about the nature of change, stating them (^{b}19–21), refuting them (^{b}21–24), and finally explaining the thought (and partly correct intuition) that lay behind them, (^{b}24–33); (3) explains why it is difficult to discover the right definition (^{b}33–202^{a}3). All three parts serve as indirect confirmation of Aristotle's own definition: (1) in an obvious way; (2) because the explanation of the motives for previous definitions requires (at the end) the correctness of Aristotle's definition; (3) because the explanation makes clear that something like Aristotle's definition is needed. In fact (3) also serves as a filling-out of (1).

To review the opinions of predecessors and the generally held intuitions about the subject of discussion is standard practice in Aristotle's dialectical method of discussion. Here the review is much abbreviated and, untypically, appears after the substantive discussion. The opinions reported are those of some Pythagoreans or of some of the early Academy, or both; one or other may be intended to represent Plato's opinion (cf. *Timaeus* 57^e, *Sophist* 256^d). The two 'columns of correlated opposites' (*sustoichiai*) were of Pythagorean origin; pairs of opposites were listed in two columns, the 'positive' twin in one column and the 'negative' one in the other. Aristotle associated the list with his own 'form-privation' polarity, and to some extent adopted it. (See *Metaphysics* I, 986^{a}22–^{b}2 for the list; *Physics* I.7 on form and privation.) It is the *Physics* I.7 analysis that lies behind the trichotomy 'privation or potentiality or (simple) operation' on which the remarks of this section are based.

Why does Aristotle say that that which potentially is, is incomplete, and that a change is an 'incomplete operation'? A first point is that, for Aristotle, potentialities are dependent on their actualities in every important respect: *Metaphysics* IX.8 argues that actuality is prior to potentiality both logically ('in definition') and ontologically ('in substance'), as well as teleologically. In the sense that it does not include the actuality on which it depends so completely, the potentiality may be said to point beyond itself; likewise the change points beyond itself to its own completion. This shows up in the way changes are to be classified, and individuated, and in a difference Aristotle is elsewhere concerned to explain between changes and operations (*energeiai*). For this difference see *Metaphysics* IX.6, 1048^{b}18–35, *Nic. Eth.* X.3, 1173^{a}32–^{b}4, and X.4, 1174^{a}14–^{b}14, and of recent discussions, esp. Ackrill (2), Penner. See also Introduction 2(*c*).

202^{a}3. More on the topic of 201^{a}19 ff.: the relations between agent of change and changing thing. 202^{a}3–7 argue that every agent of change which is capable of changing will itself be changed by a reaction from the changing thing. 202^{a}9–12 add that it is the agent's 'form' which is the principle of, and responsible for, change. The section uses explicitly or implicitly some important theses of Aristotelian physics (see further Introduction, 2(*d*)).

(1) *The necessity of contact.* This is the famous principle of 'no action at a distance'. It is argued for by induction at *Physics* VII.2, and often assumed elsewhere. (Like the other principles of physics it is either abandoned or severely modified by Aristotle when he comes to deal with the movements of the heavens and with psychological action.)

(2) *The sufficiency of contact.* The general principle is implicit here, and is stated at *Physics* VIII.4, $255^a34-{}^b1$: 'Invariably, whenever that which is active and that which is passive are together, the potential comes to be in actuality.' In the examples following this statement, a proviso is added: 'unless there is something preventing it'. Again, there are exceptions in the realm of psychology: *Metaphysics* IX, $1047^b35-1048^a8$.

(3) *The agent's 'form' is the origin of change.* Though all action is by individual agents, no individual acts simply in virtue of being that individual, but in virtue of falling into one or other of the categories of substance, qualification, or quantity: it is this that confers a 'form' which explains agency. Which kinds of 'form' explain which kinds of change is then a general problem to which Aristotle has no solution in general, but for the simplest physical changes the rule is given by the next principle.

(4) *The agent's 'form' is propagated in change.* This principle is not explicitly stated here, but is suggested by the example of human generation. The principle is that if A acts on B, and 'A is F' gives the form which is the origin of B's change, then B changes so as to become F. It is stated e.g. at *Physics* II.7, 198^a26-7, with the same example. But it is everywhere surrounded with exceptions and qualifications: for a more developed position see *Gen et Corr.* I.5, 320^b17-21 and Joachim, 119–21; *Metaphysics* VII.7 and 9. The propagation of form is important for Aristotle (*i*) in the account of substantial change between the four elements, worked out at *Gen. et Corr.* II.1–5; (*ii*) in the account of animal reproduction, worked out at *Gen. Anim.* I.17–23: in this the agent is the father, the changing thing is the material supplied by the mother; (*iii*) in sense-perception, in which the sense-organ receives the form of the perceived object (*de Anima* II.12, 424^a17-28); and something analogous happens (*iv*) in thinking (*de Anima* III.4, 5).

(5) *Ambivalence of 'forms'.* Where the 'forms' involved in change pair off into opposites linked by a continuum of intermediate states, they are 'ambivalent' in the sense that actual presence of such a 'form' F confers both potential agency—the power to change other things to become F—and changeability—the power to be changed be become the opposite of F. So *de Caelo* II.3, 286^a33-4, *Gen. et Corr.* 1.7, $323^b29-324^a14$. It seems this has application only to the simplest physical changes.

(6) *Action and reaction.* Here it is stated crudely that, since there is contact in action (1), there must also be a reaction of the changing thing upon the agent. Clearly further steps are needed: they can be constructed if we may assume that contact is a symmetric relation (which Aristotle later denied in certain cases, *Gen. et Corr.* I.6, $322^b29-323^a34$) and that all the principles (1)–(5) apply.

Even here the principle is restricted to agents which are themselves changeable (so that the unmoved mover is excepted). Since it depends on the ambivalence of 'forms' it can in general have no wider application. So e.g. *Gen. et Corr.* I.7, 324^a24-^b22.

'For to operate on this, *qua* such, is just what it is to produce change' ($^a5-6$). This appears to constitute a definition of *producing change.* 'This' and 'such' are presumably to be filled out as 'that which is changeable'. There are two different ways of attaching the *qua*-clause: to produce change is *either*:

(*a*) to operate-*qua*-changeable on what is changeable; *or*

(*b*) to operate on what is changeable, and on that *qua* changeable.

Against (*a*) it seems fatal that to operate-*qua*-changeable is to be changed (cf. 201^a28-9) and not to produce change.

CHAPTER 3

202^a13. Aristotle sets out in outline his own position on the question to be discussed in this chapter. (For convenience, in the notes on this Chapter, the term 'the patient' will be used in place of 'the changing thing'.) Cf. in general *Metaphysics* IX.8, 1050^a23-^b6.

(1) *The change is in the patient.* There is nothing to suggest that anything other than a local sense of 'in' is intended (for the various senses of 'in' see IV.3, 210^a14-24). If a change is to be localized, it must be in what is changing; that is where the change is occurring. But, both in Greek and in English, 'the change' or *kinēsis* has a transitive as well as intransitive use. (My change of clothes is an action, not a being-changed.) As soon as this point is seen, as Aristotle sees it here, there arise the two further questions: (*a*) where is the 'transitive change' (change-(T), to adapt the notation of Hornsby)? (*b*) how are the changes—the change-(T) and the change-(I) —related? These are the questions at issue; it is not further disputed that the change-(I) is in the patient. But Aristotle's reason for locating the change-(I) in the patient—namely, that it is an actuality of the patient—is inadequate on his own showing, since he locates the change-(T), an actuality of the *agent*, in the patient.

(2) *The agent's operation is the same as the patient's operation.*

Aristotle here seems to put: 'agent's operation = agent's actuality = change-(T); and patient's operation = patient's actuality = change-(I)'. Nothing here turns on the conceptual difference between actuality (*entelecheia*) and operation (*energeia*).

'There must in fact be an actuality of both.' It is hard to know how to translate and punctuate here. The words could mean (*a*) 'there must be some one actuality which is the actuality of both'; or (*b*) 'each must have an actuality' (possibly not the same one); or (*c*) 'it, [the agent's operation], must be an actuality of both'; or (*d*) 'an actuality [i.e. any actuality occurring in change] must indeed be [an actuality] *of both.*' Since *amphoin* ('both') is not usually distributive, (*b*) is less likely: and (*a*), (*c*), and (*d*) amount to much the same. But the exact sequence of thought is unclear. What follows ('for it is productive of change . . .') shows that the operation of the agent is the change-(T) and that this is an operation *on* the patient as changeable. This shows that there cannot be a change-(T) without a patient and a change-(I), but does not get Aristotle to the conclusion he wants, that the changes are the same.

What then *is* Aristotle's positive argument to show that the changes are the same? It might be just that an operation must be something that *happens* over a period of time, and that if we look at a minimal case of change, in which the agent is completely unaffected, there *is* 'nothing happening' except the change-(I) of the patient. Hence the operation of the agent must be the change-(I). This may be the force of the argument he actually gives lower down at ^a25–36: see on that.

(3) *The two operations are the same, but different in definition.* On sameness and difference 'in definition' (*logōi*) or 'in being' (*tōi einai, tēi ousiai*) and on Aristotle's notions of 'sameness' and 'difference' generally see on 202^b5 ff. What is indicated by 'the same' here is straightforward identity.

'Similarly with that which produces and undergoes change' (^a21): this probably adds a fresh example: when something is both an agent and a patient, the agent and the patient are the same thing but different in definition.

202^a21. A dilemma is set up: there are objections both to identifying and to distinguishing the operations of agent and patient. As emerges from Aristotle's solution in the next section, Aristotle in fact rejects the arguments of a 33–4 and ^a36–^b5; but it does *not* follow that he accepts any of the rest of the argumentation of this section. The fact that the problem is called 'formal' (*logikē*) indicates that the arguments used are of a very general kind and do not appeal to facts or principles peculiar to any particular science.

In settling the first principles of a science, 'formal' arguments may be indispensable. On questions internal to a particular science, as here, they may have a diagnostic and didactic value, but Aristotle clearly thinks that they are then secondary and perhaps that they have ultimately no independent value. On 'formal' arguments generally, *Gen. Anim.* II.8, 747^b27-30, and Barnes (1), 165 f.; cf. 204^b4-10 below.

One implication of calling the present argument 'formal' is that since it does not involve anything peculiar to physics, it does not in particular involve the definition of change given in ch. 1. (or any of Aristotle's other reasonings in chs. 1 and 2). This is important for the understanding of the arguments.

The problem is set out as follows:-
- (1) Both agent and patient have an operation ($^a22-4$);
- (2) Both operations are changes ($^a25$);
- (3) The changes cannot be different ($^a25-36$):
  - (*a*) they cannot be one in the agent, one in the patient. ($^a28-31$)
  - (*b*) they cannot be both in the patient ($^a31-6$);
- (4) The changes cannot be the same ($^a36-^b5$).

(1) *Both agent and patient have an operation.* The appeal is not to Aristotle's definitions of *change* and *producing change*, but to common sense considerations: when A acts on B, we want to say that both A and B 'do something', viz. A acts and B changes. Hence the *ad hoc* terminology: what A does is 'an acting-upon' (*poiēsis*), what B does is a 'being-acted-upon' (*pathēsis*). The latter word is a new coinage of Aristotle's, and occurs only here and in a related context (*de Anima* III.2, 426^a9-10). The end-product of A's acting-upon is a 'product of action' (*poiēma*: another unusual use); of B's being-acted-upon is a 'modification' (*pathos*).

(2) *Both operations are changes.* Again, there is no appeal to Aristotle's definition of change, but simply to the ordinary intuition that both the acting-upon and the being-acted-upon, if they really occur, must be processes involving something's actually happening over an interval of time. Each of them, therefore, must consist in *something's* changing–in no other way can anything happen. (For Aristotle's own views on this see 202^b19-21.)

It would be wrong, then, to see here a *confusion* of change-(T) with change-(I); as the thesis is precisely that changes-(T) must also be changes-(I). It can also be shown directly that it would be wrong to appeal to Aristotle's definition of change: for if any agent's operation can be counted as a change under that definition, then the operation of the unmoved mover can be. But the operation of the unmoved mover is unchanging and 'complete at any moment' and therefore not a change according to the official Aristotelian distinction between operations and changes (see on 201^{b}16 ff.). The same extreme case can be used to show in another way that the agent's operation cannot possibly be brought under the definition; since the unmoved mover is pure actuality and no potentiality, it cannot have an actuality-*qua*-potentially anything.

(3) *The changes cannot be different.* If there are two different changes going on, the change which is B's operation of being-acted-upon must be in B: it is the change because of which B was said to change in the first place. But where is the other change going on? Not in the agent, since we know that the agent is not necessarily changed in the course of acting. Therefore, in the patient, which must therefore be changing in two distinct ways at the same time. To this the objections made (^{a}33–6) do not seem very strong. One is in fact quickly dispatched at ^{b}6–8. Aristotle is right to say that the supposition is 'absurd': only he does not stop to draw out the absurdity, merely appealing to the original supposition that B was to be changing in *one* way.

'If one has to call this too an acting-upon' (^{a}27–8): why should one have to do so? Perhaps a more usual sense of *poiēsis*, viz. 'productive process' is in Aristotle's mind. B's being acted upon might qualify as a productive process: but the word *poiēsis* would then be being used in a different sense by homonymy.

(4) *The changes cannot be the same.* If the changes are the same, we have to say that A's acting upon B is the same thing as B's change.

'Two things different in form' (^{b}1): for all we know, A and B may be quite disparate. Aristotle does not answer this point in the next section: perhaps he thought it too weak to be worth answering.

202^{b}5. Aristotle's own solution of the problem. Steps (1) and (2) are tacitly accepted. Of (3) only one of the two arguments for (3) (*b*) is rejected, so that the conclusion of (3) still stands. (4) therefore has to be rejected, and this section is mostly devoted to dealing with the two arguments in favour of (4): that of 202^{b}1–2 is brushed aside at ^{b}8–10, while that of ^{b}2–5 receives careful attention in ^{b}10–19. The solution is complete by ^{b}19; the conclusion at ^{b}19–22 may be either a footnote to the solution or an adumbration of a rather different solution (see below). In any case, there is a (rebuttable) presumption that the first solution represents Aristotle's own position.

(*a*) (^{b}6–8): rejection of first argument for (3) (*b*). The new point here is that an agent's operation cannot occur unless there is a particular patient, and the operation is necessarily *directed at* the patient, with effects *on* him: it cannot occur *in vacuo*.

(b) (^{b}8–10): rejection of first argument for (4). On 'the same in being' and the example here see below.

(c) (^{b}10–19): rejection of the second argument for (4). From the simple identity of the teaching and the learning, in any particular case of teaching, it need not follow that *to teach* is the same thing as *to learn*; nor, even if it did, need it follow from that that the teacher necessarily learns.

One difficulty here is with the infinitives 'to teach', 'to learn' (*to didaskein, to manthanein*). They function as noun-expressions, but are equivalent neither to the generalized *what it is to teach/learn* nor to the particularized 'the teaching', 'the learning'. Most likely 'to teach' = 'the being a teacher for a particular occasion' and 'to learn' similarly.

Aristotle's point is that both of the steps he objects to involve an application of 'Leibniz's Law' ('that all the same things are true of things that are the same') and that 'Leibniz's Law' need not be true unless there is sameness 'in being' or 'in definition', on top of ordinary identity.

(i) *The steps involve Leibniz's Law* (*LL*). Suppose X teaches Y so that Y learns. It is given that the teaching and the learning are the same thing. Then the being a teacher is the having the teaching as one's operation ('the doing the teaching'); the being a learner is the having the learning as one's operation (the 'doing the learning'). If we may apply LL it follows that the being a teacher is the same thing as the being a learner. Further, if 'Z teaches' is equivalent to 'Z is in the (state of) being a teacher' and 'Z learns' to 'Z is in the (state of) being a learner' it will follow by LL that 'Z teaches' is equivalent to 'Z learns'.

(ii) *Leibniz's Law is not unrestrictedly true.* Aristotle affirms this explicitly. Given that LL is indispensable for any coherent conception of identity, it is tempting to use that fact as evidence that Aristotle did not have any concept of identity, and in particular that his ordinary 'sameness (in number)' is not the same as identity. To conclude in this way would be mistaken. Aristotle does not abandon LL for ordinary cases, and his sameness (in number) functions in every essential way as ordinary identity, giving rise to many tacit uses of LL. The restrictions on LL are proposed only in order to deal with phenomena which need special treatment in any account. These are familiar from modern discussions, beginning with Frege. Apparent failures of LL occur, for instance, inside the scope of modal operators like 'necessarily' or in indirect speech. Frege's solution involved restricting LL in a certain way determined by his theory of reference. Aristotle does not hold Frege's theory of reference, but his notion of *sameness/*

difference in being is close to being an anticipation of part of it. Aristotle's solution likewise involves restricting LL, but unfortunately the solution was, so far as we know, incomplete: Aristotle nowhere specifies a necessary condition for LL to apply, but only a sufficient condition (which is evidently too strong to be also necessary) viz. that LL applies when there is 'sameness in being'.

(*iii*) *Sameness and difference in being or definition.* The fundamental thing here is sameness and difference of essences. From that, Aristotle derives relations which he thinks of as holding between possessors of essences: these may be individuals or universals. Thus, if *what it is to be a horse* and *what it is to be a quadruped* are different, it follows that *horse* and *quadruped* differ in definition. It is tempting to think of this as a relation between the predicates *is a horse* and *is a quadruped*; but Aristotle does not seem to treat it so.

There are plenty of examples in III and IV. At 201^a30–34 the point is put directly in terms of essences: *what it is to be bronze* and *what it is to be potentially a statue* are different; if they were the same, it would follow that being bronze and being potentially a statue were the same in definition, and thence by LL that the actuality-*qua*-bronze was the same as the actuality-*qua*-potentially-a-statue.

An attempt to justify Aristotle's sufficient condition in Fregean terms might be as follows: If X and Y are the same in definition, then (for Frege) 'X' and 'Y' have the same sense. But then 'X' and 'Y' not only have the same reference, but, if they are names of things, the same indirect reference: so that LL will hold for them in all contexts. The point of making this connection, which would have to be qualified in various ways, is simply to show that there *is* some analogy between these apparently disparate theories, and to recommend the thesis that Aristotle was concerned (to some extent) with the same phenomena as helped shape Frege's theory. On the latter, see Dummett (1), esp. chs. 5, 6, and 9.

(*iv*) *The 'road' example.* This particularly interesting example is adapted by Aristotle from Heraclitus' remark: 'A road: uphill, downhill, one and the same'. (B 60 Diels-Kranz). The road from Thebes to Athens is identical with the road from Athens to Thebes. And yet (at some independently located point) the former is uphill, the latter downhill (202^a19–20, ^b13–14). The failure of LL here shows that the predicates 'is uphill', 'is downhill' produce meaning in a way that depends on the way in which the road is specified, even though there is no indirect speech, no modal operator, or the like. For other examples of this

phenomenon see Wiggins 41 f. Aristotle is not obliged to give a
general account of the phenomenon, nor does he do so; but it is
likely, given his down-to-earth approach to ontology, that he
would have agreed with Wiggins that 'this is a circumscribed and
special phenomenon', and would have held that it could always
be analysed away. Something of the sort seems to be in his mind
at ^{b}19–22 (see below). The general form of the analysis would be
this: suppose that for some X, Y it is true that X = Y and ϕ (X),
and not true that ϕ (Y). Then we can always find a Z such that it
is true that X = Z and Y = Z, and such that there are predicates
'α' 'β' such that it is true that α (Z) and β (Z), (with no contradiction involved, i.e. α (Z) does not imply that β (Z) does not
hold) and that 'α (Z)' is logically equivalent to 'ϕ(X)' and 'β (Z)'
is logically equivalent to 'not ϕ (Y)'.

(d) (^{b}19–22). It is clear from the final words that 'the same in the
primary sense' must mean 'the same in definition'. It is odd that
Aristotle makes sameness in definition prior to sameness in number,
although sameness in definition is certainly the most restrictive kind
of sameness.

'The teaching is not the same, in the primary sense, as the
learning, nor the acting-upon as the being-acted-upon, but that in
which these things are present, the change': so a literal translation.
There are two ways of understanding the last clause; as equivalent to:

    (i) 'the change, in which these things are present, i.e. of which it
    is true that it is an acting-upon and a being-acted-upon, is the
    same as the being-acted-upon';

or (ii) 'but that in which these things are present; i.e. that of which
    it is true that it is both an acting-upon and a being-acted-upon, is
    the change'.

On either interpretation, 'that in which these things are present' will
have to mean 'that of which these things are predicated'–a possible
meaning for the verb *huparchein*. Teaching and learning are, in
Aristotle's view, predicated of the change involved, since we say that
this change is a teaching or that it is a learning. The remark, in both
interpretations, serves to supply the more fundamental and neutral
description (the 'Z') required by the reductive analysis of (c) (iv)
above. Only, in interpretation (i), the extra point is made that the
change is indeed the same in definition as the being-acted-upon (for
change has been defined as an actuality of the changing thing).

It may be objected that if the change is indeed the same in
definition as the being-acted-upon it does not supply a 'more fundamental and neutral description' of what goes on; and, more generally,
that this fact points to a strange asymmetry–*why* should the change
be defined as the being-acted-upon and not as the acting-upon? The

answer is that the change has been defined, without any reference to
agency at all, not as the being-acted-upon but as the actuality of a
certain potentiality of the changing thing. Strictly, therefore, it is
not the same in definition as the being-acted-upon, which point
favours interpretation (*ii*) above; and the description 'the change' is
indeed neutral as between the agent's and patient's operations considered as such.

Further points on the section:
(^b9−10). 'in the way that what potentially is is related to what is
operating'. Aristotle has in mind sophistic puzzles such as that about
Socrates, who, at first unmusical, then becomes musical. The
unmusical Socrates is potentially musical, the musical Socrates is
'operating' in respect of musicality. 'They' are one and the same
man: yet different, incompatible things are true of the 'two
Socrateses'. Accordingly, for Aristotle 'they' are not one in
definition.

(^b13): 'raiment and clothing'. The two Greek words are more
specific about the type of garment. It is Aristotle's stock example of
synonymy.

202^b23. Conclusion of the discussion of change. On the sentence
(202^b26−28) omitted from the translation here, see List of
divergences from the text of Ross.

THE INFINITE

CHAPTER 4

202^b30. Motivation for the study of the infinite. The fact that
'finite' and 'infinite' are predicates applying to quantities suggests
that the study of the infinite as such is properly part of mathematics.
But whether actual infinites exist, and if so in what sense, is a
question for either metaphysics or physics. Aristotle's view in these
chapters seems to be consistently that the question of the existence
of infinite quantities, of the kinds with which physics is concerned,
is a matter internal to physics, whereas questions about other
possible infinites belong to 'a general inquiry' (204^a34−^b1), i.e.
some kind of metaphysical treatment. The motivation gains force if
we can read it as implying that it is physics that studies the actuality

and possibility of the *primary* kinds of quantities (magnitudes, changes, times)—other quantities being derived from these by abstraction.

'Magnitudes' (*megethē*): actual physical quantities and bodies. Aristotle's use of this word makes it cover (*a*) physical quantities, particularly size; (*b*) physical bodies or their boundaries or powers, *qua* possessing such quantities; (*c*) abstract quantities.

'Each of which must be either infinite or finite'. Every quantity must be either infinite or finite; what is either infinite or finite is a quantity. The tie is implicit in the following discussion, explicit at (e.g.) 207^{a}7, *Physics* I.185^{a}33–^{b}3. 'Property' (*pathos*): for this sense, see *Metaphysics* V.21. Properties cannot properly be said to be quantities: *Metaphysics* V.13, 1020^{a}26–28.

'All of them posit it as some kind of principle': a generalization that requires some defence: see 203^{a}16 ff.

203^{a}4. The collection and exposition of previous opinions about the topic of discussion is an important part of the dialectical method (*Topics* I.13 and 14). (On this whole passage 203^{a}4–^{b}30 as history of philosophy, Cherniss (1), 16–22 and (2), 104–7, 165–72 (as usual excessively severe on Aristotle); Kahn (2).) The present classification is based on the Aristotelian doctrine that what is must either (A) itself be a substance; or (B) be predicated of some substance. Analogous classification of opinions about 'the one' in *Metaphysics* X.1.

(A) The infinite is itself a substance. For criticism of this thesis see 204^{a}8–34. 'The Pythagoreans': a mid or late fifth-century group, not necessarily having the same opinions as Pythagoras. See *Metaphysics* I.5, 985^{b}23–986^{b}8, 987^{a}9–27; and Burkert, 28–52, Kahn (1). On 'gnomons' and the link between even numbers and the infinite, Heath (1), vol. i, 77–84. 'They do not make number separable': they do not allow the possibility of number existing apart from and independently of ordinary things.

Plato's philosophy of mathematics is an obscure subject; good introductions are Wedberg, Annas (1), 3–26, 42–73. For 'the great' and 'the small' see also 206^{b}27–33.

203^{a}16 (B) The infinite is predicated of some substance. 'The natural philosophers' are those earlier thinkers whose primary concern was (according to Aristotle) the nature of the physical universe. They are here divided into:

(1) Those who verify the general rule, i.e. predicate 'infinite' of some one elemental body, i.e. make it infinite in extent;

(2) First exception: those who posit (more than one but) finitely many elements, none of them infinite in extent;

(3) Second exception: those who posit infinitely many elements.

Aristotle seems to be claiming that all natural philosophers said there was some substance infinite in extent. It is odd then that in (2) he recognizes exceptions; with regard to (3) he labours to show that the exceptions are only apparent. Comparison of *Physics* I.187ᵃ12–26 suggests that Aristotle might have tried to reduce (2) to (1), as he there tries to reduce Empedocles; but that would still not give an infinite in Empedocles, or in other members of class (2).

For class (3) Aristotle tries to show that these thinkers did after all recognize some infinite body as a principle of things. First, (ᵇ19–23) he claims that these thinkers 'say the infinite is continuous by contact'. That is, for them the sum of all body, being infinite, makes a weak kind of unity 'by contact' (see *Physics* V. 227ᵃ10–17, *Metaphysics* V.6). But this is a very attenuated sort of 'principle'. So Aristotle attempts to go further and show that at least for Anaxagoras and Democritus, the two most prominent members of class (3), the infinite sum of body was also homogeneous.

(*i*) *Anaxagoras* (ᵃ23–33). The point about homogeneity is made in the first sentence. All that follows I take to be a footnote designed to strengthen Aristotle's point by exhibiting certain other doctrines of Anaxagoras as consequences of the homogeneity. The passage is compressed and obscure; for a rather different interpretation see Schofield (1), 45–52.

(*a*) (ᵃ23–4) Anaxagoras posited a homogeneous mixture in any portion of stuff whatever, because 'anything comes to be out of anything'. (For if anything of whatever kind can always emerge from any portion whatever, that portion must always be a mixture of all different kinds of stuff.)

(*b*) (ᵃ24–5) It is (it seems) because of the homogeneity that Anaxagoras also holds that there was an initial state of complete mixture.

(*c*) (ᵃ25–6) The thesis of initial mixture is reached in two steps. *First*, consider the example of two differentiated packets of stuff, this bit of flesh and this bit of bone. They originated from a relatively undifferentiated mixture (the unformed embryo). So too with anything else that may be taken, and therefore with everything. Hence all things were once part of an 'undifferentiated mixture.

(*d*) *Secondly*, everything must once have been in the undifferentiated mixture *simultaneously*, because the alternative would be that separation-out has been going on for an infinite time. There must be some starting-point which is a starting-point of *all* separations. (*Archē*, usually 'principle', must here be 'starting-point'.)

(e) (^{a}28–30). Why there must be a starting-point. Step (1): what comes to be does so from a homogeneous body, but variously at various times, so that a moving cause (a 'principle') is needed to explain the coming-to-be in each case.

(f) (^{a}30–1). Step (2): But Anaxagoras recognizes only one moving cause, namely Mind.

(g) (^{a}31–2). Step (3): Mind needs an initial state to start its operation from, because its operation is thought, and thought starts from some initial state.

(h) (^{a}32–3). Step (4): Hence for Anaxagoras there must be an initial state of the physical universe, one of undifferentiated mixture.

On Aristotle's reading of Anaxagoras as evidence about Anaxagoras see in general Schofield (1), 52–67. The precise nature of Anaxagoras' mixture and of the 'homoeomeries' is highly controversial; see also e.g. Vlastos (1), Strang, Barnes (2), vol. ii, ch. II.

(ii) *Democritus* (^{a}33–^{b}2). Democritus held that there were infinitely many (finite and indivisible) atoms moving in an infinite void. (Presumably the void is regarded by Aristotle as too negative to be a 'principle' for Democritus.) Aristotle claims that Democritus' infinite principle is 'the body common' to all the atoms. All the atoms are made of the same sort of matter, which in sum is infinite; so the claim is that this matter is an infinite material cause for Democritus.

203^{b}3. First (203^{b}4–10), Aristotle's reasons why, if there is an infinite, it must be a principle. Then (^{b}10–15), a brief and interesting footnote on the role of the infinite in the natural philosophers (in confirmation of Aristotle's deductions).

Archē (literally 'beginning') is here and mostly elsewhere best translated by 'principle'. Some of the uses Aristotle recognizes are listed at *Metaphysics* V.1. Generally it is that from which other things originate, in all possible uses of 'originate'; thus there is a rough correspondence with the uses of 'out of' (*Metaphysics* V.24). Here it is 'principle' used for 'basic factor in explanation'. What is infinite, the thought is, cannot arise by accident and at random (it is too important a feature of the universe), nor can it be explained by anything outside itself, since its unlimitedness allows nothing outside itself. Nor, even, can one explain it by giving an account of how it came to be, since what is infinite never comes to be nor ceases to be. For a coming-to-be or ceasing-to-be of an infinite would take an infinite time (cf. *de Caelo* I.7, 274^{b}33–275^{b}4), which is impossible since all coming-to-be (or ceasing-to-be) is bounded by time.

'Those who do not provide other explanatory factors besides the infinite' i.e. those classed by Aristotle as 'material monists' (see *Metaphysics* I.3, 983^{b}6−984^{a}29).

203^{b}15. The prima facie case for the existence of something infinite. The arguments are not necessarily endorsed by Aristotle; as turns out in ch. 8, some are completely rejected and some accepted only with qualifications. But the prima facie arguments are part of the material on which Aristotelian dialectic goes to work.

(*i*) Time: it is intuitively plausible that time should have neither beginning nor end. (Aristotle holds that this is true and argues for it at *Physics* VIII.1, 251^{a}8−252^{a}5.) So time is infinite in the sense of having no temporal boundaries, and so (another plausible step) in the sense of being of infinite extent.

(*ii*) In Euclidean geometry every line can be divided *ad infinitum* and it is plausible to suppose that this holds good in principle of physical objects. Even if not physically, anything extended can be theoretically divided into two, if geometry applies to the physical world. So it is plausible to conclude that, both in the abstract and in the concrete, every line (or solid) contains infinitely many sub-stretches (or portions).

On the ways in which Greek mathematics 'used the infinite' see on 207^{b}27 ff.

(*iii*) The notion of an infinite reservoir of possibilities, from which new things perpetually emerge, goes back at least to Anaximander and is characteristic of the cosmological tradition founded by him or by Thales.

(*iv*) An appeal to ordinary intuitions about space. A spatial limit seems to imply the existence of something beyond, and so of something spatially extended beyond. So the sum of what is spatially extended cannot have a spatial boundary.

(*v*) The appeal is to what we can conceive of. For any number we can always conceive of a greater, and perhaps of there being infinitely many; for any geometrical figure, likewise; for any given finite size for the whole cosmos, we can always conceive of there being something beyond, of any arbitrary size and perhaps infinite, and for any such size, a 'beyond' even greater. (See further on 208^{a}5 ff.) In the absence of arguments justifying a stop at a particular place, conceivability supplies a prima facie case for existence.

For the final dispatch of these arguments see 208^{a}5−22.

^{b}25−30 is a footnote to (*v*): two arguments from infinite spatial extension to infinitely extended body and infinitely many world-systems. One appeals to the principle of Sufficient Reason, and is probably due to an early Presocratic. The second is Aristotle's own:

an infinite void entails the possibility of an infinite body (cf. *de Caelo* I.9, 279^{a}11−17); but the possibility of an infinite body is a structural fact about the universe, and therefore everlastingly and unchangingly true, if true; but there cannot be unrealized possibilities in the realm of immutable truths. (On the last step here see esp. Hintikka, ch. 5.)

203^{b}30. The case for the existence of some infinites has been stated; the case against is nowhere stated in any generality. In ch. 5 only certain particular kinds of infinite are attacked. Formally, therefore, the difficulty is not a real one. For suggestions about the roots of Aristotle's finitism see Introduction 3(*c*).

As a preliminary to discussion, Aristotle first recalls the relevant uses of 'be'. The infinite might 'be' (*a*) as a substance, cf. 203^{a}4−16, 204^{a}8−34; (*b*) as 'an accident in itself of some kind of thing'; (*c*) in some other way. According to *Metaphysics* V.30, 1025^{a}31−2, an 'accident in itself' is 'whatever holds good of a thing in its own right without being in its substance, as for instance possessing (an angle-sum of) two right angles does of a triangle' (see Kirwan 180−2, and on 'in its own right', 'in itself' (*kath'hauto*), Barnes (1), 113−19).

The distinction of the uses of 'infinite' itself is in accord with dialectical method: *Topics* I.15. The distinguishing descriptions are not necessarily meant as formal definitions: if there is a formal definition of 'infinite' (in the primary sense), it is at 207^{a}7−8.

Aristotle here distinguishes four uses of 'infinite' in terms of the notion of 'going right across' or 'traversing'.

(1): Something may be 'impossible to traverse' just because the notion of a journey or series through or across it makes no sense; an example at 204^{a}12−13 (anything indivisible).

(2): Something may be traversable but the traverse may be unending: i.e. one *can* 'get right across it' but never come to any natural end-point. Here Aristotle is bringing in such phenomena as the circumference of a circle or the surface of a sphere. Circular formations were called 'infinite' in Greek (see Liddell-Scott-Jones under *apeiros, apeiron*): an example at 207^{a}2−7.

(3): Something may be 'difficult to get through': as e.g. a boring lecture might be said to have 'gone on for ever'. Perhaps this case is meant to take care of the usage thus reported by Liddell-Scott-Jones: 'In Tragedy, frequently of garments, etc. in which one is entangled past escape', on which see Fraenkel (on Aeschylus, *Agamemnon* 1382), vol. iii, 649−50.

(4): Something may be impossible to get right across, although the notion of a journey through or across does make sense. This is the primary use for Aristotle (cf. 204ª14: 'untraversable'), and is akin to the definition at 207ª7−8 ('that of which some part is always beyond'). The fact that one can never say of an infinite series or extent that it has been traversed is important for Aristotle's finitism and his answer to Zeno's paradoxes; see Introduction 3(*c*), and on 204ª34 ff.

'With respect to addition' and 'with respect to division': the successive steps of the 'journey' involve adding something or dividing something: see 206^b3 ff., 12 ff.

CHAPTER 5

204ª8. Attack on the Pythagorean-Platonist thesis of a self-subsistent Infinite. This is closely akin to the criticisms of a self-subsistent One (*Metaphysics* X.2) and of self-subsistent numbers and other mathematical objects (*Metaphysics* XIII and XIV) and of Platonic Forms (*Metaphysics* XIII, XIV, and elsewhere). 204ª17−20 appeals explicitly to the criticism of self-subsistent number.

'Just-infinite': a term of Platonic type, indicating something of which the essence is just to be infinite.

First argument (204ª9−17)

(*a*) If the infinite is as such a substance, it must, as such, be indivisible; for it is only as quantities that things are divisible (ª9−12).

(*b*) But what is not divisible can be infinite only in the sense (1) (204ª3−4), which is not in point (ª12−14).

(*c*) (A footnote). What is infinite not as a substance cannot, as such, be an element of things even if some element should accidentally be infinite in that sense (ª14−17).

Second argument (204ª17−20).

(*a*) It has been argued (in *Metaphysics* XIII, XIV) that there are no such things as self-subsistent numbers or magnitudes (see esp. XIII.2, 6−9, XIV.2−3).

(*b*) But being infinite is a 'property in itself' of numbers and magnitudes. That is, if there are such things as infinite numbers or magnitudes, their being infinite is an attribute closely linked to their being the particular number or magnitude they are.

(*c*) Hence, *a fortiori*, if numbers and magnitudes are not self-subsistent, the infinite is not either.

Third Argument (204ª20−34)

(*a*) Either a self-subsistent infinite is divisible or not;

(*b*) But if it is divisible it is a divisible substance, and so each of its parts will be just as much infinite as the whole.

(This step is supported (*i*) by the example of air: every portion of air is just as much air as any other; (*ii*) by the doctrine that every substance is identical with its essence—for which see *Metaphysics* VII.6, where it is used to attack Platonic Forms and other self-subsistent entities. On this doctrine see Woods.)

(*c*) But 'the same thing cannot be many infinites', so that the infinite cannot be divisible.

(It is unclear why the same thing cannot be, in the sense of 'be composed of', many infinites.)

(*d*) But if the infinite is indivisible, the same argument applies as at $^{b}12-17$; it can be infinite only in some special sense.

(*e*) So the infinite is not self-subsistent but an accident of something else and therefore not, as such, a principle.

204ª34. The question of whether there is a self-subsistent Infinite is not germane to physics and has to be treated with 'formal' arguments i.e. ones not drawing on any particular science. If there were such an infinite it would have to be classed among 'mathematical entities and things which are objects of thought and have no magnitude', since it could not inhabit the ordinary physical world. Aristotle therefore narrows the discussion to the questions of interest to a physicist; the first of which, which occupies the rest of the chapter, being the question of the existence of an infinitely extended body.

Among the arguments offered, those of $204^{b}4-205^{a}7$ seem to be put forward as prima facie only ('it would appear' $204^{b}5$) while those of $205^{a}8-206^{a}8$ are put as clinching ('it is clear', $205^{a}9$, 'it is manifest', $205^{b}24$).

The present section presents two arguments of a 'formal' kind (see on $202^{a}21$ ff.), one only in parenthesis.

(*i*) *There cannot be an infinite body.* The more usual Aristotelian definition of 'body' is 'three-dimensional magnitude'. But a magnitude by definition has a definite measurable size, and such a size cannot be infinite. As stated, the argument is too quick, but represents one of the motives of Aristotle's finitism.

(*ii*) *There cannot be an infinite, separated number.* What is meant by 'separated' (*kechōrismenos*)? It cannot mean, as *chōristos* ('separable') often does, anything like 'self-subsistent' or 'existing independently of ordinary things'. Apart from the variation of terminology, that sense bears no relation to the argument. The sense required is, rather, 'existing as the number of an actually realized totality' and hence 'separated out' from a mere potentiality, cf. *Metaphysics* IX.6, $1048^{b}9-17$, and $207^{b}13$ below. The claim is that there is no actually realized numbered totality which is infinite in number. The argument is the only argument Aristotle ever offers directly on this question. It may be filled out as follows:

(1) Any actual numbered totality is countable (taken as self-evident).

(2) For any countable totality it is possible for someone to have counted that totality (by definition of 'countable').

(3) To have counted an infinite totality is to have traversed an infinite.

(4) What is infinite cannot have been traversed (by definition, 204ᵃ5–6).

∴ (5) No infinite totality can have been counted (by (3) (4)).

∴ (6) No infinite totality is countable (by (2) (5)).

∴ (7) No actual numbered totality is infinite (by (1) (6)).

Again, this represents well Aristotle's finitist intuitions. The argument was probably present in essentials in Zeno (B3 Diels-Kranz).

204ᵇ10. The first physical argument. On the physical arguments generally see Introduction, Sec. 5(*b*) and cf. *de Caelo* I.5–7.

(A) *An infinite body cannot be composite* (ᵇ11–22). By 'composite' is meant 'composed of more than one element'. What Aristotle does is to assume that there are only finitely many elements (but more than one) and argue that it cannot be that any of them is infinite in total extent. Note (*i*) the assumption that the 'powers' of the different elements are measurable quantities which act proportionately to their amounts; (cf. Additional Note B). (*ii*) the strange (and badly based) conclusion that an infinite body is infinite in all directions.

(B) *An infinite body cannot be simple* (ᵇ22–205ᵃ7). The argument runs: (*i*) there is no simple body other than the elements, for if there were it would be observable, but it is not (ᵇ24–35); (*ii*) but no one of the elements can be infinite (for the reason given above, ᵇ14–19) (ᵇ35–205ᵃ1); (*iii*) and in general no one element could ever be the whole sum of body, for that would mean an end of elemental change (205ᵃ1–7). The argument for this is compressed into one sentence: for physical changes we need different things with opposed qualities (some thing hot to be cooled, something cold to do the cooling), cf. 202ᵃ3 ff. The theory of (*i*) is probably that of Anaximander.

205ᵃ8. An argument from the Aristotelian principle that every physical body has a natural place to which it naturally moves and in which it naturally rests. Moreover, any portion of the total body must be naturally at rest anywhere within the natural place of the whole, and the natural place of the whole must be large enough to accommodate the total body.

(A) If (^{a}12–19) there is an infinite homogeneous body, its place is likewise infinite in extent. Consider any arbitrary portion of that body. Either it will be naturally at rest everywhere, in which case there will be no natural motion (and therefore no motion at all, since forced motion is dependent on natural motion). Or it will be naturally at rest nowhere, in which case its natural motion would have to be unending. But this too is impossible since in an infinite extent there can be no privileged places or directions to determine the motion.

(B) If (^{a}19–^{b}1) the infinite body is not homogeneous, each of its components will have its different natural place, and the body will be a unity only 'by contact' (cf. 203^{a}22–3). In any case, there cannot be finitely many components of an infinite body, for reasons explained before (204^{b}11–22), nor infinitely many because that would mean infinitely many different elements (which is ruled out at *de Caelo* III.4).

205^{b}1. Criticism of a reason given by Anaxagoras why the infinite (i.e. the infinite sum of material body in Anaxagoras' theory) remains at rest as a whole.

According to Aristotle, Anaxagoras held (1) that the infinite was not contained in anything else, hence (2) that it was in itself; hence (3) that it kept itself still; and hence (4) that it was at rest. Aristotle agrees that (2) and (3) together imply (4), but disallows the inference of (3) from (2); and goes on to explore further the notion of natural motion in this context.

The objection to deriving (3) from (2) (^{b}4–10) is that the expression 'keeps itself still' must be interpreted as meaning 'in its own natural place'; but it does not follow from a thing's being in itself that it is there *naturally*. So Anaxagoras ought to have given further reasons why the infinite is its own natural place.

At ^{b}10–18 the objection is enlarged. If a body stays at rest there are three possibilities: (*a*) it has no natural motion; (*b*) it has a natural motion but is in its natural place; (*c*) neither (*a*) nor (*b*), but it is prevented from moving naturally by some external force. In the case of Anaxagoras' infinite, (*c*) is inappropriate, but whether (*a*) or (*b*) is correct, Anaxagoras has not given the right reason. To make this point Aristotle imagines an infinite universe full of earth which tends towards a 'central' point (i.e. an example of case (*b*)).

A further objection at ^{b}18–24: if Anaxagoras opts for case (*b*), then every portion of the infinite must be, of its nature, at rest 'in itself', and therefore will not naturally move.

205^{b}24. Further arguments:

(1) (^{b}24–31). The supposition of an infinite sense-perceptible body is incompatible with the Aristotelian thesis that every such body moves naturally either upwards (away from the centre) or downwards (towards the centre). For this thesis see esp. *de Caelo* III.2, IV.1–5.

(2) (^{b}31–5). In an infinite extent there is no ground for the absolute distinctions between 'above' and 'below' and 'left' and 'right' and 'forwards' and 'backwards'. On these distinctions see on 208^{b}8 ff.; Aristotle takes them to be indispensable for motion.

(3) (^{b}35–206^{a}7). The argument is: (*a*) every body is in place (for every body is capable of motion and what is capable of motion is in place; cf. 205^{a}10–11); (*b*) but an infinite body would have to be in an infinite place; (*c*) but there cannot be an infinite place; hence (*d*) there cannot be an infinite body. Most of the space is taken up by an argument for (*c*): what is in place is in some particular place, just as what is a quantity is some particular quantity. But we cannot specify particular places without the six distinctions of place mentioned in (2), and these can refer only to a finite region.

'What is somewhere is in place' (^{a}2): not generally true, see on 212^{a}31 ff.

CHAPTER 6

206^{a}9. The recapitulation of the problem, in the first half of this section (^{a}9–18), is not wholly satisfactory. What Aristotle claims to have demonstrated is that there cannot be a body actually infinite in extent. He does not claim, in ch. 5, to demonstrate that there cannot be an actual infinite plurality of things (unless 204^{b}7–10 is to be taken seriously). But the problem he is now faced with, though he does not say so here, is how to save some kinds of infinity without the support of actual infinite *pluralities* of any kind. Time, the divisions of magnitudes, and number, create series, pluralities which in some sense must be infinite; but not actually, therefore potentially. (For Aristotle's rejection of a beginning or an end of time, see *Physics* VIII.1 251^{a}8–252^{a}5, and cf. 222^{b}6–7 below; for his rejection of indivisible magnitudes see *Physics* VI.1, 2 and 4.)

The explanation of 'potentially' (^{a}18–25). A confusing passage. There are three different distinctions, all germane.

(1) We may distinguish

    (A) a totality of which all the components are, or have already been, actually present; and

    (B) a totality of which, as yet, not all the components are or have already been actually present.

(2) We may further divide case (B) into

(B*i*) a totality of which the components yet to be realized will of necessity be realized; and

(B*ii*) a totality of which the components yet to be realized may possibly, but will not necessarily, be realized.

(3) Both (B*i*) and (B*ii*) may be subdivided into

(*a*) the case in which there is (necessarily or possibly) some time at which all the components will have been realized; and

(*b*) the case in which there is, for any component, a time at which (necessarily or possibly) it will have been realized.

The examples of 'the day' and 'the contest' ($^a21-23$). The point of the examples might be to illustrate distinction (1) ('by one thing's always happening after another') or distinction (2). What follows, i.e. the distinction of the Olympic Games case into 'potential' and 'actual', can hardly be distinction (3), so must be distinction (2). Hence 'the day' and 'the contest' should be making distinction (1). This yields a coherent account, as follows:

(I) ($^a18-21$) We are looking for a sense in which the infinite 'is potentially'. It must not be the sort of potentiality that it is possible to realize fully at some one time.

(II) ($^a21-23$) To find the required sense, recall that 'to be' has many senses. Some things 'are' (actually) even when not all their components are as yet actualized, e.g. a day or a games-festival.

(III) ($^a23-25$) This sense of 'be' admits a distinction ((2) above) into 'actually' and 'potentially'. Even if it is not certain that the next Olympic Games will be held at the proper time, still it is right to say that the Olympic Games are in existence, taking that as a claim as to potential existence.

See further on 206^b12-14 below, and Introduction, 3(*c*). (Another difficult passage on the same subject is *Metaphysics* IX.6, 1048^b6-17; on this see Hintikka, 131–4, Lear, 192–3, Ross (2), vol. ii, 252–3.)

Examples of infinites ($^a25-29, 33-206^b3$; cf. $^b10-12$). In this conclusion Aristotle omits to mention the infinity of numbers, on which see further 207^b1-15.

(1) *Time* can be taken to be a series of unit time-stretches (it does not matter what the unit is). Only one such stretch can be in existence at any one time; each such stretch 'perishes' with the advent of its successor. But the advent of its successor is for Aristotle not only possible, but necessary, since it can be proved that time cannot have an end.

(2) *The human race.* The individual members of the race form a series being realized in time. Each individual member perishes within a finite term which is fixed. But the race can, and in fact must,

continue for ever. (For the *necessary* immortality of the race see *Gen. Anim.* II.1 731^{b}24–732^{a}1; and cf. *Gen. et corr.* II.11, 337^{a}34–338^{b}5; *de Caelo* I.12.)

(3) *The division of magnitudes.* The series here is a series of acts of division. There is no necessity for any such series to continue beyond any given point, but there is always a possibility that it may do so. It is true here (as it is not in cases (1) and (2)) that each member persists in the sense that its consequences persist: a magnitude, once divided at some point stays divided at that point (in default of special intervention).

206^{b}3. A close connection is demonstrated between 'the infinite by addition' and 'the infinite by division'. Actual physical magnitudes, Aristotle holds, must be finite, and less than a certain quantity which is fixed for all time. So there is not even a possibility of producing an infinite series of magnitudes of which the total sum eventually exceeds any given magnitude. The only 'infinite by addition' in this case, therefore, is an infinite series of magnitudes of which the total sum is never greater than some fixed magnitude. Such a series can be produced by a series of divisions of the fixed magnitude.

As an example, Aristotle takes the case where the quantities produced by successive divisions are in geometrical progression. If the series of quantities is $a_1, a_2, \ldots, a_n, \ldots$ then with a fixed ratio $r = a_n/a_{n+1}$ (less than unity), the partial sums are all less than $a_1/1 - r$ (Aristotle has in mind the case where $r = 1 - a_1$). If the ratio is taken as unity, the partial sums will increase without limit, and exhaust any given finite magnitude. For 'every finite quantity is exhausted by any definite quantity whatever': i.e. for any two quantities A, B there is an integer n such that $nA > B$. (This is a form of the 'Axiom of Archimedes': on the early use of the Axiom, see Heath (1), vol. i, 326, 328–9).

Aristotle ultimately wishes to 'reduce' all infinites in some sense to the infinite in the divisions of magnitude. On this programme see on 207^{b}21 ff. The present section is a small beginning to the business of reduction.

206^{b}12. Recapitulation with a few extra points.

'And actually too . . .': This remark is apparently at variance with the interpretation offered of 206^{a}18–25. It must be making the point that, though an infinite never actually exists, as such, it is true to say that potentially infinite processes are actually occurring. Does it follow that the same point should be read back into 206^{a}18–25? Not necessarily, for there Aristotle is concerned with establishing the sense of 'potentially' which is relevant, and it is in his manner to introduce new points by means of the same examples, in a recapitulation.

'Potentially in the way in which matter is': on the infinite as 'matter' see on 207^{a}15 ff.

The impossibility of a potential infinite in respect of unbounded addition (^{b}20−27). The reasoning here is faulty. If it is granted that there cannot be an actual infinitely extended body, as Aristotle claims to prove in ch. 5, it still does not follow that there cannot be a corresponding *potential* infinite. That would involve the continual, unbounded, expansion of an always finite universe. So Aristotle needs the extra premiss that the size of the universe is not only finite but fixed, or at least of bounded variation. This, perhaps, he takes for granted: cf. 207^{b}15−21, where the point is made explicitly. (Here, the derivative infinites such as those of time and the human race are ignored; these, of course, do involve unbounded expansion of a kind.)

Plato's opinions: see on 203^{a}4 ff.

206^{b}33. A definition of 'infinite' is given, and contrasted with the meanings of 'whole' and 'complete'.

(1) 'Whole' *and* 'complete'. The explanatory or defining clauses contain an ambiguity, paralleled in the definition of the infinite:

(*a*) (^{a}8: *hou mēden exō*) (*i*) 'that outside which nothing is'; or (*ii*) 'that of which no part is outside'.

(*b*) (^{a}9−10: *hou mēden apestin*) (*i*) 'that from which nothing is absent'; or (*ii*) 'that of which no part is absent'.

In both cases (*i*) can hardly be the right rendering, since it would have the consequence that only the universe could be whole or complete. The rendering with 'part' is further supported by *Metaphysics* V.26, 1023^{b}26−7. 'We call a whole . . . that of which no part (*meros*) is absent out of those of which we call it a whole by nature'; and by *Metaphysics* V.16, 1021^{b}12−13: 'We call complete . . . that outside which not even one portion is to be found.' (Kirwan's translations; see Kirwan, 167, 175−7). These passages make clear that the genitive *hou* has in effect two roles, and that the (*ii*) versions should be expanded to read: 'that of which no part is outside *itself*', 'that of which no part is absent *from itself*'. The definition appears already in Plato *Parmenides* 137^{c}7−8, with *meros*.

The notions of *whole* and *complete* can thus be applied to members of a class having a natural 'specification': every human being will have a right ear, barring some special, accidental intervention, although human beings without right ears are just as much human beings as others. The application to the universe is rather different.

There are two strands to the 'wholeness' of Aristotle's universe: (*a*) that it is all-embracing (here sense (*i*) comes in); (*b*) that it is a satisfactory organic unity—not lacking anything it needs to function as such. This is more like sense (*ii*); though the notion of a 'natural specification' for the universe may seem odd, it is in line with Aristotle's teleology. (The analysis of *Metaphysics* V.26 distinguishes the senses of 'up to specification' and of 'making up a unity'.) Teleology is more clearly in view in the notion of 'complete', here and at *Metaphysics* V.16. *Telos*, here rendered 'end', is said to be a 'limit' (*peras*): the thought being that what is complete is up to specification and therefore sharply defined (unlike the infinite—on the formlessness of the infinite see 207^{a}15—32 below).

'That outside which absence is . . .' (^{a}12): possibly aimed at a theory of a world-system suspended in a void, such as that of 'the Pythagoreans': see IV.6, 213^{b}22—7. The point is that saying that there is a void outside is different from denying that there is anything outside (a void entails e.g. at least the possibility of movement through the void).

(2) *The definition of 'infinite'* (206^{b}33—207^{a}8). Again there is an ambiguity in the defining clauses:

(*i*) 'that outside which there is always something (it is always possible to take something)'; or (*ii*) 'that of which some part is always outside (it is always possible to take some part outside)'.

There are various reasons for preferring (*ii*) to (*i*). First there ought to be a parallel between these clauses and the corresponding ones about 'whole' and 'complete'. Secondly, the characterization of the infinite, as involving a series which can always be continued, is given more precisely by (*ii*) than by (*i*). Thirdly, the clause has been anticipated at 206^{b}17—18. Taken by itself, the phrase at 206^{b}17—18 tells neither way, but it is repeated here in connection with the ring (207^{a}3). Here the point is obviously not that 'it is always possible to find something outside', since that would apply to any ring whatever; but that 'it is always possible to find some part beyond' the part already reached. It may be objected that (*ii*) produces a false opposition, namely between 'that of which no part is outside *itself*' and 'that of which some part is always outside *the parts so far considered*'. But Aristotle need not be implying that there is an exact opposition; merely that there is a neat contrast.

Circular things called 'infinite': see on 204^{a}4—5.

207^{a}15. Further points arising from the definition of the infinite. Parmenides and Melissus: Parmenides B 8, 42—44; Melissus' monolithic universe was infinite in size, B 3, and in time, B2.

'It is from this that people derive . . .', cf. 203^{b}10—15.

The infinite as matter. The characterization here of the infinite as 'the material of the completeness of magnitude' (^{a}21−22) should be taken together with 206^{b}14−15 (the infinite is potentially as matter is) and 207^{b}34−208^{a}4 (the infinite is a material cause). 'Potentially as matter is' is a recognized sense of 'potentially' at *Metaphysics* IX.6, 1048^{b}6−17, where the application to the infinite is explained: 'The infinite is not potentially in the sense that it will *actually* be separate, but in knowledge [it will be separate].' The position is the same with the matter of any substance. That is not the sort of thing that can ever actually *be* a substance in its own right. But it can be separated in thought; we can think away everything that makes the matter some determinate substance and what is left by this thought-experiment is the matter itself. Just so, in thought we can separate an infinite series from its successive partial realizations. 'Potentially' means 'potentially separate in thought'. But 'potentially' in this sense also conveys the thought that the matter is the matrix of a whole range of possibilities, some of which will be successively realized as the matter receives different forms. Analogously, an infinite series makes an unending pilgrimage through successive definite but partial realizations.

If, then, the infinite is a kind of matter, of what is it the matter? At this point Aristotle is clearly considering only what he regards as the primary kind of infinity, namely the divisibility *ad infinitum* of physical bodies. Any physical body of a definite size may be considered a whole, from which divisions start. What is 'potentially whole', in this context is the infinite series of pieces created by an infinite division-process; or, correspondingly, the infinite series of partial sums of pieces in an infinite addition process. What is being said, then, is that, when an infinite division-process occurs in a physical body (*a*) the infinite, i.e. the infinite collection of parts, exists only potentially in a way analogous to that in which matter does; (*b*) the infinite is 'potentially whole' in the sense that it potentially constitutes a whole by addition; and therefore (*c*) the infinite is the material out of which the completeness of the magnitude is constituted. All this is still true, of course, even if no division takes place; the various infinite series that might have come about then are present in a doubly potential way. At some points it seems as though Aristotle does not distinguish between particular infinite division-processes and the general potentiality for being divided *ad infinitum*, when he uses the phrase 'the infinite'.

'Not in itself but in respect of something else' (^{a}24): it is not as being infinite that the infinite could constitute a whole, but only as inhering in some particular body that was in fact a whole.

The infinite as formless, unknowable, and surrounded. Since the

infinite is a kind of matter, it is formless and therefore unknowable
(^{a}25–6). Connected with this point is the remark that it 'does not
surround but is surrounded': i.e. does not constitute a defining
boundary but is the undefined matter which is detachable in thought
from the boundary. These are Aristotelian commonplaces about
matter (e.g. *Physics* I.7, 191^{a}7–12, *Metaphysics* VII.10, 1036^{a}8–9;
11, 1037^{a}27, *de Caelo* IV.4, 312^{a}12–16). On the infinite as unknowable, cf. *Physics* I.6, 189^{a}12–13; *Post. An.* I.22, 82^{b}38–83^{a}1. (See
also Introduction 3(*c*).)

The parenthesis of ^{a}29–32 ('If it surrounds . . .') is directed
against Plato's theory, for which see 203^{a}15–16, 206^{b}27–33.

CHAPTER 7

207^{a}33. The infinite's being like matter makes it reasonable that it
should be found only within a spatial boundary supplied by a form.
See on 207^{a}15 ff., above. Again the possibility of unbounded expansion is not considered.

207^{b}1. The section professes to explain the contrast between the
ways in which number is infinite and magnitudes are infinite.

(1) *Number* (^{b}5–15). Aristotle is concerned with the positive
integers, the only numbers he recognized. There is a least positive
integer, which cannot be divided into two positive integers, namely 1.
But the series of positive integers is infinite, in some sense which has
not yet been explicitly given. Assuming that the general ideas of
206^{a}9–^{b}15 must govern numbers as well, one would expect that the
series of positive integers is infinite in the following precise sense:
for any given integer *n*, it is possible for there to be an integer *n* + 1.
This is the *minimum* sense that can be given; it might be that
Aristotle intended something stronger, e.g.: for any given integer *n*,
there exists an integer *n* + 1. Against this stronger sense, it is an
objection that if that were so, infinitely many integers would exist,
at once, which would be incompatible with Aristotle's finitism.

In the present section Aristotle makes various restrictive remarks,
which in sum confirm that he wishes to deny the stronger claim.

(*a*) 'in the direction of more it is always possible to conceive of
more–since the halvings of magnitude are infinite' (^{b}10–11). The
introduction of conceivability here is confusing, since Aristotle later
agrees (208^{a}14–19) that what is conceivable is not in general a guide
to what is actually the case. In the case of numbers it may be that to
be conceived of is to be; see on 208^{a}5 ff. and Additional Note A.

In any case, no more is being claimed here than that there always *can* be a greater number than any assigned number; and that this fact is shown by the divisibility *ad infinitum* of magnitudes. Clearly, if a magnitude has been divided into n magnitudes, its further divisibility entails at least the possible existence of some number large than n.

(*b*) 'It (the infinite in number) is potentially, but not in actual operation' (^{b}11–12). This affirms that there cannot ever actually be (at one time) infinitely many numbers.

(*c*) 'This number is not separable (*chōristos*)' (^{b}13–14). 'this number' presumably means 'the sort of number we are talking about'. 'Separable' standardly means 'existing or capable of existing independently of ordinary objects' (cf. 203^{a}6–7). In Plato's theory there were separable numbers; and, in general, if numbers are separable it is hard to avoid supposing them to constitute an actual infinite totality (cf. 'separated' and 'infinite' 204^{b}7–8). Aristotle is therefore emphasizing that, in his view, there are no *abstract* numbers. (On Aristotle's general theory of numbers, see Additional Note A.)

(*d*) 'The infinity does not stay still, but comes to be, in the same way as time and the number of time' (^{b}14–15). An infinity that 'stayed still' without change would be a co-present infinity. This is ruled out; the infinity of numbers depends on the existence of increasing series in time, just like that of time itself. The reason is that the very existence of numbers depends on the existence of countable totalities of which the numbers can increase *ad infinitum*, but only progressively, in time.

From (*a*) (*b*) (*c*) (*d*) a consistent minimalist position on the infinity of numbers emerges. To make it fully coherent, we require an account of what it is for an individual number to exist. The two most plausible solutions for Aristotle, given that he has abandoned abstract numbers, are (*i*) that for a number to be is to be conceived of by some mind; or (*ii*) that for a number to be is to be the number of some actual totality. On this problem see Additional Note A. Either solution will provide a potential infinity of numbers, but no actual co-present infinity. On the 'reduction' of one infinity to another see on 207^{a}20 ff.

Further points on number:

'The one is indivisible' (^{b}6). The number 1 cannot be represented as the sum of two positive whole numbers. But that arithmetical fact is (in Aristotle's theory of numbers) based upon a more fundamental philosophical fact. Whatever can be counted as 'one X' cannot also be counted as 'many X's': for any concept X which was such that whatever was one X was also many X's would not allow there to be any determinate number of X's at all; and hence it would not even be true that there was one X or five X's. (At most what is one X might *potentially* be many X's.) The existence of numbers derives from the existence of determinate counting-concepts under which 'the one is indivisible'. In counting a plurality we have to establish a correspondence which makes each member 'one X'; so the plurality is 'many ones'. For more on this subject see 220^{b}18–22, *Metaphysics* X.1; and Additional Note A.

"'Three' and 'two' are derivative names" (^{b}8–9). 'Derivative' (*parōnumos*) signals a relation of derivation between two words, which corresponds to a logical dependence between the things signified. 'When things get their name from something, with a difference of ending, they are called *derivative*.' (*Categories* 1, 1^{a}12–5, Ackrill's translation modified, see Ackrill (1), 72–3.) The point here is that the numbers 2 and 3 (for example) are *not* so called in the primary sense of the words 'three', 'two'; rather, they get their names by derivation from the use of the words 'three', 'two' as applied to actual totalities. This derivation rests on a logical dependence going the same way. The existence of, and our understanding of, the number 3, is derived from the existence of, and our understanding of, actual trios. This is in accord with Aristotle's doctrine of abstraction in mathematics (on which see Additional Note A). The point of this parenthesis here is presumably to remove the air of circularity from the claim that a number is 'many ones'. If 3 is to be understood as 'three ones' we must already understand the adjectival use of 'three'; so that that understanding must be not derived from the understanding of 3, but the other way around.

(2) *Magnitudes* (^{b}15–21). Most of this is recapitulation, but there are two new points:

(*a*) 'The continuous is divided' (^{b}16–17). Here for the first time it is mentioned that it is because they are continuous that magnitudes are divisible *ad infinitum*. Cf. 208^{a}2 and 200^{b}16–20. See on 207^{b}34 ff.

(*b*) The argument at ^{b}17–21 is curious. The premisses are apparently:

(*i*) for any size S, if it is possible for there to be a body potentially of size S, it is possible for there to be a body actually of size S;

(*ii*) no sensible magnitude is infinite;

(*iii*) nothing can be greater than the world.

and the conclusion is:

(*iv*) it is not possible for there to be (a body) exceeding every definite size.

Here (*iv*) is ambiguous in a familiar way. If it means:

(*iva*) it is not possible for there to be an infinitely large body, then the conclusion is not novel, and is contained in premiss (*ii*). If we suppose that premiss (*ii*) is a mistaken interpolation, then (*iva*) might follow from (*iii*), which would leave (*i*) redundant.

If we interpret (*iv*) more interestingly as

(*ivb*) it is not possible for some body to exceed every definite size at some time or other (but not necessarily all at once).

then we have, at long last, an argument against the possibility of expandibility *ad infinitum*. Such an argument seems particularly necessary in the present section, since the contrast is with numbers which *are* 'expandible'. Moreover, we can now construct an argument using both (*i*) and (*iii*). Here (*iii*) must be understood to imply

(*iiib*) nothing can actually be greater than some *fixed* finite size W.

Then from (*i*) and (*iiib*) it follows that it is not possible for there to be a body potentially of size X, where X is any size greater than W. Hence, obviously, no body is expandible *ad infinitum*, since it is not even expandible to (say) 2 W.

The presence of (*ii*) in this argument is still unexplained and there is also the obvious objection that it has not been shown that the world is of fixed size. For this point see *de Caelo* I.3, 270^{a}22–5. Perhaps (*ii*) is used to show that the world must be of finite size, and the fixity of the size is taken for granted.

207^{b}21. The different uses of 'infinite'. The claims are:

(*a*) that 'infinite' has different uses in each of its principal spheres of application (to magnitudes, to changes, to times etc.);

(*b*) that these uses are related by derivation: 'infinite' as applied to time has a use derived from 'infinite' as applied to change, and that in turn from 'infinite' as applied to magnitude.

The detection of different but related uses of the same word is frequent in Aristotle, and often structurally important in his thought. (See on this particularly Owen (2).) As to 'infinite' Aristotle has already tried to show that the infinity of numbers is somehow grounded in the infinite divisibility of magnitudes (207^b 10–11, cf. 206^{b}3–12): but that does not of itself indicate either a difference or a derivation of the use of 'infinite'.

In IV.11, at 219^{a}10 ff. and subsequently, Aristotle partly unfolds a 'grand design' in which all metrical and topological properties of time-intervals are to be defined in terms of, and shown to be dependent on the corresponding properties of changes, and these in turn are to be similarly derived from those of magnitudes. This grand design is here extended to the property of being infinite, with the same chain of dependences. Probably Aristotle intended a systematic treatment which was never completed. (See on 219^{a}10 ff.)

There is thus a cluster of related but distinct theses in the air here: (a) the difference of uses of 'infinite'; (b) the derivability of some uses from others; (c) the dependences (ontological, logical, epistemological) of some infinites on others; (d) the correspondences in structure between different infinites, owing to the dependences. The central thesis is (c), from which (b) and (d) follow more or less easily.

Thesis (a): *the difference of uses.* The primary use is 'divisible *ad infinitum*' applied to a finite magnitude. It is reasonable to claim that this is a different use from that in which 'infinite' is applied to an unending series in time. But it is less easy to understand the supposed differences between the senses of 'infinite' as applied to numbers, changes, and time. Moreover, Aristotle has previously given, 207^{a}7–8, what appears to be a perfectly general definition of 'infinite'. To this objection, the reply must be that the definition is in fact multiply ambiguous in a way that turns it into a definition-schema, the ambiguity residing in the word 'outside', which has different but related meanings in each type of case. Thus, 'capable of increasing *ad infinitum*' has different meanings as applied to change, time, and number, if and only if 'more' or 'increase' does. Since time is here being thought of as a kind of number (on this see 219^{b}2 ff. and the succeeding sections of the discussions of time), the cases of time and number may be merged. Perhaps then the point is that change increases continuously, while number, and therefore time, increases discontinuously. (On the sense in which time is continuous see on 219^{a}10 ff.)

The point of stating thesis (a) is (at least partly) to dispel the Platonist assumption that there could be a quite general treatment, mathematical or philosophical, of all infinites at once. Rather, Aristotle wishes to insist, the study of the infinite breaks down into (i) the study of the infinite divisibility of magnitudes, which is part of physics and, abstracting from physics, geometry; (ii) the study of the infinite continuability of changes, which is another part of physics; (iii) the study of the infinite increasibility of totalities, which is yet another part of physics and, abstracting from physics, arithmetic.

Thesis (b): *the derivations of uses.* These are to be exhibited entirely in terms of the dependence-relations.

Thesis (c): *the dependence-relations between infinites of different kinds.* The grand design has been begun by the statements at 206^{b}3–12, 207^{b}10–11. But a full treatment is lacking in these chapters. The promise here 'later we shall say what each (of the infinites) is' seems to promise a full treatment of theses (*a*), (*b*), and (*c*). The promise is nowhere redeemed, unless indirectly in those parts of *Physics* IV and VI that treat generally of the structural relationships between magnitudes, changes, and times, with occasional remarks about infinity. On these relationships generally, see on 219^{a}10 ff. To mention only the most obvious difficulty about thesis (*c*) and correspondingly (*b*): in what sense does Aristotle suppose that the infinite in change, i.e. the unending continuability of change, is dependent upon the infinite in magnitude, i.e. the divisibility *ad infinitum* of finite magnitudes? For similar and related difficulties with other parts of the grand design see on 219^{a}10 ff.

Thesis (*d*): *the structural correspondences between different kinds of infinites.* Here too a beginning has been made, at 206^{b}3–12, in exhibiting the structural correspondence between the infinites 'by division' and the infinites 'by addition'. Again, there is no further treatment: but cf. again on 219^{a}10 ff.

'Why every magnitude is divisible into magnitudes': on this see *Physics* VI.1 and 2. It looks as though *Physics* VI is part of the projected systematic exploration of the correspondences between magnitudes, changes, and times.

207^{b}27. In these brief remarks Aristotle considers only geometry, not arithmetic: and the geometry of his day was plane and solid Euclidean geometry, developed about as far as in Euclid's *Elements*, plus the beginnings of the theory of conic sections.

(1) Aristotle claims that geometers do not use, and therefore do not need, infinitely extended lines (or planes, or solids, *a fortiori*). He implies that such lines did occur in the geometry of his day; his claim is that they can always be replaced, without damage to the reasoning, by suitably long finite ones.

It is helpful to test the claim against the geometry of Euclid's *Elements*. Euclid, notoriously, speaks of lines as being produced *ad infinitum*. The crucial cases occur in book 1, in connection with the theory of parallel lines: *Elements* I, Def. 23, Post. 5, Prop. 29. (Prop. 12 is a non-essential case.) It is clear enough that in all these cases mention of infinity can be avoided, but only at the cost of quantifying over all lengths. Thus, for Def. 23 we may substitute: 'Parallel lines are straight lines lying in the same plane and such that, for all lengths L, if both are produced to be of length L, the lines do not intersect'; and in Post. 5: 'there is a length L such that if the two lines are produced to that length . . .'.

But quantification over all lengths, when combined with Aristotle's finitism and his doctrines about the existence of mathematical objects, is also problematic. At any time, the lengths available to be quantified over cannot constitute an infinite totality, since for Aristotle there are no infinite totalities. So there will be a longest length; which fact will cause Def. 23 to bring out as parallel too many pairs of lines and to falsify Post. 5.

This example shows that Aristotle's underlying philosophy of mathematics requires careful handling. The subject is explored further in Additional Note A, which suggests a way in which a consistent arithmetic on Aristotelian finitist lines can be set up. The corresponding construction for geometry turns out to require such substitutions as the following:

Euclidean Def. 23: Parallel straight lines are those which, being in the same plane and being produced indefinitely in both directions, do not meet in either direction.

Aristotelian Def. 23: Parallel straight lines are those which, being in the same plane, are such that it is not possible that there should be a length L such that, if the lines are produced in either direction to a length L, they meet.

Here, modal operators such as 'it is possible that' are an essential part of the structure of definitions and propositions; and quantification over all lengths may occur within the scope of modal operators. (For further details see Additional Note A.)

(2) If this finitist reinterpretation of geometry is carried through, it does not follow that there exist arbitrarily long lines, but it does follow that, for any line, the existence of a longer line is possible, and, on any reasonable interpretation of Aristotle's view as to the existence of geometrical objects, the geometer can actually bring it about that such a longer line exists. In this way, the words 'they require that there should be an arbitrarily long finite line' describe a requirement which would still be met by the finitist reformulation.

But there is a further complication. For Aristotle, the universe is necessarily of fixed finite size. It therefore becomes doubtful, in view of the close link between the actual world and mathematical objects, whether for Aristotle it is possible to admit that there could exist a line of greater length than the diameter of the universe. This is one of the implications of the remark at 207^{b}15−21 that there cannot be even a potential infinite in the direction of increase of spatial extension.

As a consequence, Euclidean geometry would have to undergo a further reformulation, in which, for instance, there would be no room for the 'Aristotelian Def. 23' suggested above. The demand that there should be a fixed finite upper limit even to possible lengths brings about a thoroughly 'localized' formulation, in which all mention of how lines etc. behave at 'sufficiently great distance' is absent. Euclid's Def. 23, even in the finitist version, is essentially a definition in terms of behaviour 'at sufficiently great distance'. The interesting question is: how much of the geometry of Aristotle's day can be reformulated, as he seems to demand, in 'localized' terms?

(3) The theory of parallel lines, as it happens, is quite simply localizable. We may substitute, for Def. 23 and Post. 5, (i) a localized definition of 'parallel' in terms of, for instance, the equal angles property; (ii) a localized postulate equivalent to the parallel postulate: e.g. 'all triangles have the sum of their angles equal to two right angles.' We know that there was debate in Aristotle's day as to which propositions should figure as postulates and which as theorems derived from them (*Prior An.* II.16, 65^{a}4–9; 17, 66^{a}11–15; and Heath (3), 27–30). Such debate must have been essentially philosophical; there is therefore nothing implausible in supposing that Aristotle supported a version different from the one that later became enshrined in Euclid's *Elements*.

With these formulations, the elementary geometry of Euclid *Elements* I to IV can easily be presented in a localized form. For its theorems are all in essence 'local', in the sense that they do not depend essentially on the behaviour of lines etc. at sufficiently great distances. Indeed, they prove theorems about figures which may be taken arbitrarily small. This is the further point made here by Aristotle when he remarks that, for the purposes of proof, any geometrical diagram may be scaled down arbitrarily small. The existence of similar figures of arbitrarily small size is a consequence of the 'two right angles' postulate.

Was there, one might ask, any geometry in Aristotle's time which was not 'localizable'? Only, it seems, some of the elementary theory of conic sections. Much of this is 'local'; but the asymptotic properties of the curves are obviously not. Yet even here, 'localized' theorems can be proved which for many purposes are acceptable substitutes for theorems about asymptotic properties. Thus, instead of saying that a hyperbola approaches a straight line as it tends to infinity, one may say that, taking sufficiently small-scale models of the original hyperbola, we shall find the scale models approaching arbitrarily closely to the corresponding lines.

Once the 'scaling-down' trick is thoroughly understood, it is convenient for geometers to forget about it, and to talk as though there existed arbitrarily long lines. Such 'loose talk' Aristotle recognizes, implicitly here, and explicitly at *Metaphysics* XIV.2, 1089^{a}21–25, as not detracting from the truth of what is proved.

(4) Another use of infinity in geometry is not covered by what Aristotle says here. There is use of actual infinites, and quantification over them, in Eudoxus' theory of ratios, as set out in Euclid *Elements* V, and in the applications of that theory to the proofs

using the 'method of exhaustion', also due to Eudoxus, which appear in *Elements* XI and XII. Here it is infinitely large totalities that appear. Once, again, a finitist reworking is possible, saving the essential features. For the key idea of the method is that any plane or solid figure may be approximated with arbitrarily great accuracy by a large enough number of rectilinear figures. There is nothing here to disturb an Aristotelian finitist. For example, the claim that the series 1, 1/2, 1/4, 1/8 . . . approaches arbitrarily close to zero may be reformulated as follows: for any line AB, and any segment AX of AB, there can be a finite sequence of successive bisections yielding segments AB, AC, AD, . . . AN such that the last segment is less than AX. This is provable, with the help of the 'Axiom of Archimedes', which provides the crucial fact that, for some finite n, n.AX is greater than AB. And Aristotle knew and accepted the 'Axiom of Archimedes'. In fact, he knew Eudoxus' work generally, recognized its importance, and made use of it in his ratio-propositions in physics. (See Heath (3), 41–4, 223–4 on *Post. An.* I.5, 74^{a}16–^{b}4, *Metaphysics* VI.1, 1026^{a}23–27; XIII.2, 1077^a 9–10, ^{b}17–22.)

207^{b}34. The infinite as 'material cause': see on 207^{a}15 ff. Its use as a material cause by others: 203^{a}16–18, and, for Plato, 203^{a}15–16 with *Physics* I.4, 187^{a}16–18.

'Its being is privation': it is in its essence not anything positive or form-like.

'What in itself underlies it is the continuous and perceptible by sense': in its primary sense, 'infinite' applies to physical magnitudes. But it applies to them in virtue of their being spatially extended and accessible to sense-perception (otherwise they could not be physically divided), and whatever is such must be a *continuum* (there cannot be extension if there are only points).

On the four 'causes', i.e. types of explanation see generally *Physics* II.3, and Hocutt.

CHAPTER 8

208^{a}5. Final clearing-up of points raised in favour of actual infinites at 203^{b}15 ff. The numbering used here corresponds to that of the earlier section.

(*iii*) This solution is incorporated into Aristotle's own theory of the elements: *de Caelo* III.6, 305^{a}14–32; *Gen. et Corr.* I.3, 318^{a}9–319^{b}5.

(*iv*) A spatial limit seems to imply the existence of something beyond itself. Aristotle's counter, that there is a conceptual difference between being limited and being in contact (with something outside), though correct, is hardly sufficient as a reply. Whatever force the original intuition had is left unimpaired. The same is true of his other remark, that it is not the case that anything whatever can be in contact with anything whatever.

Possibly Aristotle is thinking not so much of the original common-sense argument as of a problem relating to his own conception of the universe. He wants the outermost sphere of the heavens to be moved by the unmoved mover, which is to be 'on the circumference' and in contact with the sphere, yet it is not to have any location or spatial extension, and the sphere is not to be in contact with it. (See *Physics* V.3, 226^{b}21–3; VIII.10, 267^{b}6–9; *Gen. et Corr.* I.6, 322^{b}29–323^{a}33, Joachim, 141–8; *de Caelo* I.9, 279^{a}6–18.)

This kind of theory can be extended into a general reply to the original argument. Aristotle can concede that a spatial limit implies the existence of something beyond, and then deny the next step: what lies beyond need not itself be spatially extended, and what is limited need not, then, be in contact with it.

(*v*) The original claim was that certain things, e.g. the number series, 'do not give out in thought' and are therefore infinite.

The possible meanings for 'they do not give out in thought' can be conveniently exhibited, for the paradigm case of the number series, as follows. We use a sentential operator C ('it is conceivable that'): (quantification over existing numbers)

(A) $\neg$ C $\neg$ (x) (Ey) ($y > x$): 'it is inconceivable that there is a greatest number';

(B) C (x) (Ey) ($y > x$): 'it is conceivable that there is no greatest number'.;

(C) (x) $\neg$ C $\neg$ (Ey) ($y > x$): 'for any existing number it is inconceivable that there is not a greater';

(D) (x) C (Ey) ($y > x$): 'for any existing number it is conceivable that there is a greater'.

It is natural to suppose 'C' subject to the following axioms: (a) $\neg$ C $\neg$ $p \rightarrow p \rightarrow Cp$; ($b$) $\neg$ C $\neg$ (x) (ϕx) $\rightarrow$ (x) $\neg$ C $\neg$ (ϕx). If so, these are the implications.

$$(A) \rightarrow (C) \rightarrow (x)\,(Ey)\,(y > x) \quad \begin{cases} \rightarrow (B) \\ \rightarrow (D) \end{cases}$$

Now Aristotle cannot admit (A) or (C) to be true, since they both imply (x) (Ey) ($y > x$), which he rejects. So it is not (A) or (C) that he is assuming his opponents to use here, since he is willing to admit that 'they do not give out in thought'. The choice is between (B), which makes the existence of an actual infinity conceivable; and (D) which makes a potential infinity conceivable, and indeed is a consequence of Aristotle's own theory. What Aristotle is controverting is not (B) or (D) itself, but the inference from (B) or (D) to the actuality of what is conceivable. Aristotle's point is simply that this is not in general valid. But this point alone is hardly enough to deal with (B); for it might well be argued on Aristotelian lines that, at least in the case of mathematics, what is conceivable is also possible. (B) would then yield $\Diamond (x) (Ey) (y > x)$, 'it is possible that there is no greatest number', which Aristotle has to reject. Probably, therefore, 'they do not give out in thought' is to be interpreted as (D).

Even (D) gives an un-Aristotelian result for spatial magnitudes, if the principle $Cp \rightarrow \Diamond p$ is allowed to hold unrestrictedly. For, with quantification over magnitudes, $(x) \Diamond (Ey) (y > x)$ 'for any actual magnitude it is possible that there is a greater' is not acceptable to Aristotle. Hintikka, 124–30 has supplied reasons for thinking that Aristotle would have barred the inference $Cp \rightarrow \Diamond p$ in such cases. On Aristotle's general doctrines about existence of numbers and geometrical objects see Additional Note A.

(*i*) Time and change: these have been brought in as potentially infinite. (On the problem of past time, see Introduction 3(*c*).) 'Thought' here may just mean 'the thought of them'; thinking about such things as infinitely proceeding time is itself a (potentially) infinite process in time. In other words, there cannot be a *simultaneous* conception of the whole of infinite time; that would involve the existence of an actual infinite. If so, even Aristotle's God cannot see the world *sub specie aeternitatis*; though it may see all the essentially timeless aspects present at any one time.

(*ii*) Magnitude, too, is only potentially infinite: hence, in particular, no magnitude contains infinitely many actually existing points or substretches. On the 'increase in thought' see on (*v*) above.

BOOK FOUR

PLACE

CHAPTER 1

208ª27. (*a*) Motivation for the study of place (ª27–32). This motivation is more to the point than that given at 200ᵇ20–1.

'About place': Aristotle's use of the noun *topos* ('place') is variable in the same ways as ordinary English use of 'space'. (1) 'Place' as a count-noun: e.g. 'every body is in a place', 'the place of this body'. (2) 'Place' as an apparent mass-term: e.g. 'place is something', 'place has some power'–cf. e.g. 'space is not electrically conducting'. (3) 'Place' as the name of a unique individual, i.e. 'the common place in which all bodies are' (209ª32). The distinction between (2) and (3) is in some cases blurred. Ultimately, use (1) will turn out to be the primary use for Aristotle, but to begin with no priority can be assumed.

'Everyone supposes that things that are, are somewhere': not strictly true; the Platonic Forms are not supposed to be anywhere (209ᵇ33–5: cf. Plato's criticism of the axiom, *Timaeus* 52ª8–ᵈ1; the axiom itself appears at *Parmenides* 145ᵉ1). Nor does it follow from 'what is not, is nowhere' that 'what is, is somewhere'. But Aristotle is merely indicating the outline of common-sense intuitions on the subject (cf. 208ᵇ30–33). (Aristotle himself would probably accept that every substance must be 'somewhere' in the sense of having a spatial relationship to others, but not that every substance is in place–for the unmoved mover is not. For the location of the unmoved mover *Physics* VIII.10, 267ᵇ6–9: for its placelessness, *de Caelo* I.9, 279ª11–18.)

'Of change, the most general and basic kind': arguments that locomotion is the primary kind of change, in various senses, at *Physics* VIII.7, 260ª26–261ª26. It is the 'most general' (*koinē*) perhaps because even the otherwise changeless celestial bodies are subject to it.

(*b*) The difficulty of the study of place (ª32–ᵇ1). The conflicting views of place may be those set out at 209ª31–ᵇ11.

99

Aristotle does in fact use materials on place from previous thinkers (Zeno A24 Diels-Kranz: see 209ª23–5, 210ᵇ21 ff.; Plato, *Parmenides*: see on 209ª2 ff., 31ff., 210ª25 ff.; Plato's *Timaeus* theory and that of his 'unwritten doctrines', see on 209ᴰ6 ff.; perhaps also Gorgias B3 Diels-Kranz, (69)–(70)). Presumably he means that none of these had provided any useful discussion; cf. 209ᵇ16–17.

208ᵇ1. First prima facie argument for the existence of place. Aristotle is concerned with place as something distinct from mere locatedness; see Introduction 4(b) 1, and cf. 208ᵇ27–8: 'something over and above (*para*) bodies'. 'Over and above' seems to imply at least logical independence: cf. the examples of Aristotle's use of *para* in Bonitz, 562ª31–44. The argument of this section, from replacement, purports to show that the place of a particular body may persist as a place even when that body no longer occupies it. As stated, it takes us from

(1) X now is where Y previously was

or

(2) X now is in that in which Y previously was

to

(3) X now is in the place in which Y previously was

with X and Y two different bodies. But if we start with (1) it is not clear how we get to (2), and even (2) does not yield places as distinct from surrounding *bodies*. Once more the argument is little more than a sketch of certain common-sense notions; in locating bodies relatively to one another at various times, we do usually think and talk as though there were persisting slots, representing locations, into which different bodies fitted at different times. From (3) Aristotle draws the conclusion that no place is identical with any of the bodies of which it is temporarily the place, which agains needs a little extra work. The argument is used by Aristotle, speaking in his own person, at 209ᵇ22–30.

208ᵇ8. (*a*) Note on the absolute senses of the six dimensions (ᵇ12–25). The six 'dimensions' are six directions—above, below, left, right, ahead, behind—which Aristotle takes to be definable in an absolute sense everywhere. Absolute 'above' and 'below' are straightforwardly defined as respectively far from and near to the centre of the cosmos. Aristotle's attempt to define an absolute, cosmic sense of the other two pairs is one of the more curious parts of his cosmology: see *de Caelo* II.2 and 5, *Inc. Anim.* 2 and 4; Joachim, 144–6.

Aristotle begins with the point (ᵇ15–18) that in ordinary usage 'above', 'below', etc. are defined by the orientation of the speaker.

The word *thesis* here translated 'position' (i.e. orientation) can also bear the meaning of 'convention' (so 205^{b}34). As the speaker's orientation changes, so his 'above', 'below', etc. change in terms of fixed directions.

With this state of affairs is contrasted (^{b}18—22) the absoluteness of cosmic 'above', 'below', etc. and the conclusion is that these cosmic directions differ in *power*. The parenthesis on mathematical objects (^{b}22—5) seems intended to confirm the claim that ordinary 'above', 'below', etc. are determined by orientation. In the case of such objects their 'left' and 'right' is derived from the left or right of someone studying the diagram representing them. It is obvious in this sense that the designations are conventional; there can be nothing in the objects themselves to determine a left and a right, as they are not in place at all. (All this argument really shows is that 'left', 'right', etc. when applied to geometrical objects are conventional, not that their ordinary use is conventional.)

(*b*) The absolute difference of 'above' and 'below' as proof that place exists and 'has some power' (^{b}8—12, cf. 20—22). Heavy bodies, if not hindered, move naturally downwards; light bodies upwards. Thus these two directions are distinguishable in a non-conventional way, by the natural behaviour of bodies. Bodies also tend to rest by nature when located in certain ways. It hardly follows from this, as Aristotle claims, that there must be natural places which not only exist independently of their bodies but have 'power'. Aristotle in fact later denies (209^{a}22) that a place can be an agent of change. But the general metaphysic of change does suggest that end-states of changes ought to enjoy some sort of independent or semi-independent existence: see Introduction, 4(*b*) 1.

208^{b}25. For this definition of void, see 213^{a}12 ff., 213^{b}30 ff., and notes.

208^{b}27. Conclusion of the prima facie case for the existence of places. 'Over and above bodies': see on 208^{b}1 ff.

'Every body perceptible by sense is in a place': this might be argued for on the basis of the arguments already used, since they apply indifferently to all sense-perceptible bodies.

The arguments given do not clearly reveal Aristotle's own reasons for holding that there are semi-independent places: see Introduction 4(*b*) 1.

The quotation from Hesiod is *Theogony* 116—17. (On the nature of Chaos in Hesiod see West, 192—3.) Aristotle's interpretation makes Chaos an empty space which exists independently of all else, showing that Aristotle recognized the existence of 'common-sense' notions of independently-existing space as providing places for things. But the rest of the dicussion of place completely ignores 'space-based' theories of place (except for Plato's *Timaeus* theory).

'For place does not perish' . . . .: the comment seems pointless, except as a maladroit partial explanation of 'itself is without the others'.

209^a2. Six problems about place. (1), (2), (5), and (6) reappear at 212^b22 ff. (5) is also briefly treated in 210^b21 ff., (6) perhaps at 211^a15−17. See on those sections.

(1) (^a4−7). It is natural to think of the place of a three-dimensional body as being itself three-dimensional. But then a place ought itself to be a body, since an Aristotelian characterization of body is 'what is extended in three dimensions' (e.g. *de Caelo* I.1, 268^a7). In that case, a body's occupying a place would constitute a coincidence of two distinct bodies—assuming that the place of a body is not identical with the body. But two distinct bodies cannot coincide.

(2) (^a7−13). If the argument from replacement, 208^b1−8, is sound, it will apply equally well to the surfaces, lines, and points on the boundaries of physical bodies. Thus, for instance, any vertex-point of some actual cubic body will have to be in a place, distinct from itself, at any moment. But 'we have no distinction between a point and the place of a point'. Why not? The implied argument may be that the place of a point would have to be without extension, like the point itself, and therefore itself a point; but two distinct points cannot coincide. Or the argument may be, as at Plato *Parmenides* 138^a3−7, that what has no parts cannot be 'in' any other thing, in the sense of being surrounded by it: 'If it (the One) were in another thing, it would presumably be surrounded all around by that in which it was, and that would be in contact with it, with many parts, at many places; but it is impossible to be in contact all around in many ways with something that is one and without parts and that does not partake of a circle.'

(3) (^a13−18). The classification of things into 'perceptible by sense' (*aisthēta*) and 'intelligible' (*noēta*) (i.e. to be apprehended only by the intellect), and particularly the suggestion that anything is either an element or composed of elements, suggest a Platonic background (compare the criticisms of Platonic ontology in *Metaphysics* I.9, particularly 992^a10−24, 992^b13−18 on the inability of Plato's theory to account for points, lines, and surfaces; and 992^b18−993^a10 on the mistake of an undifferentiated search for 'the elements of things'). Perhaps this 'argument' was originally formulated as an objection to Platonism. It is not referred to again.

(4) (^{a}18–22). For the four Aristotelian 'causes' (types of explanatory factor), see *Physics* II.3. Prima facie place will not figure as an explanatory factor of any type, and so will be superfluous in science. The puzzle is hardly more than a reminder that one must look at the actual work the notion of *place* does in physics (cf. 211^{a}12–14). It is not referred to again: but cf. on 214^{b}13–17.

(5) (^{a}23–5). From (*a*) 'a place is' and (*b*) 'whatever is, is in a place' (208^{a}29), we have (*c*) 'a place is in a place'. To construct a Zenonian infinite regress we need also (*d*) 'nothing is in itself' and (*e*) the transitivity of 'in'. On the problem see further on 210^{b}21–7; on (*d*) see 210^{a}25–^{b}21.

(6) (^{a}26–9). The problem seems to be constructed as follows (so Simplicius):

(*a*) every body is in a place (208^{a}29);

(*b*) every place contains a body (assumed by those who deny void);

∴ (*c*) the place of each body is neither smaller nor greater than the body itself

(if it were smaller, part of the body would not be included; if greater, part of the place would stand empty);

∴ (*d*) the place of a body growing in size itself grows in size; But

(*e*) a place does not change size (common assumption).

So there is a contradiction from (*a*), (*b*), and (*e*). As interpreted, the argument depends essentially on (*b*), so may have originated as an argument in favour of void. But (*a*) (*c*) (*e*) could equally well be taken as the common assumptions.

CHAPTER 2

209^{a}31. In this chapter Aristotle presents as plausible two lines of thought about place, one of which identifies the place of a body with the shape (the present section), and one of which identifies it with the matter of the body (209^{b}6–17); and then, speaking in his own person, argues against both identifications (209^{b}17–210^{a}13).

Place as a first surrounder (^{a}13–^{b}2). Assume that the place of a body is that which it is most properly said to be *in*. *Being in* is a transitive relation, and as a result there are some statements of the form 'X is in Y' that do little, if anything, towards *locating* X: e.g. 'you are in the universe'. This suggests that the properest, most truly locating sense of 'in' is the most restrictive. So we must look for a 'least surrounder' for X, i.e. some Y such that (*i*) X is in Y and (*ii*) there is no Z such that X is in Z, Z is in Y (with Z ≠ X, Z ≠ Y).

'In respect of themselves . . . in respect of another thing': in general, 'X is F' is 'said in respect of another thing' if the ground for saying it is that (*i*) X is G and (*ii*) X is F *because* X is G and not vice versa. Various kinds of explanation may come under the 'because'; see, for the corresponding senses of the distinction, *Post. An.* I.4 with Barnes (1), 113–19, *Metaphysics* V.18 with Kirwan, 168–70. Here the asymmetry of explanation is grounded very simply: if Y is in Z, then 'X is in Y' implies 'X is in Z' but the converse does not hold.

'Surround' (*periechein*) means 'circumscribe without including as a component part', i.e. it corresponds to sense (8) of 'in' at 210^a14– 24, not to sense (1). ('You are in the earth' with sense (8) of 'in' may seem to imply 'you are in a subterranean position'; more likely 'the earth' is loosely construed to include the area above the earth's surface. The Greek is idiomatic in the sense 'you are on the earth'.)

First surrounder as shape ($^b2$–6). The outer boundary or surface of the body is a surrounder of it and thus the first surrounder. (For a boundary as a surrounder cf. Plato, *Parmenides* 145^a1.) But this boundary may be identified with the 'form and shape' of the body. The 'form' (Aristotelian) of an extended body considered simply as such is its form or shape in the ordinary sense.

'By *which* the magnitude . . . are bounded; for *that* . . .': the antecedent in both cases must be 'the form and the shape' (not 'the place'). 'The magnitude', i.e. the extended body: on Aristotle's use of 'magnitude' (*megethos*) see on 202^b30 ff.

209^b6. If a place is taken to be coextensive with, rather than surrounding, its body, then instead of being a boundary it will be surrounded and bounded by the outer boundary. If we look for something that is so bounded and has nothing but mere extension, it looks as though it must be the matter of the body. For if we remove from the body everything other than extension, only its matter is left.

On this view, the thought experiment proceeds as follows. We start with some ordinary physical body, say a bronze sphere. We abstract the 'limit', i.e. the outer boundary; then the thing has no size or shape, but mere extension: it is an indefinite extension of bronze. We now abstract the 'properties' (*pathē*), i.e. everything that makes it a determinate kind of stuff. (On Aristotle's use of *pathos* see Kirwan, 171–2, on *Metaphysics* V.21.) What is left is mere corporeal extension, which is the matter of the body considered merely as a body.

The point of the 'experiment', then, is to show that the only thing we can extract from the body itself which satisfies the requirements for place in this section is 'the matter of the magnitude'. (For an apparently similar thought-experiment see *Metaphysics* VII.3, 1029^{a}10−27.)

The connection with Plato is stated by Aristotle to be as follows:

(1) In the *Timaeus*, Plato's 'participative' (what Plato in fact calls 'the receptacle of all coming-to-be': *Timaeus* 49^{a}5−6, see in general 48^e−52^d) is what Plato also calls 'space' (*chōra: Timaeus* 52^{a}8);

(2) But the 'participative' is obviously matter, on the *Timaeus* account;

(3) So, in the *Timaeus*, Plato identifies space with matter;

(4) And his reasons for so doing were those just suggested (^{b}6−11).

(5) In his so-called 'unwritten doctrines' he used 'the participative' as a name for something different from the space of the *Timaeus*;

(6) But even here he identified place and space.

This account of Plato's views is rather careless. (1) Plato in the *Timaeus* does not actually use the term 'the participative' (*to metalēptikon*), though the corresponding verb 'participate' does occur in an important characterization of the receptacle: 'A certain invisible and shapeless kind of thing, all-receptive, participating, in the most difficult sort of way, in what is intelligible' (*Timaeus* 51^{a}7−^{b}1). (2) Aristotle interprets Plato's receptacle as playing the same role as Aristotelian matter. If this is understood as 'intelligible matter', the equivalence is close, but not perfect. In particular the existence and whereabouts of a piece of Aristotelian matter are always dependent on those of the body of which it is the matter, whereas the Platonic receptacle seems to be an independent entity of which the parts cannot change their relative positions. (3) Correspondingly, all we can reasonably extract from this claim is the story that Plato wanted to give an account of space which would make it pure extension, and therefore made it something like Aristotelian matter. Perhaps the claim can be substantiated from the remarks of Plato at *Timaeus* 52 ^{a}8−^{d}1. (4) On the 'unwritten doctrines', a controversial subject, little is known for certain; see e.g. Vlastos (4) for one moderate view. For the different use of the 'participative' see below 209^{b}35−210^{a}1. (5) 'Still' seems to mean 'even in the unwritten doctrines'. 'He still declared that place and space were the same thing', is surprising, perhaps a mere mistake of the pen for 'he still declared that matter and space . . .'. Alternatively: 'he still declared that the same thing (viz. the participative) was place and space.' This would fit 209^{b}35 below, where 'place = the participative' seems to be the fixed equation in both of Plato's accounts. On Plato's *Timaeus* theory in general see Introduction 4 (*b*) 6.

209ᵇ17. Arguments against the identifications suggested in the previous two sections.

(1) (^{b}22–31). The argument from replacement, if it shows anything, shows that a place may continue its career as a place though the occupying body leaves it and is replaced by another. This is presumably what is meant by saying that the place is 'separable' from its body, or 'can be separated'. Aristotle's point seems to be that a body's matter and form are logically tied to the body in such a way that they could never have any independent career. Not only could they never exist independently of any body (that is true of places too); they could never exist except as the matter or form respectively of the particular body. (At ^{b}30–32 the phrasing may seem to suggest that the separability argument applies only to the form; but both ^{b}22–23 and 211^{b}36–212^{a}2 contradict that impression.) How far matter and form are logically tied to *a particular individual* in other works of Aristotle is a difficult question.

'Not anything appertaining to the object': literally 'nothing of the object'; on this use of the genitive see on 210^{b}32 ff.

(2) (^{b}31–33). Affirms the view of place as a 'surrounder'. Cf. Plato, *Parmenides* 138^{a}2–^{b}6.

(3) (^{b}33–210^{a}2). A parenthetic thrust at Plato: see above on 209^{b}6 ff.

(4) (210^{a}2–5). A number of different objections seem to be compressed here. (*i*) A body must be able to change its place. This excludes matter as place; a body cannot remain the same body and change its matter. (*ii*) A body must have a natural place to which it naturally moves if not hindered. This of itself does not exclude form (in the sense of 'shape') as place: it might be that every body did have a natural shape in this way. (*iii*) The natural movements in respect of place must be upwards or downwards, i.e. must have 'above' 'below' as their termini. This rules out shape, and anything that does not have, at least relatively to the immediate environment, a specific location.

(5) (210^{a}5–9). The argument may be taken in one of two ways: (*i*) the shape and the matter of any X are in X, and X is in the place of X; hence the place of X is in itself, by transitivity of 'in', if the place is either the shape or the matter. Against taking it this way is the dubious use of transitivity, since it is not clear that 'in' has the same sense throughout (cf. 210^{a}14–24 below). If it does then the sentence 'For both the form . . .' is irrelevant. At best it could be used to show that the shape and the matter are just where X is, not that they are *in* X.

(*ii*) The shape and the matter of any X are in X, in some sense of 'in' upon which nothing turns, in the sense that they always travel about with X. Hence, since they can change places whenever X does, they too are capable to locomotion and must have places at any one time. On this view, then, the place of X will be in a place, and this will lead to an infinite regress or to some other absurdity (the place of the place of X will have to be the matter of the matter of X, and so on).

(6) (210^{a}9−11). This too may be taken in one of two ways: (*i*) In substantial change, e.g. of air into water, both the matter and the form of the air perish, being logically tied to the substance (air) that ceases to be. But how can a *place* perish? The water may be in just the same location as the air was, and we shall want to say that it is in the same place.

(*ii*) In substantial change, e.g. of air into water, both the matter and the form (in the sense of 'shape') of the air may survive; but the location will naturally change, since the natural place of water is different from that of air.

It is difficult to choose between (*i*) and (*ii*) without knowing what account of substantial change is presupposed. In some later writings Aristotle seems to postulate a kind of matter that survives substantial change.

It is difficult not to feel dissatisfied with these arguments. If the point of having a concept of *place* is that it is needed in any account of the locations and locomotions of objects, then all Aristotle needs to say is that there can be locomotion without change of matter or form. (4) comes nearest to making the point.

CHAPTER 3

210^{a}14. Enumeration of different uses of a key word: cf. 203^{b}30 ff. and notes on that section. There are close connections with *Metaphysics* V.23 and 25, on the uses of 'have' (*echein*) and 'part' (*meros*). *Metaphysics* V.23, 1023^{a}23−25, notes that the uses of *en* ('in', 'on') correspond systematically to those of *echein*, i.e. whenever A may be said in some way to 'have' B, B may be said in a corresponding way to be 'in' A. But the *Metaphysics* list makes fewer and coarser distinctions than the present one, finding only four distinct uses (*a*) 1023^{a}8−11, corresponding to (6) here; (*b*) 1023^{a}11−13, to (5) here; (*c*) 1023^{a}13−17 to (1) and (8) here; (*d*) 1023^{a}17−23 without correspondence here. As might be expected with a preposition, not all the uses of *en* can be idiomatically rendered by a single English preposition; and even this list of eight uses is far from complete, as the Greek commentators note, if considered as pure lexicography. But Aristotle is concerned only with philosophically important uses.

(1) 'part' cannot be meant in the widest possible way, otherwise (3) would be subsumed under (1), for 'the form is a part of the genus', *Metaphysics* V.25, 1023ᵇ24. Perhaps 'part' is meant in just the first way of *Metaphysics* V.25: 'We call a part, in one way, the result of any kind of division of a quantity; for what is subtracted from a quantity *qua* quantity is always a part of it.' (*Metaphysics* V.25, 1023ᵇ12–14, Kirwan's translation.)

(2) 'The whole is in the parts', i.e. *consists of* the parts.

(3) 'Man is in animal': 'man' is treated as the name of the species (form), and 'animal' as the name of the genus.

(4) Compare *Metaphysics* V.25, 1023ᵇ22–24: 'Whatever is in the formula indicating each thing is also a portion of the whole; that is why a genus is also called part of its form' (Kirwan's translation). The proper definition of the form *man* states genus and differentia; so the definition contains a term giving the genus *animal*.

(5) 'Hot and cold things' are the matter of a healthy body, because in the theory of health alluded to here it consists essentially in the bodily components' having the right temperatures; *Topics* VI.2, 139ᵇ21, and other passages in Bonitz, 781ᵇ26–28. 'In a subject' of *Categories* 2, 1ª20–ᵇ9, belongs here. The corresponding use of 'have' in *Metaphysics* V.23, 1023ª11–13, is given more generally: 'that (is said to have), in which, as receptive, something is present'. Such a 'receptacle' use could cover not only the relationship of matter to form, but e.g. that of void to occupying body. It is striking that Aristotle does not here explicitly recognize the use of 'in as in a receptacle' as distinct from 'in as in a surrounder' (sense (8)). See further on (8) below.

(6) It is not clear whether 'the first thing productive of change' is the proximate agent of change or the ultimate one. The examples of *Metaphysics* V.23, 1023ª10–11 perhaps suggest the proximate agent; but the King of Persia here (legendary for his remoteness) suggests the ultimate one.

(7) It is obscure what uses Aristotle has in mind here.

(8) A vessel surrounds what is in it; but it may also be said to 'receive' or be occupied by what is in it. So, on the face of it, Aristotle does not here distinguish the 'receptive' from the 'circumscriptive' aspects of being in a vessel or a place; and the discussion in ch. 4 proceeds as though the issue had not been prejudged. Possibility the 'receptive' use is meant to be taken care of by (5).

In what sense is (8) the 'most basic' (*kuriōtaton*) use? Where there are many uses, Aristotle likes to suggest that all but one are derivative, by analogy or metaphor, from one original sense, which is usually of a down-to-earth kind. Controlling, comprising, composing, may all be thought of as analogous to surrounding. (The verbs *echein* and *periechein* apply to most uses.) On this view (8) is chronologically the first use, and probably epistemologically (we understand the others by first grasping (8)).

210^{a}25. Discussion of the problem: can anything be in itself? The problem arises naturally from the analysis of Zeno's puzzle: see on 209^{a}23–25, 210^{b}22–27. Zeno's puzzle in turn may have arisen from those who objected to Parmenides' universe that 'it must be in something'. Puzzles about how 'what is' or 'the one' can be in itself or not in itself, appear also in Gorgias (B3 Diels-Kranz (69–(70)) and in Plato, *Parmenides* 138^{a}7–^{b}5, 145^{b}6–^{c}7. The problem arose for Aristotle's own universe or for the outermost moving celestial sphere, since that was not surrounded by any body or spatially extended container.

(*i*) Aristotle invokes the distinction between 'in (respect of) itself' and 'in respect of something else' (on which see on 209^{a}31 ff.) and applies it to *being in*. X is in Y, in respect of something else, if there is some part or aspect of Y, say Z, such that X is in Z in a primary sense. In Aristotle's examples, we have X = the colour white, Z = the surface of the man, Y = the man *or* the man's body; or again X = knowledge, Z = the reasoning part of the soul, Y = the soul.

(*ii*) Aristotle uses the distinction to construct a case in which X is in X 'in respect of something else', i.e. there is some part or aspect Z of X such that X is in Z; but the point is complicated by the fact that X is in Z, in turn, 'in respect of something else', say Y, which is such that Y is a part or aspect of X, and Y is in Z in the primary sense. If X = the jar of wine, Y = the wine, and Z = the jar, the jar of wine (i.e. the jar filled with wine) is in itself in respect of the wine's being in the jar.

This tortuous construction is applied to the problem of the universe at 212^{a}31–^{b}22. It does not seem to correspond to any natural idiom in Greek, though in English 'self-contained' applies to something partly isolated by its own natural boundaries, and perhaps that is all Aristotle has in mind.

(*iii*) Aristotle next (210^{a}33–4, 210^{b}6 ff.) claims that 'in respect of itself' or 'primarily' nothing can be in itself. In the first place (^{b}8–9) a look at the eight senses of 'in' shows this impossible (e.g. nothing can *surround* itself, which involves being outside itself). (A counter-example is suggested at Plato, *Parmenides* 145^b–^{c}: an indivisible unity is both a whole and all its parts: but the parts are

in the whole or vice versa (senses (1), (2)): so, in either sense, the
unity is in itself; but of course 'parts' has to mean 'proper parts' for
senses (1) and (2).

(*iv*) There follows (^{b}9–21) a tangled argument for the same conclusion. The stages appear to be as follows:

(1) (^{b}16–17). *Being in* is different in definition from *being that
in which*; otherwise, for X to be in Y would be the same as for Y to
be in X, in all cases. For this point, using Leibniz's Law, and
'different in definition' see on 202^{b}5 ff.

(2) (^{b}10–13) Absurd consequences if (1) is denied. In that case,
whenever the wine is in the jar, the jar is in the wine (in exactly the
same sense of 'in') and so the wine and the jar will have to be
identified.

(3) (^{b}13–16) It follows that (1) is true, and hence, even if, *per
impossibile*, the wine and the jar were in each other, the wine's being
in the jar would be conceptually distinct from the jar's being in the
wine. It would not be possible to identify the one state of affairs
with the other, nor the respective roles of the two *relata*. Accordingly, it would just be 'accidental' that the one thing had two different roles, container and contained; as when a physician heals himself
(*Physics* II.1, 192^{b}23–27).

(4) (^{b}18–21) But even the 'accidental' case is impossible. Here
Aristotle does not rule out accidental reciprocal containing (which
he seems to admit at 212^{b}13), but accidental self-containing. The
argument seems to be: a jar is always capable of containing wine, so
long as it is a jar. Put the jar into itself, if that is possible, and then
put wine into the jar. Then the wine and the jar are both in the jar at
once, which is impossible. The argument is defective and obscure,
at best.

210^{b}21. Zeno's puzzle: see on 209^{a}23–25. To make an infinite
regress, Zeno needs at least four assumptions: (*a*) every place is;
(*b*) whatever is, is in a place; (*c*) nothing is in itself; (*d*) 'in' is
transitive (to block reciprocal or cyclic containing); Aristotle's
solution is to deny (*b*): there can be a place which is not itself in a
place, though it may be in something else, in some other sense of
'in'. Thus there need be no infinite series of *places*, which may be
adequate *ad hominem* against Zeno. But Aristotle still ought to
explain how there is not an infinite progression all the same. There
must be something which is not itself spatially contained in anything
outside; for Aristotle this is the bounded universe: see on 212^{a}31–
^{b}22.

210^{b}27. 'The primary "what" and "in which" are different':

whenever X is in Y in the primary sense (in respect of themselves), X is distinct from Y.

'The vessel is nothing pertaining to that which is in it' (literally 'nothing of that which is in it'): on 'pertaining to', see on 210^b32 ff. From distinction of X and Y, Aristotle here infers separability of X from Y, a dubious step.

On the inseparability of the form and the matter see 209^b22-24.

CHAPTER 4

210^b32. Introduction to the substantive discussion of place.

The six axioms ($^b32-^a7$). In Aristotle's method, the first principles of the sciences must be established by dialectical argument from possibly less basic but more immediately evident principles. The six axioms are extracted from the discussion so far as being general principles which cannot be abandoned without the collapse of the whole notion of *place*, i.e. it is taken by Aristotle as more or less obvious that their truth is built into that notion. The procedure is in line with Aristotle's practice elsewhere, though the 'axioms' are not usually stated so explicitly. (See in general, Owen (3), Wieland (2).)

'All things that are thought truly to belong to it in respect of itself': It is unclear whether 'truly' qualifies 'are thought', 'belong' or 'in respect of itself', and however taken the phrase seems slightly odd. Two possibilities: (*a*) 'truly' qualifies 'are thought' emphasizing both that the axioms are held true by some, and that Aristotle is now claiming them as true; (*b*) 'truly' qualifies 'belong' and is explicated by 'in respect of itself'—'are thought to belong *genuinely*, i.e. in respect of itself'. On 'in respect of itself' see on 209^a31 ff.

The six axioms have all appeared previously. (1) See 209^a31-^b2. It is odd that Aristotle should here give in to the 'circumscriptive' view of place, as against the 'receptive', without further argument; even odder, that 'receptive' views of place are reintroduced at $211^b14-212^a2$ and there argued against without the use of this axiom (except just at 212^a2). (2) 'Not anything pertaining to the object', literally 'nothing of the object'. The idiom has already occurred in this connection at 209^b30, 210^b27-31. Other occurrences: 219^a3, 9, 10. The genitive is partitive, and perhaps the best way to take it is as covering all the senses of 'part' given at *Metaphysics* V.25. At 209^b22-30 'X is nothing of Y' allows the inference 'X is separable from Y', so that part of (4) here is redundant, given (2); but Aristotle is simply listing axioms gleaned from what precedes, without being concerned as to the precise logical relation-ships between them. (3) 209ᵃ28–9, cf. 209ᵃ31–ᵇ1. (4) depends on the replacement argument, 208ᵇ1–8, cf. 209ᵇ22–33. (5) (6) 208ᵇ 8–25, 210ᵃ2–5. The use of (5) and (6) might seem to involve circularity; if they bring in theses peculiar to Aristotelian physics they ought not to be used in setting up the foundations of that physics. But Aristotle clearly considers them to be given by common observation, independently of any physical theory.

The aims of the inquiry. (ᵇ7–11). The construction of the sentence is awkward, but the sense is clear. The aim is to provide a definition, a 'what-is-it', in such a way that three further tasks can be achieved: (*a*) to solve the problems that have been gathered and stated (at 209ᵃ2–30), which is not done in detail, but see 212ᵇ22–29, where at least a hint or two is given; (*b*) to bring out as true the stated assumptions, which is shown for some of them—for (1) at 212ᵃ28–9, (3) at 212ᵃ29–30, (5) (6) at 212ᵃ21–8, and for (5) (6) see also 212ᵇ29–213ᵃ10; (*c*) to make clear the reasons for the difficulties—something is done towards this at 212ᵃ7–14, cf. also 211ᵇ10–212ᵃ2.

The whole section is interesting because Aristotle is here unusually self-conscious and explicit about the methodology of such an inquiry.

211ᵃ12. Preliminary points about change in respect of place. 'Place would not be a subject for inquiry if there were not change in respect of place': on this point, see Introduction, 4(*b*) 1.

'The heavens' (*ouranos*): the sphere carrying the fixed stars, the outermost part of the world-system. On the problem of its being in place see 212ᵃ31 ff.

Increase and decrease: Aristotle's point is that this type of change too will have to be accounted for satisfactorily by any theory of place, since it involves change of place. 'Changes position . . . into a smaller or a larger': ambiguous, meaning either (*i*) 'so as to become smaller or larger' or (*ii*) 'into a smaller or larger region'. To make the point, (*ii*) seems necessary. The remarks are perhaps meant to serve also as the solution of the puzzle of 209ᵃ26–29.

Change 'in (respect of) itself' and 'accidentally'. The distinction is a particular case of that between 'in respect of itself' and 'in respect of something else', on which see on 209ᵃ31 ff. The things moved 'in themselves', i.e. of which the motion is primary in explanation, are single sense-perceptible substances (e.g. a man, an amoeba, a con-tinuous volume of water) and artificial unities (e.g. a boat). It is to such things if to anything, that any theory of place must apply; it is these only that can be 'in themselves' in place. The distinction is recalled at 212^{b}7−13, where an important application of it is made to the question of the place of the heavens. Aristotle does not remark that some motions would naturally be described as *mixed*, partly in 'themselves' as being real motions relative to the surroundings, and partly 'accidental' as being due to the motion of the surrounding body: on this kind of situation, Aristotle has only a hesitant comment at 212^{a}14−20. What the distinction, above all, shows is that for Aristotle locomotion is, in the primary sense, change of position *relative to immediate surroundings*, not relative to any absolute landmarks. See further below on 212^{a}14 ff., 212^{a}31 ff., 212^{b}3 ff.

211^{a}23. This section introduces a different distinction based upon a dichotomy: a body is either (*a*) 'divided from' or (*b*) 'continuous with' the surrounding body. The dichotomy is unclear, and is not fully elucidated either by 212^{b}3−6 below, where it is recalled, or by other passages elsewhere (of which the most helpful are *Metaphysics* V.6, 1015^{b}36−1016^{a}17, X.1, 1052^{a}19−27). Nor is it clear exactly how this distinction is related to that of the previous section, though the relationship must be close. What follows is a necessarily tentative account of the distinction and its importance for Aristotle's account of place.

To judge by what is said here and elsewhere, the word 'continuous' (*suneches*) may cover any or all of the following cases: A and B are continuous when they are bodies in contact and (1) are parts of one and the same unitary substance, whether this is (*a*) an organic unity, like an animal; or (*b*) a unity 'with like parts' like a volume of water; *or* (2) are incapable of motion independently of one another; *or* (3) have no physical division separating them. The concept of a 'physical division' however, is elusive. According to Aristotle the various naturally occurring kinds of stuff, even if they are compounds of the four elements, do not have any internal 'fine structure'. Within a given mass of water or of rock there may be no physically defined boundaries; within water there cannot be, but within rock and other solids there may be cracks or faults or lines along which physical splitting has occurred. Between two bodies of different stuffs there is always a physically defined boundary, by definition. It would seem that, for Aristotle, senses (2) and (3) would coincide, apart from some inessential qualifications. Thus, two lumps of rock might be glued or tied or clamped together, making something 'continuous' in sense (2). But the glue or string or clamp is an *external* constraint, nothing to do with the rocks themselves, and if it is removed, there is no continuity in either sense (2) or sense (3). (Cf. *Metaphysics* X.1, 1052^{a}19−25.) Conversely, within a given volume of water, some smaller volume would be continuous in sense (3), but might seem to be not so in sense (2), being capable of independent motion. But it could only, in fact, move in a way independent of the whole if, once again, particular and external causes were operating.

If we take it that sense (3), then, is the sense of 'continuous' here—which is borne out by 212^b3-6 so far as that goes—the first points Aristotle makes are (a) that when a body A is physically divided from the surrounding body B, it is in B as in a place, and primarily in the boundary of B; (b) that when A is not physically divided but continuous with B, it is not in B as in a place (and therefore cannot be used as a counter-example to any proposed definition of place). This claim, that only physically divided bodies can have places (in the strict sense) is compatible with the previous section, since all sense-perceptible substances will be physically divided from their surroundings (the converse does not hold). Throughout this section Aristotle assumes the 'circumscriptive' nature of place (see on 210^b32 ff.), and shows that the primary place of a divided body must be the boundary of the surrounding body, thus anticipating the conclusion of 211^b5-212^a7.

A further point, at $211^a34-{}^b1$, is that a physically divided body moves *in* its container, a continuous one *with* it. Again, the qualification must be understood: that the motion is not caused or checked by external intervention. (At 211^b1-5 occurs in the manuscripts a passage inconsistent with the above interpretation. The passage was known in antiquity, but already questioned then, and there are grounds for suspecting it independent of the general interpretation. See Ross (1), 572, who omits the lines; the present translation follows Ross in doing so.)

On the present reading, the effect of the whole section is to exclude certain (physically not realized) parts of substances from being in place at all. This makes it easier to formulate a definition of place, but thereafter difficulty elsewhere: see on 212^a31 ff.

Difficulty may also seem to threaten what Aristotle says about *contact*. 'The extremes of things which are in contact are in the same spot' (*literally* 'in the same'); compare *Physics* V.3, 226^b21-23: those things are in contact of which the extremes are 'together' (*hama*), and 'together' means 'in one primary place'. Yet (a) on the definition of place to be given, it will turn out that boundaries cannot themselves be *in* places at all, since they are themselves the only places that they could be in; (b) it seems circular, here, to justify an account of what the place of a body is by a concept of *contact* which presupposes the notion of place. These difficulties suggest that Aristotle needs a notion of location which is wider than that of place: cf. Introduction, 4(b) 1.

211^{b}5. From 211^{b}5 to 212^{a}14 Aristotle purports to arrive at the definition of place by a procedure of elimination. The procedure has its puzzling aspects. Thus, Aristotle does not explain how his list of four candidates is arrived at, nor how it can be shown to be exhaustive. It contains two candidates already disposed of (form and matter). In the section in which form is once again rejected, the eventual result is assumed already known. The only really new arguments in the whole passage occur at 211^{b}19–29 and are extremely obscurely expressed.

No doubt the occurrence of such oddities may be satisfactorily explained by the unfinished state of Aristotle's draft or drafts. But they are still obstacles to the understanding of Aristotle's intentions. On the list of four candidates see Introduction, 4(*b*) 3. On 211^{b}19–29 see below on 211^{b}14 ff.

211^{b}10. On place as form see 209^{a}31 ff., 209^{b}17 ff.
'In the same spot': see on the same phrase at 211^{a}34 above.

211^{b}14. The theory of place here considered has not been mentioned before. According to this theory the place of any body X is the extension 'in between' the extremes of the body surrounding X. For example, if X were a wooden sphere immersed in water, its place would be a coextensive spherical extension bounded and defined by the inner surface of the water.

Against the theory, Aristotle states, ^{b}18–19, that the only extensions are the extension of actual bodies (which, of course, if true, reduces the theory to an identification of X's place with X itself as X's extension).

What follows, ^{b}19–29, is a confused passage out of which it is hard to extract any satisfactory over-all sense. If the text given by Ross at ^{b}19–20 is accepted (it contains a plausible conjecture based on the evidence of Themistius), the argument or arguments which follow are directed only against one variant of the 'extension' theory, one in which the extension is 'such as to exist in itself'. This would be an attack, in effect, on a theory of self-subsistent space. The objections to Ross's text are: (1) that at least part of what follows is hard to interpret as an argument against self-subsistent space (^{b}23–25); (2) that it represents an unnecessary alteration of the manuscript tradition, which even the Greek commentators confirm. Accordingly, the tradition should be retained.

Construed as an attack on *any* 'extension' theory of place, ^{b}19–29 still does not make much sense. It is necessary to suppose (and this is also required by the theory about Aristotle's list of four candidates put forward at Introduction, 4(*b*) 3) that the 'extension theory' is of a particular kind, in which the existence of the exten-sion is tied to that of the boundary that surrounds and defines it. The extension is thus dependent upon the surrounding body, and must move when the body moves.

^{b}19–25 may then be taken as supplying one or two arguments:

(*a*) Two arguments: (*i*) (^{b}19–23). If we argue from replacement of water by air, in the whole vessel, that there is an extension existing independently of either, we can equally argue that, since (e.g.) half the water is replaced by air, there is an extension occupy-ing the region occupied by half the water; and so on, giving infinitely many overlapping extensions.

(*ii*) (^{b}23–25). Since the original extension is defined by the surrounding body, it has to move when that does; hence it changes place, so that a place has a place and again we have overlapping places.

(*b*) One argument: The place of a body X is supposed to be the extension occupied by X within the surrounding body. But the parts of a mass of water are to the whole mass as the water in sum is to the vessel, i.e. since the parts may mutually replace one another within the whole mass, the parts are in the whole as the whole is in the vessel. So the place of any part is an extension which moves about inside the whole, and so places can changes places, giving over-lapping places as before.

On either view, ^{b}25–29 constitute an appended note. This is even harder to interpret satisfactorily as part of Aristotle's treatment. The situation envisaged seems to be that the surrounding body is moving and that, inside it, either water or both water and air are circulating. This kind of case is difficult for Aristotle's theory: see on 212^{a}14 ff. Aristotle's view is that movement of the surrounding body does not in itself constitute change of place, and perhaps we have here (*a*) a statement of that view (^{b}25–26); (*b*) a quick argu-ment for it (^{b}27–28). if what is inside a moving vessel were changing its place, *where* would the mutual replacement inside the vessel be occurring? But even on this interpretation, ^{b}28–29, ('That place . . . world system') is impossible to accommodate; in any case the world-system as a whole does not have a place, see on 212^{b}3 ff.

211^{b}29. On place as matter see 209^{b}6 ff., ^{b}17 ff. The motivation suggested here is a new one; if we consider mutual replacement within a fixed surrounding body, then the argument for the existence of a persisting place is compatible with the place's being a fixed material substratum.

'Not separated but continuous': the point of this addition, and its exact meaning, are unclear; on 'continuous' see on 211^{a}23 ff.

212ᵃ2. Place as the limit of the surrounding body. Why does Aristotle add that the thing in place must be a body, and capable of locomotion? If it is not such a body, it cannot be a primary subject of locomotion, and hence not primarily in place, see on 211ᵃ12 ff. The qualification is relevant to the questions of whether the universe is in a place (see on 212ᵇ3 ff.), and of whether places are in places (212ᵇ27–29).

'Some extension which is always present' (ᵃ4): not 'present for all time', but 'present on every occasion (when a body is surrounded by another)'.

212ᵃ14. On the relation of this section to the general tenor of Aristotle's account of place see Introduction, 4(*b*) 4. Although the whole of the section suggests that places 'ought' to be immobile, it is only the concluding revised definition that makes the condition absolute. The difficulties are very much reduced if we may take the revised definition (ᵃ20–21) to be an interpolation. (1) The definition as it stands is apparently circular, and yet almost useless as well, if 'the first unchanging limit of what surrounds' means what the river example suggests. If the river banks constitute the place, on this definition, of the boat, then the boat is not in locomotion at all, whether it is drifting downstream or being rowed upstream. Moreover, there is no guarantee that we shall find any such limit that is not very remote. For these reasons the definition is deeply suspect. (2) If the definition is to be rescued, one way is to suppose that 'unchangeable' (*akinētos*) is here to be understood as 'having a fixed location relative to the whole universe'. This sense does not involve reference to places or to locomotions, since 'fixed' location is defined in terms of fixed spatial relationships to fixed landmarks. Then 'unchangeable limit' will signify a kind of limit which is by definition such that it has a certain fixed location built in. Then, for example, a body moving, relative to the universe as a whole, and surrounded immediately by water, will be in a different 'unchangeable limit' of the surrounding water at each moment. The difficulties with this interpretation are: (*a*) it is not naturally extracted from the statement and fits badly with the remarks about the river; (*b*) the sense attributed to 'unchanging' has no support in Aristotle's general theory of change; (*c*) it does not even work in all cases, since when a body is at rest relative to the universe as a whole it may still be being moved relative to the surroundings, and it is motion relative to the surroundings that Aristotle in general sees as prior in explanation. If we take 'unchangeable' as 'having a fixed location relative to the surrounding body as a whole', difficulty (*c*) vanishes, but (*a*) and (*b*) remain. Moreover, it is not always easy to decide when a location is so fixed. If, in a circular tank of water, the water is all rotating round the central axis, is a fish drifting with the current changing its location relative to the body as a whole or not? How is this case to be differentiated from the case where the water is by and large at rest, and the fish is swimming in a circle round the tank? (3) If, on the other hand, ^{a}20−21 (the revised definition with 'unchangeable') is rejected as un-Aristotelian, everything is much easier. In the rest of the section Aristotle does not say that places are unchangeable, but only that they are 'meant to be'. This can be taken as saying that if there were only natural motions of bodies having natural places, all places would be unchanging, for there would be a layered, static arrangement of elements. As it is, that is the arrangement towards which there is a tendency, and that is partly preserved by certain permanent features of the universe (see ^{a}21−28). *Bouletai* ('is meant') often indicates a natural tendency that is not always fulfilled: see Bonitz, 140^{b}37−55.

212^{a}21. The account of place just given yields, as it should, the truth of the assumptions about place (see 210^{b}32 ff.). Here Aristotle seeks to show how (5) (6) (1) (3) are deduced:

Above and below. Assumption (5) was that 'every place has "above" and "below" ', i.e. there are natural up and down directions everywhere. (6) was that 'each body should naturally move to and remain in its proper places . . . either above or below'. The present section (^{a}21−28) shows that there are natural places, kept immobile by the permanent structure of the world, which define an 'above' and a 'below' satisfying the conditions. They are places, because limits of surrounding bodies. This hardly fits the centre of the world, which is a point; presumably 'the surrounding limit towards the middle' means the inner limit of body immediately surrounding earth, whereas 'the (surrounding limit) towards the extreme' must be the inner limit of the celestial region surrounding the region of fire. The natural places are in turn defined by natural motions, as is proper.

Place as surrounding. Because place is a limit, it is a surface and therefore 'circumscribes' rather than 'receives' the object: see assumption (1).

Place as 'fitting' the object. Because place is a bounding limit, it is 'together with' (*hama*) the object and so extends just as far as the object does. On 'together with' and coincidence of boundaries see on 211^{a}23 ff.

CHAPTER 5

212^{a}31. Aristotle uses his results to attack the problem of whether the world-system as a whole has a location or a place. Some terminology: 'the universe' (*to pan*) is the sum of all that there is; 'the world' (*ouranos*) is the whole Aristotelian world-system, comprising sublunary and celestial regions, and bounded on the outside by the sphere of the fixed stars; 'the heavens' (also representing *ouranos* in some of its occurrences) may cover the whole celestial region, or be restricted to mean the outermost sphere of the fixed stars. In the present section the word *ouranos* appears several times, and it is not always clear in which sense it should be taken.

Aristotle holds that the unmoved mover is 'at' the outer circumference of the world, though it cannot be said to have an extension or a place. Since it is not part of the world, though, that cannot (strictly) be identified with the universe. In this passage Aristotle seems to disregard this point, and to use 'the universe' loosely as an equivalent for 'the world'.

Aristotle's problem is best taken as focused on the sphere of the fixed stars. Since there is no body containing it, it has no place according to his definition. But (*a*) it *is* subject to locomotion, for it rotates; (*b*) it has a location within the universe, namely, at the outside. Aristotle is concerned to show that there is no contradiction. The structure of the section is: (*i*) outline of solution (^{a}31–^{b}1); (*ii*) footnote to (*i*) (^{b}1–3); (*iii*) recall of the distinction made at 211^{a}23–^{b}1 (^{b}3–6); (*iv*) recall of the distinction made at 211^{a}17–23 and application to give solution in more detail (^{b}7–13); (*v*) conclusion (^{b}13–17); (*vi*) footnote to (*v*) (^{b}17–22).

In (*i*) Aristotle begins by generalizing the problem (to test his theory) to the case where the body not in place is not even rigid, but composed of water, and so homogeneous and capable of internal movement of parts. The parts do move, i.e. change place; they are capable of so doing, because, though derivatively (211^{a}29–31), they are in places, since 'they are surrounded by one another'. But can the whole body move? It cannot change its place as a whole, because it has no place to change. This is not just a verbal point; Aristotle means that there is no content to the supposition that it might move away. For it is surrounded neither by another body nor by a void (since it is assumed there is no such thing); so there is nothing for it to move away through.

The only possible movement of the body as a whole, then, is one involving no change of place of the body, but only exchange of places between parts in a concerted way, e.g. rotation. Rotation in general is a problem for Aristotle's theory of change. It cannot be a

locomotion of the whole body, for the reason Aristotle gives at ª35
(At *Physics* VI.9, 240ª29–ᵇ7 he remarks that the whole body does
change in some respect in rotation, namely in respect of *orientation*;
but this remark is *ad hominem* against a sophistic puzzle). So it must
be concerted locomotions of the parts of the body, or of some of
them. (This has an obvious application to the sphere of the fixed
stars. Its rotation must consist of concerted circular movement by
some of its parts. Is it the stars that are the primary subjects of
movement?)

The parts of the rotating body may be said to have places, in a
modified sense, even if the whole body does not. The parts are
indeed not all fully 'surrounded': a part which reaches to the outer
boundary cannot be surrounded on that boundary. But even
peripheral parts will share boundaries with other such parts. The
point is made at ª33–34, ᵇ1, ᵇ10–11, 12–13. It even serves to
provide a way in which, via its parts, the whole world or the heavens
are 'accidentally' in place. (The place of parts even in a homogeneous
body: to justify talking of 'places' here, in spite of the apparent ban
at 211ª29–31, Aristotle recalls the distinction there made, and
rephrases it as a distinction here, ᵇ3–6, between 'being in place'
(*a*) potentially (*b*) in actual operation.)

In (*iv*) and (*v*) Aristotle introduces *being somewhere* as apparently
equivalent to *being in a place*. That this is not in fact an equivalence
is shown by 212ᵇ27–28. To be somewhere it is indeed necessary to
be 'in' something which 'surrounds'; but 'in' and 'surround', as in
212ᵇ27–28, may be taken in derivative senses.

The 'footnotes' or parentheses (*ii*) (212ᵇ1–3) and (*vi*) (212ᵇ17–
22), are troublesome. (*a*) 212ᵇ1–3. There are two ways of punctu-
ating the Greek text here. The traditional punctuation, followed
by Ross, yields the sense: 'Some do *not* move up and down, but
in a circle: while others . . .'. This is objectionable: (1) the Greek
is harsh; (2) we get a classification of components of the world
into those that move in circles and those that have *both* up and
down, leaving out those that move naturally only up or down. To
remove the objection one might suppose that 'others move both
up and down' refers to all four elements collectively, with 'condensation and rarefaction' affording the elemental transformations
(cf. *Physics* VIII.7, 260ᵇ7–12). But this seems strained. It is better
to take 'others move both up and down' as referring to the middle
elements, water and air: cf. similar expressions at *de Caelo* IV.3,
310ª17, *Physics* III.5, 205ª25–29. If so, it becomes necessary to
punctuate in the way presupposed in the present translation. But the
point of the whole remark is, on any view, obscure. It might have
been added by someone who thought all the main components of

the world ought to be mentioned here, not realizing that Aristotle was concentrating on the sphere of the fixed stars. (*b*) 212^{b}17–22. Here there is confusion, redundancy, and an un-Aristotelian word. *Ouranos* switches from being 'the world' (^{b}17) to 'the heavens' (^{b}21, 22). The definition of place is repeated unnecessarily in a confusing formulation: 'the extreme part . . . in contact'. The word 'ether' (*aithēr*) is not elsewhere used by Aristotle as a term referring to a component of his own world-system, let alone to fire.

212^{b}22. The problems about place cleared up: see 209^{a}2 ff.

(*i*) refers to (6) of the earlier section. With the lettering of the notes on that section, it is obvious that since Aristotle accepts (*c*) and (*e*), he must reject the inference from (*c*) to (*d*), which depends on the assumption that a growing body does not exchange its original place for a different one. But this is false; cf. 211^{a}15–17.

(*ii*) refers to (2). Aristotle denies that the argument from replacement yields places of points, but does not explain how it is that it does not do so. Perhaps the explanation is simply that, while the argument does yield locations of points, for there to be places there must be not only locations but *surrounding* locations. (Points have locations: *Metaphysics* V.6, 1016^{b}25–26.) Points perhaps cannot be said to move 'into' and 'out of' their locations as bodies do (208^{b}7, 8). That points cannot be 'surrounded', i.e. be in contact with a surrounding area along an extended boundary, is already argued by Plato, *Parmenides* 138^{a}3–7, quoted on 209^{a}2 ff. above.

(*iii*) refers to (1). Places have turned out to be two-dimensional, and so cannot be bodies.

(*iv*) refers to none of the problems stated at 209^{a}2 ff., but as it would seem to a fuller version of (1) which ran thus: If what is three-dimensional is a body, then *either* place is three-dimensional, in which case there are two bodies overlapping; *or* place is two-dimensional, in which case it defines a three-dimensional extension inside itself, which will be a body, and again there will be two bodies overlapping.

(*v*) refers to (5). Aristotle denies that places are themselves in places, although they have locations: cf. (*ii*) above. It is still true of course that places, in a derivative sense, will be 'in' (inside) other places, giving a regress which would threaten to be infinite were it not for the finitude of the world.

212^{b}29. The purpose of the section is to show that Aristotle's account of place brings it out 'reasonable' that there are natural places, to which bodies move naturally, and in which they rest naturally. This is part of Aristotle's programme (see on 210^{b}32 ff.)

and something has been done towards it at 212^a21 ff. But Aristotle has not shown any essential connection between places and natural motions and rests. This section gives a rapid and, as Aristotle admits, obscure sketch of the metaphysics of natural places. The promise of a clear exposition is redeemed, if at all, in *de Caelo* IV.3–5.

There are two general principles given here: (1) if X is *naturally* in contact with Y, then X must be of the same kind as Y. This ensures that there will be a natural arrangement in which similar bodies are grouped together. (2) The natural persistence of this natural arrangement is explained by the analogy of the natural rest of the part within the whole. This in turn is tied to the form-matter relationship, so that there is analogy between: (*a*) X is naturally contained in Y; (*b*) X is part of Y; (*c*) X is the matter of Y (*or* potentially Y). The analogies are already implicit in the list of senses of 'in' at 210^a14 ff., cf. also on the infinite as 'formless' 'matter' and 'surrounded', 207^a15 ff. For the metaphysical background, *de Caelo* II.13, 293^b1–15, IV.3; 4, 312^a12–21; *Gen. et Corr.* I.3, 318^b12–33, II.8, 335^a14–21 with Joachim, 98–102, 246.

It is the link between place as 'surrounding' and form and whole as 'surrounding' that gives Aristotle what he needs here. Smaller points:

(*a*) *Contact and fusion.* (^b31–32, 213^a9–10) For this distinction, not of much point here, cf. *Metaphysics* V.4, 1014^b22–26, *Physics* V.3, 227^a23–27.

(*b*) 'As when one produces change . . . or of air' (212^b35–213^a1): an obscure remark, the point of which may just be that even in a homogeneous mass one can make a small portion move independently and be as it were a detached part of the whole.

VOID

CHAPTER 6

213^a12. Connection of the topics of *void* and *place*. Aristotle claims that in theories of void, the void is a kind of place. The content of the claim seems to be that the void, as generally hypothesized, is a (non-bodily, three-dimensional) spatial extension which is (*a*) independent of any bodies that may happen to occupy it; (*b*) *receptive* of occupying bodies, i.e. remaining in position even when occupied. It is point (*b*) which is expressed at ^a16–19: 'it is thought to be a plenum . . . their being is not the same.' On 'their being is not the same' see on 202^b5 ff. It is the same X, viz. the non-bodily extension, which is void at one time and full at another, but what it is to be void is different from what it is to be full. So to call the extension 'the void' is misleading; in itself it is capable of being either void or full, but is not either.

It is this type of space-like void with which Aristotle will be mainly concerned. On the relation between the concepts of *void* and *space* see further Introduction, 5(c).

In calling a receptive void 'a kind of place' Aristotle does not mean that it fits his own account of place, but that because of its receptivity and independence it resembles the 'receptive' account of place which he has considered at 209^b6-17, 211^b14-29.

Aristotle implies that the Atomists' void was receptive: whether he is correct is uncertain: see Introduction, 5(c).

Methodology: on the method of beginning from previous theories and common intuitions see on 203^a4 ff. The rival arguments are stated at 213^a22 ff., 213^b2 ff. 'The common opinions': those held by people generally, e.g. those reported at 213^a27-31 and in 213^b30 ff.; cf. the common opinions about location and place at 208^a29-31, $^b27-33$.

213^a22. The account of ordinary opinions given here, 213^a27-31, is puzzling as it stands. We have:

(1) A void is by definition an extension containing no sense-perceptible body ($^a28-29$);

(2) Whatever is, is body (and sense-perceptible) ($^a29$);

∴ (3) (from (1), (2)) A void is an extension containing nothing whatever ($^a30$). But from that it does not follow that what contains only air is a void. We need a further explanation of why it should be thought that air is nothing, and this can be found at $213^b34-214^a3$, a passage which sits badly in its present context and was presumably transferred there by mistake. Using $213^b34-214^a3$ we have further:

(4) All body is tangible and therefore heavy or light ($213^b34-214^a2$).

(5) (from (1), (4)) An (extension) in which there is nothing heavy or light is a void (214^a2-3).

(6) Air is neither heavy nor light (understood as a common opinion: cf. 205^a28, 212^a12-14).

(7) (from (5) (6)) An extension in which there is only air is void.

In this argument, (2) is superfluous for reaching the conclusion, but Aristotle presumably wishes to exhibit the full structure of ordinary intuitions, and the mistake made by the attempted refutation. From (6), (4), and (2) it follows that air is nothing; and the demonstration that air is something merely refutes the conjunction

of (6), (4), and (2); but since only (1), (4), and (6) are needed for
the argument, it would, strictly, suffice to drop (2) to preserve the
argument. But even if the argument is destroyed, (i.e. if the demonstration of the strength of air is taken to refute either (4) or (6)), we
still only have one particular kind of presumed void refuted, and
nothing has been done to advance the general question.

The classification of void-theories ($^a32-^b2$) is as follows:

A void is a non-bodily extension which, either actually or
potentially, contains no body, whether (*a*) inside the sum of body
(Atomists etc.), (*b*) outside. Here, void is not assumed receptive.
(*b*) is the Pythagorean version, see 213^{b}22–27. 'Separable' must
here be 'capable of existing without an occupying body': cf. on
209^{b}17 ff.

213^{b}2. Arguments for a void. These are probably due to the early
Atomists.

(1) *The argument from locomotion.* (^{b}4–15). The claim is that
movement through a plenum would have to be movement *into* a
plenum, and that that in turn would involve dual occupancy of some
locations. But dual occupancy would have absurd consequences:
(*a*) many bodies in the same places; (*b*) small volumes being occupied
by arbitrarily large ones.

Melissus: see B7(7) Diels-Kranz, and cf. 214^{a}26–28.

Aristotle's answer is at 214^{a}22–32.

(2) *The argument from compression* (^{b}15–18). Wine was carried
in skins and stored in jars. The alleged fact is that a wine jar can be
made to contain *both* the normal quantity of wine *and* the wineskins
it was carried in. But there were, of course, better-attested instances
of compression; nothing turns on this particular case. The argument
is that a fixed quantity of matter must always occupy the same total
volume; if it can contract into itself, there must have been unoccu-
pied volume, i.e. void, in it. Aristotle gives a general reply at
214^{a}32–^{b}1, and takes up a particular case in ch. 9.

(3) *The argument from growth* (^{b}18–20). The argument is that
the nutrition of living things can be explained only by assuming the
existence of void. For there must be channels to convey the nourishment to all parts of the body, and if they contained no void nothing
could travel along them. Aristotle's answer is at 214^{b}1–9.

(4) *The 'ashes' argument* (^{b}21–22). It is not clear here whether
Aristotle counts this as a full-scale argument, as something weaker,
or as a variant of, or supporting evidence for, (3) or (2). As stated
here it looks like another case of compression, but at 214^{b}3–10 it
seems like a variant of (3)—perhaps water seeping through ashes in a
way that seemed impossible without the existence of void.

At *Problems* XXV.8, 938^{b}14–16, 24–26, the 'wine jar' and the 'ashes' are both examples of compression. (*Problems* was compiled in the Peripatetic school but not necessarily by Aristotle).

Pythagorean theories: see on 203^{a}4–8 on these 'Pythagoreans'. 'It was what was primary in numbers': or possibly 'it was present in numbers primarily'. This group held the structure of the universe and its contents to be explicable in terms of numbers, see *Metaphysics* I.5, 985^{b}23–986^{b}10, 987^{a}13–27.

CHAPTER 7

213^{b}30. Distinction of uses of void (for distinction of uses generally see on 203^{b}30 ff.). The procedure seems to be that Aristotle starts with a plain man's definition of void, 'a place in which there is nothing', and refines it into his first sense: 'That which is not full of body perceptible by touch' (214^{a}7); he then adds (^{a}11–16) a second use.

The popular account of void (213^{b}31–214^{a}1). As it stands, the account of popular intuitions is confused. There are two pieces of reasoning:

(A) (213^{b}31–34): (cf. 213^{a}27–30).

    (1) Void is place in which there is no body (^{b}33).

    (2) All that is, is body (^{b}32).

    (3) All body is in place (^{b}32–33).

by (2); (4) Where there is no body, there is nothing (^{b}33–34); by (1) (4);

    (5) Void is place in which there is nothing.

The argument is straightforward, though (3) is unnecessary; it leads from the intuition (1), which Aristotle accepts as roughly correct, and the mistaken (2), to the 'popular' definition (5) which Aristotle is trying to refine. His account thus enables him to replace (5) by the accurate (1). The presence of (3) may be explained by the wish to represent fully the structure of common opinion (cf. on 213^{a}22 ff.).

(B) (213^{b}34–214^{a}3).

    (6) All body is tangible (^{b}34–^{a}1).

    (7) All that is tangible is heavy or light (^{a}1–2).

by (6) (7);

    (8) All body is heavy or light (understood).

    (9) Void is that in which there is nothing heavy or light (^{a}2–3).

or: (9a) Anything in which there is nothing heavy or light is void.

On the first interpretation of $^a2-3$ (9), the missing premisses are
> (10) Void is that in which there is no body (i.e. roughly (1)).

and (2) All that is, is body.

On the second interpretation, we need only
> (10a) Anything in which there is no body is void.

If this is the correct account of (B), the point of it is hard to see, since it is proceeding in the wrong direction, *towards* Aristotle's own definition, instead of away from it like (A). Hence (B) cannot be understood as explaining anything here, and is suspect. It has already been shown that it fits very well at 213^a27-31.

If we remove (B), (A) can be understood as a partial refinement of popular ideas, and to complete the process two further steps are necessary. First there is one which might be represented by the argument:
> (11) Void is place in which there is no tangible body.
> (6) All body is tangible ($^b34-^a1$).
> ∴ (1) Void is place in which there is no body.

Finally, Aristotle needs to make precise the notion of 'place' involved here, which is a 'receptive' rather than 'circumscriptive' one. It will not do to say merely 'Void is that in which there is not tangible body'; which, by dropping the requirement of receptivity, would allow a point to count as void. So the final refinement is to
> (12) Void is that which is not full of tangible body (i.e. that which is capable of receiving tangible body but does not in fact contain any).

The second use of void (214^a11-16). Since any body is an individual (a 'this') and a corporeal substance, it is clear that the second sense includes the first. But this second sense is not heard of again, and it looks as though it was constructed merely in order to account for the use of 'void' by Plato in a derived sense: the 'receptacle' is void in that, considered in itself, it is indeterminate and so does not have 'in' itself any particular individual or kind of body. The derived sense corresponds to a derived sense of 'in'. Aristotle's criticism is the one already made of Plato at 209^b17 ff.

214^a16. (*a*) ($^a16-20$). 'Void must be place deprived of body.' Here 'place' is not to be understood in Aristotle's official sense, but in a wider sense including that and others. In the previous section it has been shown that the core of the notion of a void is of a receptive extension not actually containing body. Aristotle remarks that this notion has already been considered and rejected in his account of place, at 211^b14-29.

'Neither separated nor inseparable': on 'separable' see on 213^a 22 ff. The dichotomy seems not to be exhaustive (what of separable but non-separated void?), and not to the point, since inseparable void is not in question. Possibly we should read 'separable' for 'inseparable', giving the same dichotomy as at 213^a32-33. If 'inseparable' is kept, it must be understood as meaning a receptive extension which always and necessarily contains bodies but which exists independently of them; such theories may be among the targets of some arguments in ch. 8. For other theories of 'trapped' or non-isolable void see on 217^b20 ff.

(*b*) ($^a21-26$). Further reflections on void as receptive place.

(*c*) ($^a26-^b11$). Answers to the arguments of 213^b2 ff., in favour of the existence of void.

(1) *The argument from locomotion* ($^a26-32$). Movement through a plenum need not be movement into a plenum, since there is the possibility of 'mutual replacement'; the air in front of the moving arrow can give way and move into regions left free by the corresponding inrush of air behind the arrow. The rotation of a rigid body, e.g. a solid sphere, is an example in which mutual replacement occurs, as also the vortex movement of a liquid; and all that is needed here is to show that it is possible.

(2) *The argument from compression* ($^a32-^b1$). Again it is sufficient to note that 'squeezing out' is possible. But in Aristotle's own view not all expansion and contraction involves squeezing out or the reverse: see ch. 9.

(3) *The argument from growth* ($^b2-3$). Aristotle disputes the assumption that growth necessarily entails addition of body: increase of size might be produced in another way, e.g. by substantial change. This is adequate only *ad hominem*, if at all. There is still the problem raised in ch. 9; and a complete theory of nutrition is needed.

'Qualitative change': the change of water to air is not usually so labelled by Aristotle, but as 'coming-to-be'.

(4) *The 'ashes' argument.* The fact that this is not separately answered suggests that it is a variant of (2) or (3).

Why are (3) and (4) said to be 'self-obstructing'? Apparently because they prove too much: not just that there is void, but that a body capable of growth must be everywhere void. Similarly, a heap of ashes which can be permeated by water must be everywhere void. The objection seems without force, if we think of growth as accretion of particles: only a number of void channels are needed. But for Aristotle's non-particulate theory of matter it is a serious problem, discussed at *Gen. et Corr.* I.5, 321^a2-322^a33, how growth is possible at all. This is why Aristotle here calls it 'a common difficulty', and his objection to void theorists is that they simply do not begin to meet the real difficulty. To say this is to assume, as

Aristotle does, that a particulate theory of matter is untenable on
other grounds.

CHAPTER 8

214^b12. Further arguments against the existence of void occupy the
whole chapter. On these generally see Introduction, 5(*b*) and (*c*).

'Separated void': i.e. a receptive extension actually free of body,
see on 214^a19.

The arguments of the present section are miscellaneous but
clearly 'physical'.

(1) (^b13–17). 'Responsible for' (*aition*) might also be translated
as 'an explanation for'. In any case, the natural first hypothesis is
that Aristotle is thinking of his list of four types of explanatory
factor; cf. the similar puzzle about place at 209^a18–22, where the
list is made explicit. The solution to that puzzle is not given but is
presumably that natural places (at least) are *final* causes of movement.

Why then does Aristotle think it clear that a void cannot be an
explanatory factor for natural locomotion? Presumably, a void, as
such, cannot be a natural place: if a natural place were void, it would
not be *qua* void that it functioned as a final cause, but *qua* located in
a particular way. But no other sort of explanatory factor will fit.
Hence void cannot be an explanatory factor for locomotion in
general. But there is nothing else it could plausibly be used to
explain.

'It is thought to be responsible for change in respect of place':
this picks up 214^a24–25: 'they think that the void is responsible for
change in the sense of being that in which change occurs.' If a void
were an essential adjunct to any change (of place) in this way, it
could perhaps be classified as a 'material cause'. But in any case the
need for void in change has already been refuted at 214^a28–32.

The implication of the argument is that a void which is not an
explanatory factor of anything is pointless and therefore cannot
exist; there is a tacit use of the principle that a permanent feature of
the universe cannot be completely idle in explanation.

(2) (^b17–24). Aristotle uses a thought-experiment: what will be
the motion of a 'test particle' placed in a void? The particle cannot
move 'into all the void', i.e. in all directions in the void. Either it
rests, or it moves in one particular direction. But for it to move in
any particular direction would violate symmetry. Nor can it move in
its natural direction, for a reason not explained here, but suggested
at 214^b31–215^a1, 215^a9–11: there is no intrinsic distinction

between 'up' and 'down' in a void, so that there is nothing to guide the particle in its proper course. So it remains at rest, which shows that motion is impossible in a void. The strategy of this argument is repeated at length, with variations, in 214^{b}28–216^{a}21.

(3) (^{b}24–27). This is a problem about how the occupancy of a void or of 'unsupported' place, is to be envisaged. The thought seems to be: suppose we have a receptive void which persists even when occupied. Then every part of the occupying body ought to be occupying a corresponding part of the void. But a part of the occupying body, if not actually physically separated, exists only potentially: it is 'in the whole'; and so has no actual location more determinate than that. A clearer exploration of the problems of void-occupancy is given at 216^{a}26–^{b}21; cf. also the obscure passage 211^{b}19–29 on the occupancy of extension.

(4) (^{b}28). 'Place is not separated', i.e. there is no kind of receptive 'place' existing independently of the occupying body, since the 'extension' theory has been rejected at 211^{a}14–29. By the definition of ch. 7, void would have to be such an extension, or so similar as to fall foul of the same arguments.

These four arguments are excessively abbreviated. (2) and (3), as stated, reappear in better and clearer form in what follows.

214^{b}28. This section and the next each contain elaborate argument to show that movement through a void is impossible. They were obviously composed together, and perhaps originally as part of a polemic against the early Atomists.

(1) (^{b}31–215^{a}1). The void, as such, contains nothing to distinguish any one direction from any other. Therefore a test particle surrounded by void (a) will not be acted on by any other body— since it is not in contact with one (see 202^{a}3 ff.); (b) will not be caused by the void as such to move in one direction rather than another. If it is suggested that the void *qua* something else might distinguish one direction from another, Aristotle could reply that the Atomist void at least cannot have any other role than that of just being void. But why should not the required distinction between directions be provided by (*i*) the particle's own nature; or (*ii*) the state of motion the particle is already in; or (*iii*) some spatial relationship to the universe as a whole or to bodies in the environment? These possibilities are considered in what follows: (*i*) in (2), (*ii*) in (3) and (4), (*iii*) in (2).

(2) (215^{a}1–14). The assumption is that natural movement would be determined in direction by a spatial relationship to the universe as a whole (and perhaps conversely that movement so determined would be natural). On the ontological and other priority of natural over unnatural movement, cf. *de Caelo* II.3, 286^{a}18–20.

The introduction of the 'infinite' makes an *ad hominem* point against Atomists and others, not essential to the argument.

The void is too negative to be the carrier of distinctions of direction. Nor could a pull in one direction be conveyed by something like a field of force: both for Aristotle and for his opponents, such a thing would have had to involve bodily action. Nor can the particle be supposed to move *of itself* in its natural direction: not by the Atomists, since they probably supposed that particles move only if pushed by the impact of others, and not by Aristotle, since for him all motion involves contact with a body causing movement. (For Aristotle's theory see III.2, above, and *Physics* VIII.4. The early Atomist theory of motion is a difficult subject: see e.g. Guthrie (2), vol. ii, 396–404.)

(3) (^{a}14–19). After (1) and (2) the only possibility left is that the particle moves in a particular direction because it is already doing so. Here, Aristotle's first objection to such persistence of motion is that it itself is in need of physical explanation in terms of bodies, and so cannot occur in a void. Against the Atomists, this is a plain begging of the question. For Aristotle it follows from the principle that all change involves continued contact of an agent with the changing body, but of course this principle is one of the points at issue. Aristotle's wording ('in actual fact') suggests that the principle is supported by ordinary experience, although both of the detailed explanations he offers are hopelessly unsatisfactory, as was seen already in antiquity and shown with devastating force by Galileo in the *Dialogo*. On the weakness of Aristotle's position here and the nature of his arguments see Introduction, 5(*b*).

(4) (^{a}19–22). The second objection to persistence of motion in a given direction. Aristotle points out, rightly, that the only reasonable version of this theory is that in a void a particle will travel to infinity, in accordance with Newton's First Law, unless interfered with. For Aristotle this is a *reductio ad absurdum*, since he holds linear motion *ad infinitum* to be impossible on other grounds: *Physics* VI.10, 241^{b}9–12 claims that every motion must be completable. Once again Aristotle's finitism blights the development of physics.

(5) (^{a}22–24). An *ad hominem* thrust as an afterthought: if (as some Atomist may have said) movement occurs 'because the void yields' then why does it not occur in all directions at once, since the void ought to yield irrespective of direction?

215^{a}24. Outline of the section:

(1) (^{a}25–29). The speed of a given body though a medium is a function of (*a*) the nature of the medium, (*b*) the 'excess' (*huperochē*) of weight or lightness of the body.

(2) ([a]29–[b]12). Consider first (*a*) the nature of the medium. The speed of the body varies inversely as the resistance of the medium, i.e. as its 'thickness of texture'.

(3) ([b]12–20). A void has zero resistance, and so bears no finite proportion in respect of 'fineness of texture' to any body.

(4) ([b]20–216[a]12). Hence motion through a void is impossible (it would have to be infinitely fast).

(5) (216[a]12–21). As to (*b*) the 'excess' of weight or lightness: this can make no difference in a void, so that similar bodies will move with equal speed, which is impossible.

These arguments are hardly intelligible except in the context of an Aristotelian theory of dynamics; for one attempt at reconstructing that theory, and giving sense to this section, see Additional Note B.

(1) What is being compared with what? 'The same weight and body', seems to show that the comparisons are between the behaviours of one and the same individual body in different circumstances. This would mean that 'excess of weight or lightness' cannot mean the same thing as 'weight'; see on this on (5) below.

(2) Effect of the medium. Aristotle ascribes the different effects of different media to the fact that their resistances are different, and that in turn to the fact that they are divided more and less easily, and that in turn to the fact that they are of finer or thicker texture. So there must be a functional dependence, for each body under given initial conditions, of the speed of the body through the medium on the texture of the medium. Aristotle assumes that the texture can be measured by a quantity of thickness, and that the speed varies inversely as the thickness of texture. (There is no Greek noun corresponding to 'texture': the adjectives *pachus* ('of thick texture') and *leptos* ('of fine texture') define the continuum.)

There is no further explanation of why the relationship has to be that of a simple inverse proportion. At 215[a]25, 'we see' suggests an appeal to observed facts. Could the law have been derived from observations? Measurements of time were hardly accurate enough to allow for determination of speeds over short distances. But suppose Aristotle had compared the behaviour of bodies falling under gravity through *x* feet of water with the behaviour of the same bodies falling under gravity through *x* feet of air. He would indeed have found a roughly constant proportion between the *terminal* velocities in the two cases. But it is unlikely that terminal velocities are in question here: see Additional Note B.

(3) The void's resistance must be put equal to zero, and so there is no finite proportion between the speeds. (Understood of terminal velocities, this is correct: when a body falls under constant force

through a void, there *is* no terminal velocity: the velocity increases without limit.)

That zero bears no ratio to a finite quantity is an immediate consequence of the definition at Euclid, *Elements* V, Def. 4: 'Magnitudes are said to have a ratio to one another which are capable when multiplied of exceeding one another.' But Aristotle does not refer to this definition, and his arithmetical parenthesis serves no clear purpose.

(4) In the example using letters, letters A to E are taken over from 215^a31–^b10. The aim is to produce a *reductio ad impossibile* of resistance by a void. Let the body traverse a length of medium D in time E, and the same length of void in time G. Then

$$\frac{E}{G} = \frac{\text{resistance of void}}{\text{resistance of D.}}$$

(The next step, defining H, is pointless.) Then Aristotle assumes that there will be some medium F (non-void) such that:

$$\frac{E}{G} = \frac{\text{Resistance of F}}{\text{Resistance of D}} \, ;$$

it then follows that resistance of F = resistance of void, which is impossible since F is non-void, and so has *greater* resistance.

(5) The understanding of this reasoning depends partly on establishing the meanings of the words *rhopē*, ('preponderance') and *huperochē* ('excess'). It seems that these words have the same meaning here: cf. 'excess of weight or lightness' (215^a28–29) with, here, 'preponderance of weight or lightness' (215^a13–14). It has traditionally been supposed that these terms refer to the weight of the body (forgetting about 'lightness' for the present, and considering only free downward movement). But the traditional view (*a*) seems incompatible with the wording of 215^a25–29, as already pointed out. Further, (*b*) it makes 215^a25–29 false and contrary to ordinary experience. Everyone knows that the ease with which a body forces itself through a resistant medium depends not *only* on its weight but also on its velocity. So at 215^a25–29 'excess' ought to include both weight *and* velocity; the same conclusion is suggested here by the talk of 'force' (^a19).

Is there any prospect of taking *rhopē* and *huperochē* in a more suitable sense, viz., as meaning something like *momentum*? An examination of the use of *rhopē* in physical contexts by Aristotle provides no support for the interpretation of *rhopē* as 'weight', though in places it is closely associated with 'weight'. Rather it seems to be 'tendency to move'; at *de Caelo* III.2, 301^a22–23, the identical phrase, 'preponderance of weight or lightness' can be rendered 'tendency to move due to weight or lightness'. *Huperochē* is not used in a specialized physical sense, but 'excess of weight or lightness' can, in the light of $^a12-14$ here, be understood as 'excess of tendency to move due to weight or lightness'. So while there does not seem to be any clear attestation elsewhere in Aristotle of the concept of *momentum* there is nothing in the context to exclude its being present here. (At *de Caelo* IV.6, 313^b16-21, the 'strength' of the 'weight' which should be (on the same grounds as above) something like momentum, is recognized as the important quantity in considering fall through a medium.)

Unfortunately, there are good reasons for adhering to the usual interpretation of *rhopē* as 'weight' or 'downward tendency'. For these reasons, and for an attempt to elucidate the present passage, see Additional Note B.

The essential assumption here, that differences of weight make a difference to motion only because they make it easier to overcome the resistance of the medium, is in fact in accord with Aristotle's ways of thinking. Since there is no action at a distance, the weight can act only (*i*) on the body itself, or (*ii*) on the medium with which it is in contact. But the action of the weight on the body itself cannot make a difference in the required way, since there is also an 'inertial resistance' to action which is proportionate to the weight (*Physics* VII.5).

216^a23. Most of the section is devoted to problems arising from considering the void 'in itself' (216^a26-^b16), i.e. considering what its essential properties would have to be (rather than its effects on motion). Aristotle argues: (*a*) that the void will not be displaced by any occupying body and will therefore permeate it. ($^a26-^b2$); (*b*) that the occupying body has an extension of equal size to the void occupied ($^b2-6$); (*c*) that therefore either the body's extension and the occupied void are identical, or (if not) there will be two coextensive extensions—in either case an impossibility ($^b6-12$); (*d*) in any case, the void will be superfluous in the role of a *place* for the body, since the body's own extension will do just as well ($^b12-16$).

(*a*) Aristotle argues that since the void cannot be physically displaced it must remain coextensive with the occupying body. But even if a part of the void cannot be *pushed away*, it still seems possible that portions of the void should cease to be when their locations are occupied, and other portions should correspondingly come to be; or that the void as a whole should change its outline as a result of a rearrangement of bodies. But it is the 'receptive' theory of void, as outlined at 213^a14-19 and 214^a6-11, that Aristotle regards as the only serious theory: hence his equation of it in this section too (^{a}23−25, ^{b}8−9, 13−16) with a theory of place.

(*b*) The extension of the body is here called the 'magnitude' (^{b}3), the 'extended body' or 'volume' (*ogkos* ^{b}6, 15), and the 'body' (^{b}10): a confusing selection of terms, suggesting that Aristotle's terminology was not yet fixed. ('Body' (*sōma*) meaning 'three-dimensional extension' or 'volume' is a geometrical term, cf. e.g. 204^{b}5). Cf. on 209^{b}6 ff. On 'different in being' see on 202^{b}5 ff.

(*c*) There must be two distinct extensions, because the body's extension moves around while the void does not, or (more compellingly) because the body's extension is logically dependent on the body while the void is not. (Why did not Aristotle consider the possibility that the extensions were the same but 'different in being'?)

The objections to this theory involving two coextensive extensions are reminiscent of Aristotle's critiques of Platonic forms and numbers: the two things are indistinguishable, occupy the same region uncomfortably, and one is superfluous for the purpose it is invoked for.

Further points:

(1) 216^{a}23−26. 'In itself distinct': presumably, 'existing actually, in independence of, and empty of, bodies', cf. 'distinct' (*apokekrimenon*) again at 217^{b}20 in opposition to 'potential'. For the reduction of 'receptive void' to a kind of place see on 213^{b}30 ff.

(2) (216^{a}27) 'void indeed': one of the very few jokes in Aristotle's surviving writings.

(3) (216^{b}17−20) a further argument, unknown to the ancient commentators, appears in the MS tradition here. The present translation follows Ross in excising it as non-Aristotelian.

CHAPTER 9

216^{b}22. The subject of the chapter is 'the rare and the dense', i.e. the changeability of bodies from condensed to rarefied states and back again, and the relation of these phenomena to the existence of void. Aristotle's substantive discussion is at 217^{a}20−^{b}11. Before that, at 216^{b}30−217^{a}10, he attacks theories of internal 'non-separable' void in bodies. Of the rest of the chapter, the present section (216^{b}22−30) states, by way of introduction, an argument for the occurrence of condensation and rarefaction; 217^{a}10−20 repeats it (this is probably a mistaken addition); 217^{b}11−20 contains further points about density and rarity; and 217^{b}20−28 concludes the discussion.

The argument for condensation and rarefaction. If the universe has a finite volume, then any change involving the expansion in volume of a particular body must somehow be compensated for, if the universe is not to 'bulge'. Now such changes do occur, since, e.g., water expands when it turns to air. Either there is a compensating mechanism which arranges for simultaneous compensating changes of e.g. air to water, or, if this is not possible, other bodies must be forced mechanically to contract in volume, without substantial change. The argument is really a setting-out of what is obvious. But it is an argument for genuine, and not apparent, contraction: it cannot be answered, as Aristotle answered the argument from contraction at $214^a32-{}^b1$, by suggesting a mechanism involving no real reduction in volume. Hence it is an argument for genuine condensation and rarefaction: changes in volume of a given body which do not involve the addition and subtraction of other bodies. Aristotle does not further discuss the argument, because he is happy to accept it; he devotes himself to destroying the further inference from genuine condensation and rarefaction to void.

It may be objected that this argument, as presented, argues from an *apparent* expansion to a *real* contraction. Perhaps the expansion of water when it changes into air is only apparent, and other bodies have been added? But we can show experimentally (and very likely the Atomists did so) by boiling water in a closed vessel, that the expansion cannot plausibly be explained so.

Xuthus is said by Simplicius (*Phys.* 683.24) to have been a Pythagorean.

216ᵇ30. Differences in density not explicable by void. For 'separable' void Aristotle refers to the arguments of ch. 8, and here considers only 'inseparable' void: i.e. void which could not exist independently of the body inside which it is. This might be true in various ways: the void might be trapped as 'bubbles' inside the body, or be present as an inseparable ingredient in a mixture or compound. See further on 217^b20 ff., and cf. generally *de Caelo* IV.2, $309^a27-{}^b28$. Aristotle begins with two *ad hominem* points, which suggest that here too his opponents, who offered the argument of the previous section, are the early Atomists. These opponents want to make void 'responsible for' all motion, and in the sense that void is the medium in which motion occurs (cf. 214^a22-26, $^b16$). But an inseparable void inside bodies will be 'responsible for' only upward motion, and as a moving cause ($^b34-217^a3$).

Hereupon a transition to substantive arguments: (*i*) (217^a3-5) if void is a moving cause in upward movement, that can only be because void itself naturally moves upwards to a natural place. But that void itself should move or have a place is impossible, for 'that into which void moves comes to be void of void.' Either 'comes to be' (*gignetai*) here describes what happens when void *leaves* its natural destination—what is left behind is a region *emptied of void*; or 'comes to be' means 'turns out by reasoning to be' (as John Ackrill has suggested to me): the logical result of supposing void to have a place is that that place is empty of void when not occupied. (*ii*) (217ᵃ5–6) What will be the corresponding explanation for downward motion? Mere absence of void will not be enough, so that it will be necessary to suppose a natural downward motion of what is dense. (But this is asymmetrical.) (*iii*) (217ᵃ6–10) Another proportion sum: if upward speeds are inversely proportionate to density, a void, having zero density, will move of itself infinitely fast, which is impossible. (On the proportion of upward speed to lightness see Additional Note B.)

217ᵃ10. This section is of no use to the discussion: it merely restates, twice, the argument for genuine compression and expansion already given at 216ᵇ23–28. Probably, therefore, all but the first clause ('Since . . . rightly stated') is an explanatory addition; the first restatement (217ᵃ12–15) could be Aristotle's own, but the second is not likely to be, since it goes into unnecessary detail, and the end of it (ᵃ18–20) looks like a desperate attempt to make sense of the disjunct 'there is no change' in the original statement. (This disjunct was inserted, probably, to cover the Eleatic option of denying the reality of all change; but the writer of ᵃ18–20 supposed that it implied that *all motion* involved real expansion and compression.)

217ᵃ20. To show that condensation and rarefaction need not entail the existence of any void, Aristotle states his own theory of these processes. To answer the opponents it is of course sufficient that Aristotle's theory should be possible—it is not necessary here to prove it true—and that it should not itself involve the existence of void in any form.

(1) Opposites have the same matter (ᵃ22–26). Aristotle refers to 'what we take as true', i.e. the general physical principles laid down in *Physics* I.7. For matter as the underlying subject of change between opposites see 190ᵇ10–17; for change as the coming-to-be of what the matter was potentially, *Physics* I.7, 191ᵃ8–12; for matter as the same in number, and different in being, *Physics* I.7, 190ᵇ23–24. That matter is inseparable, cf. 191ᵃ12–13 (On 'same in number, different in being' cf. on 202ᵇ5 ff.)

(2) Application to change of density (ᵃ26–33). In any such change (Aristotle's examples here are those from water to air and

back), the matter persists throughout and is not added to (or sub-tracted from): it simply realizes one of its potentialities. If anything were to be added to or subtracted from when there is a change of density, it would have to be the matter, because that is the under-lying subject of change. But there is, according to the theory, no change of *this* kind; for it is the very same matter all along.

So far, the theory is compatible with Atomism. The Atomist could understand the 'matter' to be the set of atoms of which a body was composed, and the change involved in rarefaction as one of a rearrangement of those atoms. So Aristotle still needs to exclude the possibility that the matter could have a micro-structure such as is given by the atoms in Atomism. This he does in the next step (3) (and thereby goes beyond the doctrine of *Physics* I).

(3) There are no 'microscopic' subjects of change at a lower level (*below* that of matter) (^{a}33–^{b}7). The overriding assumption here is that it is *the matter as a whole* that is the primary subject of change. This does not follow from the logical analysis at *Physics* I.7; it is a specifically *physical* hypothesis about changes, which Aristotle does not argue here (he does not need to). (In many other places he argues indirectly for it by arguing against Atomistic accounts of phenomena.)

In the present sub-section, the example of the circles shows that some differences of degree cannot be accounted for by micro-structure; in the case of heating, Aristotle asserts that they are not to be so accounted for. If X as a whole becomes hotter, it is not true that more 'minute parts' of X have become hot than were so before.

(4) Application of (3) to change of density. If there is only one subject of change, the matter as a whole, all it can do in one change is receive one new simple form. So, then, in condensation and rarefaction, Aristotle does not deny that there can be *localized* change within a body; indeed, his account of qualitative change in *Physics* VI requires this possibility. But localized change is simply change of a certain limited extent of a homogeneous whole: it is not a change of part of a micro-structure.

217^{b}11. A footnote on the relationship of 'dense-rare' to other pairs of opposites. The examples of lead and iron were given by Democritus (A 135 Diels-Kranz). Aristotle has no general theory here, but see next section, and *Gen. et Corr.* II.2 on 'hard-soft', 'coarse-fine', and 'heavy-light' in Aristotle's general theory of per-ceptible contraries.

217^{b}20. Conclusion. 'Distinct' void has been dealt with in ch. 8; 'distinct' void in what is rarefied, in ch. 9 at 216^{b}30–217^{a}10.

Potentially existent void has not been considered, unless it is included in 'inseparable' void at 216^{b}33 ff. If any lightness were considered evidence of potentially existent void, then void would be reduced to a kind of matter; in general, if moveability is evidence of potentially existent void, void can be interpreted as 'the matter of what is heavy and light, considered as such'. On 'hard-soft', cf. *Gen. et Corr.* II.2, 330^{a}8–12.

TIME

CHAPTER 10

217^{b}29. 'The next thing': for motivation see 200^{b}15–25. 'Going through the problems' occupies 217^{b}32–218^{a}30 (problems which involve alleged contradictions in the notion of time, and so cast doubt on its existence) and 218^{a}30–218^{b}9 (previous attempts at the definition of time). For the stating of problems as part of Aristotle's method, cf. III.4, IV.1, IV.6.

'The untechnical arguments' (*hoi exōterikoi logoi*): apparently a reference to a corpus of introductory lectures or dialogues or arguments on philosophical subjects: see Bonitz, 104^{b}44–105^{a}37 and Ross (2), vol. ii, 408–10.

217^{b}32. Three arguments casting doubt on the reality of time. They are closely related to passages in Plato, *Parmenides* (details below).

(1) (217^{b}33–218^{a}3) and (2) (218^{a}3–8) present the same idea in different forms and may be taken together. (1) claims that time is made up of past time and future time, neither of which exists; (2) fills the gap by claiming that there can be no present part of time: whatever the present is, it is not a part of time.

The reasoning to show that the present is not a part of time is suppressed—presumably it had been given in 'the untechnical arguments'. Probably there was a dilemma: if there is a present part of time, either it lasts for some time (has temporal extension) or not, and (*i*) if the former, it is not wholly present; (*ii*) if the latter, it is not a part. For limb (*i*), the argument could have followed Plato, *Parmenides* 152^b–^{c}, thus: (A) if the present lasts, it may be divided into an earlier part and a later part; but (B) every part of what is present, is present; hence (C) something present is wholly earlier than something else that is present; but (D) what is wholly earlier than something that is present, is past; hence (E) something is both present and past; which is a contradiction. (Postulates (B) and (D) may also be involved *mutatis mutandis* in the claim in argument (3), at 218^{a}25−27 below, that to be together in respect of time, and neither before nor after, is to be in the same 'now'.) For limb (*ii*), that what does not last is not a part of time, the grounds given are that 'the part measures' and 'the whole is composed of the parts'. A durationless 'now' will fail to satisfy these requirements. Here Aristotle assumes that time-stretches are continua analogous to lines, with durationless 'nows' analogous to points. If time were conceived of as analogous to a discrete row of points, the argument would fail. The assumption is here justified as a common-sense one: 'time is not thought . . .', but it is also Aristotle's own view: see, on the continuity of time, 219^{a}10−14, and *Physics* VI.2, 232^{b}20−233^{a}12.

Aristotle does not advert to arguments (1) and (2) subsequently. This is a pity, since they raise fundamental questions on which it would be helpful to have an explicit statement of Aristotle's position. Aristotle rejects realism about the future, and accepts realism about the past, if at all, only in a qualified way: see Introduction 6(*g*). To give an account of what it is for 'time to exist' is for him, since time is logically and ontologically dependent on changes, to give an account of what it is for changes to occur and to be measurable. Arguments (1) and (2) can be rephrased to apply to changes: we cannot find any existing, i.e. presently occurring *part*, in the sense of 'temporally extended episode', of any change.

Aristotle's first move would have to be to distinguish for changes, between 'being', i.e. 'being in progress, occurring', and 'being wholly present'. No change is ever wholly present, yet some changes do sometimes occur. There is evidence that Aristotle did draw this distinction. At 219^{b}9−33, the passage in which he deals with argument (3) of the present section, and perhaps by implication with (1) and (2) as well, he remarks 'just as change is always different from stage to stage, so is the time' (219^{b}9−10), and the formulation recalls 206^{a}21−22: '" to be" has many senses . . . the day is, and the contest is, by the constant occurring of one thing after another.' Thus to say 'the change is' is a present-tense statement which nevertheless requires that there should be some true past-tense statements. For a change to be occurring there must already have been completed, in the recent past, some temporally extended episode of that very change (as Aristotle brings out explicitly in *Physics* VI.6).

It may be objected that such a move, attributing a special sense to the verb 'be' when applied to changes, merely leads to a rephrasing of the original problem. For now we may ask why anyone should accept the special sense of 'be' as an indication of reality. Is it not rather a tacit, or indeed an explicit, give-away, an admission that changes are not really real after all?

There is a real difficulty for Aristotle here, and it is substantially the same one as he faces in *Physics* VI.3 in the question: 'does change occur at an instant?' His answer there is that change does *not* occur at an instant but in a time-interval; the answer is as might be expected, but it only raises the original question once more: how can any change be occurring now, if it has to be occurring in some time-interval which is partly past and partly future, and present (if at all) only at a point?

If Aristotle faces up to the difficulty within the present discussion of time, it must be at 219^{b}9–33, where he draws on the analogical dependence of time on change, and change on magnitude, to illuminate the serial existence of change, time, and 'the now'. The solution that passage seems to favour is the conceding of some kind of not too tenuous reality to the past, a solution that accords with some other indications. On Aristotle's realism, with regard to the past see Introduction,. 6(*g*); on 219^{b}9–33 see notes on that section, and Introduction, 6(*d*) and (*e*).

(3) (218^{a}8–30). 'The now' is now introduced as something which 'appears to be the boundary between past and future' (cf. Plato, *Parmenides* 152^{b}2–5). The dilemma here stated is discussed at 219^{b}9–28, where Aristotle gives his solution.

(*a*) *'The now' is not different from time to time* (^{a}11–21). The argument depends essentially on the assumptions

　　(*i*) that when anything has ceased to be, there was (or is) a first 'now' at which it was (is) true that it had (has) ceased to be.

　　(*ii*) that 'nows', if all different, are densely arranged within a time-stretch, i.e. between any two there is always a third.

With (*i*) cf. Aristotle's own doctrine on changes, etc. in *Physics* VI.5, 235^{b}30–236^{a}7; with (*ii*) the continuity of time assumed in argument (2) above. These are Aristotelian rather than common-sense assumptions. Aristotle will later implicitly deny that 'nows' cease-to-be in any sense for which (*i*) holds; the ceasing to be of instantaneous 'nows' is, in fact, given Aristotle's account of 'the now' at 219^{b}9–28, only a 'coincidental' alteration (cf. in general *Physics* VI.10, 240^{b}8–241^{a}26).

(*b*) *'The now' is not the same always* (^{a}21–30). Two arguments are offered.

　　(*i*) (^{a}22–25). 'Nothing that is divisible and finite has only one limit': the general idea is that if we have (spatially or temporally) extended finite magnitude, we can 'come to the end of it' at at least two different points (instants). Exceptions can be raised: e.g. in what sense is this true of a circle? But for the application all Aristotle needs is that locally at least time-stretches have a linear ordering. We can always find a time-stretch defined by 'nows' A, B such that A is before B and therefore A, B are different. (Ultimately, Aristotle will reply that A,B are different limits, but the same something: see 219^{b}9–28.)

(*ii*) (^{a}25–30). To define simultaneity in terms of 'being in the same now' looks like a begging of the question. Aristotle's point may be just that to define simultaneity we need *unrepeatable* instants, and since 'nows' are the things we have that are most like instants there is a prima facie case for making them un-repeatable. (With the definition cf. *Physics* V.3, 226^{b}21–22.)

218^{a}30. 'Our previous discussions': the reference is unclear, per-haps to the whole of the *Physics* up to this point.

Earlier opinions: a brief and incomplete review. Time as 'the change of the universe', i.e. the revolution of the sphere of fixed stars: this is akin to Plato's position in the *Timaeus* (39^{d}1, cf. generally 37^c–39^e), which identifies time with the movements of all the heavenly bodies. Time as the celestial sphere: apparently Pythagorean (Diels-Kranz 58 B 33 = Aetius I.21, 1).

Aristotle's objections here are hardly more than debating points; his good arguments are reserved for the next section.

218^{b}9. At this point begins Aristotle's substantive discussion, though it arises naturally out of what precedes.

Aristotle uses two 'common-sense' axioms, which he later tries to derive from his definition of time: (*a*) 'time is everywhere alike': see 220^{b}5 ff. (and cf. 223^{a}29 ff.); (*b*) 'time is not fast or slow': see 220^{a}32 ff.

For the difference between change (*kinēsis*) and alteration (*metabolē*) see on 200^{b}12 ff. On the localization of change, III.3.

CHAPTER 11

218^{b}21. The arrangement of the section is odd. Aristotle uses two claims about the perception of change and time: (*a*) when we do not perceive any change to have taken place, we do not think any time has elapsed; (*b*) when we do perceive change to have taken place, we do think some time has elapsed. Of these claims, (*a*) is stated at length at ^{b}21–29 and repeated summarily twice (^{b}29–32, ^{a}7–8), while (*b*) is stated at length at ^{a}3–6 and anticipated summarily at ^{b}32–33. Moreover, ^{a}8–10 simply repeats ^{a}1–3. The simplest explanation is that the intended order was: 218^b21-29; 219^a3-8; $218^b29-219^a3$; and that, after 219^a3-8 were misplaced to their present position, 219^a8-10 were added to preserve continuity.

Aristotle is arguing here from the phenomenology of time and change: the perception and apparent perception of times and changes. This is good dialectical method. His remarks are carefully non-committal about the ontological status of time: indeed it is even left unclear (probably deliberately) whether 'time' (*chronos*) is functioning as a count-noun or as a mass-term. 'Some/any time has elapsed' is a rendering designed to preserve the ambiguity. Aristotle has not yet committed himself to any particular theory of time.

The alleged psychological facts are these. We think that some time has elapsed, between two 'nows', if and only if we have some means of distinguishing the two 'nows', and this we have if and only if we perceive that a change has taken place between them. To perceive this is to mark off the change by means of the 'nows' which bound it (elaborated at 219^a22-30).

Aristotle's conclusion is that time cannot elapse unless there is change. This seems to require the extra premiss that all lapse of time is perceptible. For what may be an attempt to supply the missing premiss see 223^a16-29 below.

'What aspect of change' (219^a3): literally 'what of change'—on the idiom see on 210^b32 ff.

(For Aristotle's developed theory of the perception of change and time, not needed here, see *de Anima* II.6; III.1, 425^a14-^b11; *de Sensu* 1, 437^a3-9; *de Memoria* 1, $449^b24-450^a25$; 2, 452^b7-453^a4 with the comments of Ross (4), (5) and Sorabji.)

219^a10. This section introduces the notion of 'following' (*akolouthein*) which plays an important part in Aristotle's theory. For the theoretical background in Aristotle's conception of 'focal meaning' see on 207^b21 ff., and Introduction, 6(*d*). The verb 'follow' incorporates the notions both of dependence and of consequent correspondence in structure. Both for the pair 'magnitude-change' and for the pair 'change-time', Aristotle's claim is twofold: (*i*) there are relationships of priority (ontological and/or logical and/or epistemological) in virtue of which the second member of each pair is in some sense dependent upon the first; (*ii*) as a result of this dependence, the second member of each pair has an internal structure analogous to that of the first, and derived from it. These claims together constitute Aristotle's 'grand design' in his discussion of time, in which his principal aim is to exhibit the structure and properties of time as wholly intelligible in terms of the structure and properties of spatially extended magnitudes. (Further details of the structural correspondences are worked out in *Physics* VI.)

(1) *Dependence of change on magnitude.* Every change involves magnitudes, according to Aristotle, in two ways. A change must be primarily a change of something having spatial magnitude and it must be 'along' something having spatial magnitude. It is the second dependence which creates the structural correspondences. (Cf. also *Physics* VII.4, 249^{a}9–29, ^{b}11–14.)

Changes are 'along' magnitudes in the following ways. Locomotion is straightforwardly along some spatially extended path. For other types of change it is less obvious what the 'path' is. In increase and decrease of size, an arbitrary point on the boundary of what is increasing or decreasing will trace out a continuous path, and perhaps that will do. In qualitative change, we might be tempted to think of the path as a continuum of *states*, e.g. in a change from white to black, a continuum of shades of grey. But such a continuum does not possess in any obvious way a natural metric, which would make it unsuitable for Aristotle's purposes. Moreover, at *Physics* VI.4, 234^{b}10–20 it is implied that there is not a continuum of intermediate states, but at most finitely many, in any qualitative change. Again, *Physics* VI.4, 235^{a}13–18 says that the 'in which', the path of change, is only accidentally divisible, not in its own right, in qualitative change, and the remark is expanded at VI.5, 236^{b}2–8. For divisibility of the path of change has to be substituted here the divisibility of the changing thing, according to the scheme suggested in 234^{b}21–235^{a}10. The idea is, roughly, that in cases of qualitative change, there being no continuous path of states, we can substitute the continuous paths along which the successive *minimal* changes spread within the changing thing; that there must be such continuous paths seems to follow from the thoroughgoing structural analogy asserted at VI.4, 235^{a}13–^{b}5. Once again, therefore, a spatial 'path' has been constructed (with its natural metric) in an indirect way.

By such ingenious means, Aristotle contrives to construct something which is a kind of equivalent of a path in 'phase space' in modern physics, without any extra existents; and each of these 'paths' is a continuum in its own right, with a natural metric. Every change demands the existence of such a path, and is necessarily a change along some such path; so there seems to be an ontological and a logical priority for the path. The logical dependence is reinforced by the doctrine of *Physics* V.4, 227^{b}3–228^{a}6, that the identity of changes depends *inter alia* on the identity of the 'in which'.

(2) *Correspondence in structure between change and magnitude* Given a spatial path involved in each change, the next step, which is implicit in Aristotle's discussion at VI.4, 235^{a}13–^{b}4, is to define a natural mapping of the path on to the change and reversely. (In what

follows it is convenient to use modern mathematical terminology to express concisely and accurately what Aristotle had in mind and could explain only more clumsily with the aid of diagrams. Aristotle does not speak of anything corresponding to a mapping, but his relation of 'following' is the same as the relation implied by the existence of a structure-preserving mapping.) The mapping must be thought of as taking actual or potential subdivisions of the change ('episodes' within the change) on to actual or potential subdivisions of the path, according to the natural principle that the section of the path corresponding to a given episode is that section which is traversed during the episode.

Aristotle's claim about 'following' is, in essence, that the mapping so defined is structure-preserving. Hence the structure of any change is analogous to, and derivative from, that of its path. For convenience we may distinguish different aspects of the structure: mereology, order, topology (which is here expressible in terms of mereology and order), metric. In *Physics* IV one of Aristotle's topics is the correspondence between changes and magnitudes (also between changes and times) in respect of mereological and topological structure. In the present chapters Aristotle is in general more interested in order and metric. Questions about metric are raised also at *Physics* VII.4, see esp. 249^{a}8–20, 249^{a}29–^{b}19. But topological questions also arise: e.g. correspondences between points, instants, and other indivisibles (indivisible slices through a change?), and, in the present section, the transference of *continuity*. Here, 'since what changes changes from something to something' is a hasty reference to the existence of the path of change. Aristotle's official definition of 'continuous' at *Physics* V. 3, 227^{a}10–17 makes it equivalent to 'not having successive parts with no common boundary'. This is just the kind of property which the natural mapping preserves; but the fact that it preserves continuity does *not* follow simply from the definition of the mapping, as Aristotle may seem to imply.

In fact, it is true in general, for each particular aspect of structure, that, while the definition of natural mapping determines the *meaning* of Aristotle's claim that the mapping is structure-preserving, the *justification* of the claim requires further argument which Aristotle does not here provide. The question of what support Aristotle supposed could be given to each particular claim will be raised in what follows. For the present section, the claim about continuity of magnitudes and changes reduces to the claim that there cannot be discontinuous change along a continuous section of the path. For example, in locomotion, if ABCD is a continuous path, there cannot be locomotion that involves moving continuously from A to B, then jumping to C and moving continuously to D, and then jumping back to B and proceeding continuously to C. Since ABC is a continuous sub-stretch, so must locomotion along ABC be continuous, i.e. with no gaps between successive parts. A stop at B would also interrupt the locomotion and make it discontinuous in the forbidden sense. Aristotle's claim is that there cannot be stops or jumps of this kind within a single change, and he would presumably base it upon the requirements for individuating changes stated at *Physics* V.4. Thus 'the time must be one and continuous' (227^{b}30–31) rules out stops, and 'the in which must be one and undivided (*atomon*)' (227^{b}29–30) rules out jumps.

(3) *Dependence of time on change.* The dependence of time upon change is ultimately given by the definition of time as 'a number of change in respect of the before and after', or something equivalent, reached at 219^{b}1–5 below. This gives a very strong dependence, logical and epistemological as well as ontological. (So far, however, Aristotle has argued (218^{b}21–219^{a}10) only for some weaker relationship.) So far, though, Aristotle has not *used* the dependence of time on change.

At this point one must begin to be careful about the way in which Aristotle's noun 'time' (*chronos*) is interpreted. So far he has used it in an untechnical way, since he has been concerned with ordinary intuitions. But from now on, it may seem, it is used in various quite different ways. First, a time as the 'number' of change is just a quantity belonging to a change, or that quantity expressed as a number. Secondly, a time as a temporally extended interval abstracted from changes is something having not merely a time-quantity but also a *date*. Thirdly, there may be an intermediate sense of 'dateless interval', something having, but not being, a time-quantity. Fourthly, there is a sense of 'time' in which it denotes the sum of all temporal intervals, and (allied to that) looser ways of speaking in which time may be spoken of as a force or an agent and so on. Aristotle never takes trouble to distinguish these senses, which is a little surprising. The reason for being pedantic about them is, of course, that Aristotle's programme of deriving everything from time as 'the number of change' requires that he should be able to *justify* his introduction in any essential role of any other sense. And this he does not show that he can do. (On all this see further 219^{b}1 ff.)

For the purposes of the present note it will be assumed that ultimately Aristotle will be able to make good the claim that a time is (in one sense of 'time') some kind of temporally extended continuum (see, on this assumption, Introduction, 6(*c*) 4, and on 219^{b}1 ff. below). Granted this, the nature of the dependence of a time, in this sense, on a change or on changes, is not yet clear, except that a general ontological dependence presumably carries over from the result of 218^{b}21–219^{a}10: there could not be 'times' of any sort if there were not changes associated with them.

(4) *Correspondence in structure between time and change.* Once again, a natural mapping may be set up, on the lines suggested by *Physics* VI.4, 235^{a}13–^{b}4, which takes actual or potential divisions of the change ('episodes') on to actual or potential divisions of the time, in such a way that the sub-stretch of the time corresponding to a given episode within the change is the sub-stretch which is occupied by the episode. And, once again, Aristotle's claim is that this mapping is structure-preserving, and once again Aristotle does rather little to justify the claim explicitly and in detail. *Physics* VI is again a helpful source of parallels.

In the present section, the only claim is about continuity. This amounts to the thesis that there could not be a discontinuous time corresponding naturally to a continuous change. This, in turn, means that a change in which there is no temporal gap between any two successive episodes cannot occupy two successive times with a temporal gap between them—a claim which is natural enough, and which can be proved easily enough if times are constructed by abstraction from changes (as will be argued below; see on 219^{b}1 ff. 220^{b}5 ff.). (The parallel argument, in *Physics* VI.2, 232^{b}20– 233^{a}12, to derive continuity of time from continuity of magnitude, uses a different definition of 'continuous', namely, 'divisible into parts always divisible' (232^{b}25).)

A difficulty in the present section is the concluding remark: 'For the time always seems to have been of the same amount as the change' (219^{a}13–14). *Amounts* of time and change are not yet in question, and in any case, a metrical correspondence would of itself do nothing to ensure the transference of continuity. Possibly the remark is misplaced, e.g. from 219^{b}1 where it would have more point; or it may be an unintelligent 'explanation' by a later hand. On metrical correspondence generally see 220^{b}14 ff.

The purpose of the present section, in any case, is to introduce the 'following' relation and to state that it guarantees the *continuity* of change: this is required for the following discussion of 'the before and after'.

219^{a}14. This section introduces and uses 'the before and after' (*to proteron kai husteron*). The grammar of the phrase is uncertain: in the text as it is transmitted, *proteron* and *husteron* are treated as adverbs at ^{a}23, but as adjectives at ^{a}24. Other occurrences of the phrase in Aristotle's works are at *Physics* VIII.1, 251^{b}10–11, *Metaphysics* III.3, 999^{a}6; XIII.6, 1080^{b}12; *Nicomachean Ethics* I.6, 1096^{a}18. These passages show that it was a technical term in the

Academy, and that it denoted something that could be present only in an ordered series.

'The before and after' ought to mean 'that which is both before and after' or 'that which is both precedent and subsequent'; i.e. it ought to pick out something (or *the* thing) that is, successively or simultaneously, present at all stages of the ordered series. And it is at least clear from 219^{b}9−28, that 'the before and after in change' is something that somehow runs through the change in its temporal order. (This cannot well be the change itself, since the change itself is not successively present at all its own stages.) In the remainder of this note, we must consider: (1) the before and after in place; (2) the application of the principle of structural correspondence; (3) the before and after in change; (4) in what sense the before and after in change is the change itself.

(1) *The before and after in place.* Places may be ordered by inclusion (cf. 209^{a}31−^{b}1) and natural places have thus a natural linear ordering (place of earth−of water−of air−of fire) in which the last is teleologically the best. Similarly, for the celestial regions, since there is a preferred direction of rotation, there is a natural sense of description of any circular orbit (which Aristotle in places tries to connect with an absolute forwards-backwards direction in the universe: see on 208^{b}12−25). So, even on a celestial circle, a non-conventional relation of 'before' can be defined, though it will not be transitive (point A is before point B, if and only if, starting from A and going in the natural direction, one reaches B before reaching the point diametrically opposite to A).

But, even if the orbits of natural motions can be ordered thus, what is 'the before and after in place?'. Something that describes the orbit? But this is to introduce changes, whereas 'the before and after in place' ought to be something intrinsic to places, in advance of any change. It ought to be something given by the very ordering. Aristotle's consciousness of the difficulty is perhaps revealed by his remark that 'the before and after' is in place *tēi thesei*−'by convention', or perhaps 'by (relative) location' or 'orientation'. The phrase is too obscure to be of any real help, and further elucidation of 'the before and after in place' will be possible, if at all, only by arguing back from the before and after in change. See below (5).

(2) *The correspondence principle.* This application is also, necessarily, obscure. It is clear (at least) how a natural ordering of a path of change will carry over to a natural temporal ordering of the change itself, by means of the natural mapping. (Even here there is the difficulty that one and the same path may be the path of two contrary changes, so that it may have two distinct natural orderings, neither intrinsically more natural, though one will be teleologically better.)

(3) *The before and after in change.* We need something that can
be said to run through the change in temporal order. Possibilities
are: (*a*) the changing thing; (*b*) the lower temporal boundary of the
change (the 'leading edge'); (*c*) the permanent present. Of these
(*a*) looks unlikely, because in the system of analogies worked out in
219^{b}9–28 the changing thing is given a different role. The interpretation that will be adopted from now on is that (*b*) and (*c*) are to
be identified with each other and with 'the before and after in
change'. It is claimed that this interpretation is justified by its
success in making sense of the whole of the rest of this chapter.

Suppose there is a change from state A to state E, with intermediate states B,C,D,. Then at different stages the history of the
change so far may be represented diagrammatically:

A   B   C   D   E
———————→
————————————→
———————————————————→

In the course of the whole change, the point of the arrow 'travels'
from A to E via every intermediate state. The point of the arrow
represents the 'leading edge' of change, the lower boundary of the
change so far.

This much shows that there is a certain intuitive plausibility
about the notion of a 'leading edge' of change. The next requirement
is that it should account for the remarks in this section about the
before and after in change, and the change itself.

(4) *The before and after in change and the change itself.* 'The
before and after in change is, in respect of what makes it what it is,
change; but its being is different, and is not change' (219^{a}19–21).
'What makes it what it is' translates *ho pote on*, a phrase of technical meaning found in two other passages outside this discussion: (*a*) *Part. Anim.* II.2, 648^{b}35–3, 649^{b}27, on the senses in
which blood is, in itself, hot or not hot. Aristotle claims that 'blood'
is a case of a word for a hot phase of some underlying X which is not
essentially hot. (Wiggins, 24 suggests *phased sortal* as a term for such
sortal concepts.) 'Blood' is to be defined as 'hot X'; Aristotle does
not identify X, but describes it as 'whatever it is that happens to be
the underlying thing' (649^{a}15–16: *ho . . . pote tugchanei on to
hupokeimenon*) and as 'the underlying thing and whatever it is by
being which blood is blood' (649^{b}24–25: *ho pote on haima estin*).
The clause with *ho pote on* is used to pick out the substantial reality
lying beneath a phased sortal concept. (*b*) *Gen. et Corr.* I.3,
319^{a}33–^{b}4. Here the question is: what, if anything, persists in

elemental change? Aristotle has just suggested that there is something which serves as 'matter' for all the elements alike (319^{a}32–33), and now asks whether the matter of each element is different or the same. He now suggests that there is some persistent X, 'whatever it is by being which it underlies' (319^{b}3–4) to serve as a basis for such phased sortals as 'X–serving-as-matter-for-water'.

In these passages, *ho pote on* clauses serve to pierce below the surface of a phased sortal and exhibit the real state of affairs. The phrase *ho pote on* itself is integrated into the construction of the sentence. In the present passage, the phrase seems to have broken loose from its original syntactical moorings and to function for brevity's sake as an independent noun-phrase. It so appears here (219^{a}20–21) and at 219^{b}14–15, 18–19, 26, 220^{a}8 and a grammatically related phrase (*ho pot' ēn*) at 219^{b}11. (On the later uses see on 219^{b}9 ff. below.)

If 'the before and after in change' is a persisting entity, as has been suggested, it cannot in itself be considered 'phased', and so does not need a *ho pote on* to be supplied. What a change underlies as a *ho pote on* is any instantaneous (or, at least, transient) phase of that change. What is being said, then, is that any transient phase of the before and after in a change is identical (though not the same 'in being') with a corresponding transient phase of the change itself. This is reasonable; if a change C is now taking place, in the course of which some X has become (and now temporarily is) F, then the present phase of the change C is just X's being F, while the present phase of the before and after in change is just the most recent state reached by the change. These two phases are identical, though differently identified (on 'different in being' see on 202^{b}5 ff.).

(5) *Remaining problems.* It is still unclear what 'the before and after in time' is: on this see 219^{b}9 ff.

To recur to 'the before and after in place'. To preserve the analogy, this ought to be something that is present at every point along a path of change, independently of any change's actually occurring. The best solution is that what is meant is the 'ubiquitous point', representing a potential division, that is present anywhere and everywhere on an undivided line. On this, see on 219^{b}9 ff., 222^{a}10 ff. On this supposition, the argument from correspondence might run as follows: Any line is divisible anywhere. But a potential division of a path of change corresponds to a potential division of the change itself (cf. *Physics* VI.4, 235^{a}13–^{b}5). So to 'the before and after in place' there naturally corresponds an instantaneous limit, which would be the end-state if the change were divided; and this is the 'leading edge' of change.

219^a22. Compared with 218^b21 ff. above, the present section makes two new points about perception of the lapse of time:

(A) To perceive lapse of time as such, it is not enough to perceive two 'nows' as different; we must also perceive (*a*) that one 'now' is before the other; (*b*) that there is something in between (cf. 218^b 25–27) different from either.

(B) To perceive (*a*) and (*b*) is to perceive the before and after in change and to mark off change by it.

Thus (A) refines the phenomenological description, (B) interprets it in terms of the before and after in change. At 219^a25–26: 'we mark off change by taking them to be different things', 'them' denotes 'the before' and 'the after' considered as two. The differentiated phases then turn out to be different 'nows' (cf. the developed theory of 219^b9–28).

219^b1. This section presents what appears to be intended as the centrepiece of Aristotle's discussion, the definition of time. But it is far from clear how the section is supposed to be arranged or related to what precedes it. The most obvious difficulties are:

(*i*) The first sentence, 'For that is what time is . . .', states the definition as if it had already been established.

(*ii*) Even if this sentence is bracketed as an aside or a later addition, the next sentence begins with an inferential particle: 'so' (*ara*). To what does this refer back? It ought to make a connection with the preceding section, but how is this to be done?

(*iii*) What is the connection, if any, with the last sentence of 219^a10–14: 'For the time always seems to have been of the same amount as the change'?

(*iv*) What is the grammar and meaning of the statement: 'So time is not change but in the way in which change has a number'?

(*v*) How does this statement lead to what is apparently the full-dress definition 'time is a number of change in respect of the before and after'? And, if the occurrence of the definition here is to be bracketed as not an integral part of the text, why is the definition not formally stated until 220^a24–25?

(*vi*) In this definition, why does Aristotle say 'a number' rather than 'the number'? The absence of a definite article is anomalous in a definition.

'Time is not change but in the way in which change has a number'. There are two possible interpretations: (A) As it stands, the sentence may be translated 'Time is not change, but is change-*qua*-having-a-number.' The Greek can bear this translation without alteration or straining of sense or grammar. (B) If we may suppose an elliptical omission of the word 'number', *arithmos*, it can be translated 'Time is not change, but is a number, in the way in which change has a number.' The ellipsis is harsh, and even if *arithmos* were present in the text the resulting expression would be distinctly odd. So (A) seems preferable, provided it is compatible with time's being a number of change.

How, then, might this result be deduced from 219^{a}14–^{b}1? At 218^{b}21–219^{a}10, Aristotle used phenomenology to show that there could be no perception of a time without perception of a change and vice versa; he concluded that there could be no time without a change and that time was 'some aspect of change'. At 219^{a}22–^{b}1 he refines the phenomenology to show that perception of time involves perception also of an *ordering*, and that time is what is 'in between' or 'marked off by' the 'nows'. This would seem to allow the conclusion that a time is a change *qua*-ordered-and-markable-off-by-nows. To get from here to change-*qua*-having-a-number, all that is needed is the general theory of measurement developed in *Metaphysics* X.1. What has an unambiguous natural ordering, and can be marked off by indivisible markers, can be measured by making off unit-stretches. Just as a line can be measured, so can a change.

This explanation has the advantage that it explains the relevance of the *continuity* of change (219^{a}10–14) and of the before and after in place and change (219^{a}14–21), as well as of the phenomenology (219^{a}22–^{b}1), to the conclusion. It may be objected that Aristotle has not yet shown that there is any such thing as a natural metric for changes, so that he is not entitled to assume that there are naturally comparable 'unit-stretches'. But the principle of structural correspondence may be tacitly invoked here (on the difficulties of deriving a natural metric in this way see on 220^{b}14 ff.). Moreover, the construction of a time-measure by means of the counting of 'nows' is made explicit at 219^{b}33–220^{a}24.

'Change-*qua*-numbered' and 'number of change'. Aristotle claims that there are two senses of 'number': the 'number counted' and the 'number by which we count'. For the background to this distinction, given by Aristotle's abstractionist theory of mathematics, see Additional Note A. Of four sheep, the 'number by which we count' is 4, but the 'number counted' is simply the four sheep considered as a numbered totality. So too with a change lasting (say) two days; the time, i.e. the 'number counted' will be simply the change itself considered as a temporally measurable thing.

It is possible, then, to give a coherent account of the present section and of its relation to what precedes it (always assuming that the first sentence, 219^{b}1–2, is excised). Aristotle's reductive intentions are clear. His aim is to show that there is nothing more to time than what is implied by this account of the time of a particular change, and to show that all the things we normally say about times and time can be understood and explained in the light of such an account.

The real difficulties with this account of time do not arise out of this section itself, but from attempts in later sections to put the account of time to work and to combine it with the theory of the 'permanent present'. In particular, in many later sections it becomes obvious that Aristotle is operating with a notion of 'abstract time', analogous to the 'number by which we count' as well as with his official notion of time. This, in itself, is not necessarily a disaster for Aristotle; as in arithmetic and geometry, he presumably thought that there was a (carefully limited) place for abstracts. (See in general Additional Note A.) But the awkwardness and muddle do at least strongly suggest that Aristotle's original intentions have become overlaid by a number of incomplete revisions. There is nowhere any explicit mention of the need for 'abstract times'. In all probability, Aristotle's original draft was written at a stage when his thoughts about the nature of mathematics were undeveloped. Later, on coming to see the need for 'abstract time', he undertook piecemeal revisions.

All this suggests that the original definition of 'time' was 'change-*qua*-numbered', as at 219^{b}3. The formulation 'a number of change in respect of the before and after' was given at 220^{a}25 by Aristotle, but not as the statement of a definition; and later, perhaps, inserted here (219^{b}1−2) by someone who thought it was the official definition and ought to be present in this section.

219^{b}9. The section falls into two parts.

(*a*) *219^{b}9−15.* An outline of the position to be taken up. One and the same change has a series of different stages ('is always other and other'). So too with one and same time (by the correspondence principle, supported by the account just given of time as 'the number of change'). And the unity-in-variety of a time is derived directly from the unity-in-variety of the now.

The now. Using the *ho pote on* terminology (see on 219^{a}14 ff.) Aristotle explains that different 'unrepeatable' 'nows', i.e. instants, are different phases of some persisting X. The X is identified later, at ^{b}22−28. 'That was what it is for it to be a now': by definition, 'nows' are unrepeatable. 'Its being is different': cf. on 202^{b}5 ff.

On the problem about 'the now' to which this section gives the answer, see on 217^{b}32 ff. On the implications of this section for the reality of the past see below (concluding remarks).

The now and time. 'It is the now that measures time, considered as before and after' (219^{b}11−12). The 'now' cannot 'measure' time as a measuring-unit does. But it provides the means of counting the number of units (cf. 219^{a}22−^{b}1), and in that sense gives the temporal ('considered as before and after') measure of time, as of change. Because the 'now' divides up times in this way, its unity-in-variety is the foundation for the unity-in-variety of times. (Remember that times here are just changes considered as measurable.) Consider a time lying between 'now A' and 'now B':

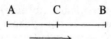

Because A and B are different phases of some X, there is some persisting X that sweeps over the whole stretch from A to B; this gives the stretch its (derivative) unity. Because A and B are different, and any intermediate 'now' (C) is different, the stretch may be said to be different at different stages with a derivative kind of difference.

The analogy between change and time still limps, because we have not learned what corresponds, for changes, to the 'now' as guarantee of unity for times: on this, ^{b}15−28 below.

(*b*) *219^{b}15−33.* The scheme of analogies is now worked out in detail.

Analogy between point and moving thing (^{b}16−22). This is implied to be a consequence of the general structural correspondence between magnitudes and changes: see in general on 219^{a}10 ff. But it is unintelligible without reference also to 'the before and after': see on 219^{a}14 ff., where it was suggested that 'the before and after in place' was the potentiality for division of a length (or other magnitude), which Aristotle conceived of as a point of indeterminate location. It is this kind of point that is needed in the present passage: call it, for convenience, 'the ubiquitous point'. (On the 'ubiquitous point' see further on 222^{a}10 ff.)

About the ubiquitous point Aristotle claims here, directly or by implication:

(1) It is the underlying X of which all particular (located) points are only different aspects (since change is not involved we cannot speak of 'phases'). Thus a particular point at location L is the ubiquitous point as realized at L;

(2) It is by means of the ubiquitous point (as realized in different places) that we come to know the line and what is before and what is after in it. This is an epistemological claim: its content is presumably that we cannot identify lines as such without reference

to particular points on them (as in geometry we speak of 'the line AB'), we cannot see a particular direction along a line without seeing the line as swept out by a moving point, and we cannot specify a particular direction along a line without reference to particular points ('from A to B').

Aristotle's next step is to claim an exact analogy: as the ubiquitous point is to its magnitude, so is the moving thing to its motion (taken as a standard type of change). In particular claims (1) and (2) above are held by Aristotle to hold good, *mutatis mutandis*, for the moving thing and motion. To make the analogy work, we need to introduce, as analogues of particular (located) points, stages of the moving thing, such as 'Coriscus-in-the-Lyceum' and 'Coriscus-in-the-marketplace'. These are the same underlying substance (Coriscus) in different 'phases'. Then the claims about the moving thing are:

(1) The moving thing is the underlying X of which all particular stages of the moving thing are different 'phases';

(2) It is by means of the moving thing that we come to know the change and what is before and what is after in it. (That is, we cannot perceive a change as such without perceiving that something is changing, and we can discern a temporal order in the change only by discerning a temporal order of particular stages of the changing thing.)

'As the point is, so is a stone or something else of that sort': the translation here, following a suggestion of G.E.L. Owen for emending the Greek text, brings out the analogy. 'A stone' is here an example of a moving thing.

'The sophists assume': there were puzzles, used by sophists, about the changes in a persisting subject. Cf. on 202^{b}5 ff., esp. on 202^{b}9–10, which see also 'for different in definition'.

Analogy between moving thing and persisting present (^{b}22–33). Aristotle now extends the analogy to times. What changing things are to their changes, that X is to times, where X is the persisting X of which all unrepeatable instants are phases. And this X is now identified as 'the before and after in change', for which see 219^{a}14–21. So the claims are:

(1) 'The before and after in change' is the persisting present, of which 'nows', unrepeatable instants, are different phases.

(2) It is by the instants that we come to know time, as it is by the changing thing that we come to know change. (We cannot identify a particular time-stretch as such except by reference to particular instants, and we cannot discern a temporal order in a time-stretch except by discerning it in a series of instants.)

The analogies in general:

The analogies of this section are shown in the following table:

Continuum	Unifying particular	'Phase' of unifying particular
Magnitude	Ubiquitous point	Located point
Change	Changing thing	Stage of changing thing
Time	Permanent present ('the before and after in change')	Unrepeatable instant

There are difficulties with this scheme. In particular, the relationships of 'unifying particulars' to 'the before and after' are not analogous throughout. In the case of magnitude, the 'unifying particular' which guarantees the unity of a magnitude is the same (on this interpretation) as 'the before and after in magnitude'. But there is no corresponding identity for changes and times: 'the before and after in change' turns out to be the unifying particular for a *time*, and 'the before and after in time' is given no role at all. In fact, it is difficult to see what 'the before and after in time' can be, unless it is identical with 'the before and after in change'. Why then did not Aristotle identify 'the before and after in change' with the changing thing, and the 'before and after in time' with the permanent present? One good reason for not doing so is that the changing thing, considered in itself, i.e. just as a stone or whatever it may be, is not necessarily involved in an ordered series at all, and therefore cannot of itself be 'before and after'. The serial ordering of change is, as it were, imposed on the changing thing from outside.

This breakdown of the analogy is not merely aesthetically regrettable; it points to a serious weakness in the whole 'grand design'. Another way of demonstrating the weakness is to ask: are the permanent present and its phases tied to a particular change or not? 'The before and after in change' ought to be tied to a particular change and to a particular time (time as change-*qua*-measurable). But then there will be many different simultaneous 'permanent presents' and many different simultaneous 'nows', and therefore an essential feature of time—that simultaneous instants are identical— has been left out. And, in fact, at 220[b]5 ff. Aristotle assumes that nows are not tied to particular changes (so too 223[a]29 ff.).

Perhaps then 'time' must be treated, for the purposes of the analogy, not as a *particular* change-*qua*-measurable, but as an abstraction from all changes, an *abstract* change-*qua*-measurable. In this case, while 'the before and after' in a particular change could be the particular changing thing, 'the before and after' in change in the abstract could be identified with the permanent present. This manœuvre will solve the difficulties just outlined, but at the price of introducing others. For the introduction of times as *abstractions* from all particular changes is not yet warranted by anything in the text, unless to call it a number is to call it an abstraction from all particulars. But abstract numbers are numbers 'by which we count', not numbers 'counted'. Moreover, if we do abstract from changes and consider them only as measurable, all changes lasting (say) two days ought to be represented by one and the same abstract time-length of two days. But Aristotle later (e.g. 220^b6) insists that times are *dated*, so that a two days' time a year ago is not the same time as a two days' time last week. Once again, the relation of simultaneity plays an essential role. But there is nothing analogous to simultaneity in magnitudes. Two lines may be said to be together if in contact, but two changes may be simultaneous even though the paths of these changes are not in contact, so that there is nothing to which simultaneity corresponds under the natural mapping.

The conclusion must be: (1) that Aristotle's 'grand design' is over-ambitious and cannot do what is required of it, namely to exhibit all temporal entities and structures as derivative from spatial ones; (2) that Aristotle's exposition is confused here between two or three different conceptions of time, according to which a time is either (*i*) a particular change considered only *qua* measurable; or (*ii*) a 'dated abstract': an abstraction from all particular changes with simultaneous end-points, considering them all only *qua* measurable; or (*iii*) a 'dateless abstract': an abstraction from all particular changes of the same temporal length. While 219^b1-9 seems to present (*i*), Aristotle later works with (*ii*). But to adopt (*ii*) here would show up the weakness of the 'grand design'.

How much can be salvaged from the wreckage? If we adopt the position that times are 'dated abstracts' from changes, the simplistic talk of times as 'numbers of changes' will have to go—and with it some of Aristotle's programme of de-mystification. But there will still be a logical dependence, and a natural structural correspondence due to the dependence, between times and changes, so that at least this part of the 'grand design' survives, and with it the account of the permanent present as 'the before and after in (abstract) change'. The most characteristic features of Aristotle's theory remain, it seems, internally coherent.

Concluding remarks: the permanent present, the reality of the past, and the reality of becoming. Aristotle's theory of the 'perma-nent present' is not a gratuitous construction. It supplies an answer to the problem about 'the now' (218^a8-30) which, it was suggested, is a way of raising doubts about the reality of the past. Aristotle does not, indeed, give any direct answer to the doubts. But he derives the persistence of the permanent present from the persistence of the changing thing. Now doubts about the reality of the past may be focused on one particular change, in progress at the time of considering the question. If Aristotle were to doubt that the previous stages of the change have really been gone through, he would have to doubt whether anything was really in a process of change at all, since he is always clear that a process of change cannot take place all at a moment. In other words, Aristotle's position on the nature of change dictates that the reality of change in the present implies the reality of at least some previous stretch of change. And by means of the everlasting changes, the rotation of the celestial spheres, Aristotle can argue for the reality of an arbitrarily long past stretch of change in this way. The 'permanent present' is a way of presenting the result of this argument in a form abstracted from particular changes.

To say that the past is real is not to say that it is really present. Aristotle's theory involves the reality of becoming: being present is really and objectively different at any moment, from being past. Moreover, what it is to be present remains the same all along, though the contents of the present vary.

To say that the past is real is, also, not to say that it exists as an *infinitely extended* totality. For the indications that Aristotle had doubts about the reality of temporal metric beyond some finite time in the past, see Introduction, 3(*c*) 3 and 6 (*g*).

219^{b}33. A corollary: time and the now are mutually dependent. Where there is a time, there is a change, by the account given of time, and therefore a changing thing. We can therefore distinguish and count phases of the changing thing, and these phases are tied to different instants, and counting them involves counting nows. Here the 'now' plays the role of an abstract unit. Conversely, if there is a permanent present, there is its analogue, the changing thing, and therefore there is a change and a time.

220^{a}4. Continua and their division discussed with special reference to time. The section is compressed and allusive, but some light is thrown by related passages elsewhere in Aristotle's work.

(1) Spatial continua. Aristotle uses, as paradigm one-dimensional continuum, a line. A point defines a line, or a sub-stretch of a line, by being a boundary point. So it 'holds together' (*sunechei*) a line and makes it one continuum, by being both end-point of one stretch and beginning-point of the next. For two different sub-stretches are by definition continuous with one another if, and only if, they have a common boundary (*Physics* V.3, 227^{a}10–15).

(2) *The continuum of change.* As before, Aristotle seeks to demonstrate a structural analogy and dependence of changes on spatial magnitudes. ^{a}9–11 gives the case of the line; ^{a}6–9 that of the change.

If we consider two sub-changes, A to B and C to D, defined by the beginning and end-states, and ask for the necessary and sufficient condition that the two together should form one continuous change, then, as before, we must be able to identify B with C. For this it is obviously not sufficient that the changing thing should be the same (e.g. Coriscus) in both cases. If Coriscus in state B is in a different state from Coriscus in state C, then there must be a gap between the two sub-changes. Hence Coriscus must be the same 'in definition' in the sense of 219^{b}19–21, i.e. in the same state. Granted this, B and C can be identified, and continuity demonstrated. It is the instantaneous states of the changing thing, therefore, that here function analogously to points, and define sub-stretches of changes.

(3) *The continua of change and time, and their division.* Aristotle further claims that the analogy extends to times, with the 'nows' in the role of points. The claim is made at ^{a}4–5. At ^{a}12 Aristotle resumes the discussion of time as a continuum with a problem: the analogy breaks down when we come to consider *dividing* the continua.

The fundamental disanalogy is this: a physical length (e.g. a thin cylinder of wood) may be physically divided and the two halves then put together so that their boundaries are continuous, and the halves themselves, though not reunited, are continuous with one another. To this physical process corresponds, in geometry, the bisection of a line at a point. To bisect the line AB at C is to make it into two lines, AC and CB, which, however, are continuous. In such a case the geometer 'treats the one point (C) as two' beause he sees it as having the two roles of 'end-point of AC' and 'starting-point of CB'. (On Aristotle's abstractionist programme in mathematics see Additional Note A.)

But there is nothing corresponding to the possibility of continuous yet not united halves in the case of changes or times. If the two sub-stretches of change are continuous as described, there is only one change, not two half-changes. Hence 'to treat one point as two' in this case is to consider the two sub-stretches as not truly continuous, and this is mistaken, if in fact they *are* continuous. Aristotle's problem therefore is: in 'marking off' stretches of a change or time, we are not straightforwardly abstracting from possible physical operations; but we understand such 'marking off' only as an abstraction; how then is it to be understood?

The statement of the problem, very compressed, is at ^{a}12–14. 'Treating the one point as two': similar expressions occur at *Physics* VIII.8, 262^{b}5–6, ^{b}24–25, 263^{a}24; *de Anima* III.2, 427^{a}13–14. (The discussion in *Physics* VIII.8, is particularly relevant to the present passage.) 'One must come to a halt': perhaps 'it must be that (the change) comes to a halt'.

Aristotle's solution follows at ᵃ14–24, but is sadly obscure. The following interpretation is tentative.

(*a*) In marking off, and counting, 'nows', we are not actually dividing the time or change that is being measured, nor asserting or assuming that it is actually divided. Hence 'time is a number not as a number of the same point is, in that it is beginning and end . . . and not as parts of the line are . . .'. It is only when there is actual division that the same point (that is counted) is both beginning and end, and that there are parts of the line to be counted. For this negative conclusion, Aristotle gives two reasons: (*i*) actual division of a change would imply a period of rest, as argued above; (*ii*) in any case, to count the dividing 'nows' would of itself tell nothing about the length of the time, since 'the now is no portion of time'. (We would need to know that the 'nows' were evenly spaced along the time; but if that were known we should already know how to measure the time.)

(*b*) From (*a*) it follows that the 'now' considered as the *limit* of a change or time is not time, i.e. not what is *primarily* counted; though 'it is an accident', i.e. it is true that measuring time involves counting 'nows', but they are not what is primarily counted.

(*c*) The positive suggestion is at ᵃ16: time is a number 'in the way in which the extremes are the number of the line'. The point must be that we measure the length of a line by seeing how far apart its end-points are. So too with a time or a change. *How* this distance is measured is not explained, but at any rate it is *this* measurement which is the primary one.

(*d*) Aristotle wishes both to assimilate time-measurement to counting, and to insist that changes and times cannot actually be divided. The only possible solution would seem to be that what are primarily counted are unit-length changes. (How we find unit-length changes is a further question: see on 220ᵇ14 ff.) If we can find a series of distinct unit-length changes which are such that the 'lower' boundary of one is the 'upper' boundary of the next (i.e. the same 'now'), then we can measure, without actually dividing, any contemporary change or time. The unit changes are what are primarily counted, but they are distinguished by their boundaries, so that they may be counted by counting 'nows'. (See further on 220ᵇ14 ff.)

(*e*) (ᵃ22–24): 'For limits are of that alone . . .': this remark is of doubtful relevance. It implies a conception of time as 'number by which we count', as used later: see Introduction, 6(*c*) 4.

220ᵃ24. A summary of results so far.

CHAPTER 12

220ᵃ27. Any continuous length can be divided in any prescribed
ratio; so if one unit of length is to be used to measure all lengths, it
will be necessary to admit fractions of a unit, and arbitrarily small
ones. Aristotle elsewhere shows signs of allowing a branch of
mathematics dealing with numbers and other quantities alike on the
model of Eudoxus' theory of proportions (see esp. *Metaphysics*
XIII.2, 1077ᵃ9–10, ᵇ17–22 and Heath (3), 222–4). Here it would
seem that, as usual, fractions are not classified as numbers. If so, to
give a length as (say) 'one-tenth of an inch' must, for Aristotle, be to
introduce tacitly a new unit, in terms of which the old unit, the
inch, is given as 'ten new units'. So Aristotle's point is that, given a
particular unit, there is a smallest possible number of those units
(two or perhaps one: Aristotle usually takes number to imply a
plurality); but that there is no smallest possible unit ('smallest'
meaning here 'smallest in length').

The point is formulated here in terms of a distinction between
'number without qualification' and 'particular number'. The distinction seems to be the same as that between 'number by which we
count' (abstract number) and 'number counted', on which see
219ᵇ1 ff., and Additional Note A. Because of the existence of different unit-lengths, lengths may be compared both with regard to
multiplicity (the multiplicity of two metres is '2') and with regard to
length. So two metres is less than four feet in multiplicity, but
greater than four feet in length. So too with times, which here are
clearly treated as 'numbers counted'.

220ᵃ32. The argument is not clear but seems to be: times are numbers counted, and as such can be 'much' (great) or 'little' (small);
times are also quantities and as such can be long or short. But there
is nothing else, in virtue of which times could be fast or slow; in
particular, abstract numbers (from which times might inherit their
properties) cannot be fast or slow.

Aristotle ought really to explain why it is that times cannot
inherit 'fast' or 'slow' from the changes they measure, the point
being that changes of different speeds may take the same time (made
at 223ᵇ6–8, on which see note).

The aim here is to justify the axiom taken as self-evident at
218ᵇ13–18, and to do it by means of the account of time as 'the
number of change'.

220ᵇ5. This is the first of two passages (the other is 223ᵃ29–ᵇ12)
on the sameness and difference of times; the note at 224ᵃ2–15, on

the sameness and difference of numbers, is also relevant. It is convenient to consider all three passages together here.

Sameness and difference of numbers. At 220^{b}8–12 the distinction between the two types of number is used. Two different sets of a hundred have the same (abstract) number, viz. 100; but they are, or have, different 'numbers counted': these hundred men are a different 'number counted' from those hundred horses, because the unit-objects making up the totality are different.

At 223^{b}4–6, 11–12, the only point made is that 'the numbers of things equal and together is everywhere one and the same'; this can only refer to abstract number, but the addition of 'together' is puzzling.

At 224^{b}2–15, there is a more elaborate discussion. The general criterion suggested is: A is the same X as B if, and only if, A and B are both X's, and A does not differ from B by the difference of an X. 'To differ by the difference of an X' seems to mean 'to differ in respect of a *differentia* falling immediately under X', and to presuppose, therefore, that a system of classification is given (cf. *Metaphysics* V.6, 1016^{a}24–32).

Thus, if under *plane rectilinear figure* the immediate *differentiae* are: 'three-sided', 'four-sided' etc., two triangles will not differ by such a *differentia*, but may differ by the *differentia* of *triangle*, e.g. scalene, isosceles; they will therefore be the same plane rectilinear figure but not the same triangle. It is an objection that two distinct isosceles triangles would hardly be said, either in English or Greek to be the same triangle, viz. an isosceles one. But this fact may merely indicate that *triangle* is an *infima species*, under which the only differences are differences in number.

The application to numbers is that two tens or sets of ten may be the same number, and yet not the same ten nor the same ten things. This suggests that *number* is a genus, with species *two, three, . . .* etc., each species having as its particular members (e.g.) these two sheep, these two horses, . . . etc. The suggestion that a particular abstract number is to the correspondingly numbered collections as species to its members seems coherent with the notion that abstract numbers are abstracted from predicates of collections. Once again, the test for difference of numbered collections is the difference of the members of the collection.

224^{b}2–15, then, may be regarded as in agreement with 220^{b}8–12, while 223^{b}4–6 and 11–12 is puzzlingly different.

Sameness and difference of times. The doctrine of 220^{b}8–12 and 224^{b}2–15 is supposed to be applied to times in 220^{b}5–14. The times are 'numbers counted', as at 219^{b}5–9; hence times are the same or different according as the basic units counted are the same or different. But the basic units counted are 'nows' (as at 219^a25- 30, 219^b25, 220^a3-4; even if this position is modified as at 220^a $14-24$, the end result is the same). Hence two times are the same if, and only if, they are the same number of the same nows, i.e. are not only equal but *simultaneous*. The fundamental point is that any two simultaneous changes can be measured by the same set of unit changes.

One trouble with this simple-minded application is that it would seem to follow that one and the same change may have two different times. Whether or not the unit is changed, a different set of unit-changes will result, on this view of number, in a different 'number counted' and therefore in a different time. (And with a change of unit, even the 'nows' counted will be different.) The solution may be that Aristotle (*i*) would insist that unit-changes are the basic things counted, (*ii*) would claim that the choice of unit-changes was not arbitrary. For (*i*) see on 220^a4 ff. above; for (*ii*) see on 220^b14 ff., 223^b12 ff. below.

The fact that two distinct changes may have, or be, the same time, is not immediately evident from the characterization of time as 'a number of change in respect of the before and after'; it uses the fact that 'the before and after' in this case, is something *abstracted* from particular changes (see on this 219^b9 ff.). So it is that a time, in this account, turns out to be something not tied exclusively by logic to any one particular change, but a kind of universal that may be common to many changes. And as a universal it is susceptible to abstraction by the mind, even if, in fact, it cannot subsist independently of the particular changes. At this point, then, another clear hint occurs of an abstract conception of time (cf. again on 219^b9 ff. above).

At 223^a29-^b12 it is likewise stated that time is 'simply a number of continuous change, but not of a particular change'; but the justification given is feeble and confused (see on that section— probably this is the remains of an early draft).

A wider sense of 'the same time' is recognized at the end of the present section, at 220^b12-14. Changes 'repeat themselves', not in the sense that the identical change occurs, but in the sense that the same type of change recurs; analogously, times equal in length may recur.

The upshot of the whole section is to justify the axiom that 'time is everywhere the same', taken as self-evident at 218^b13.

220^b14. More on time-measurement; as before, Aristotle's theory of numbers and counting and the 'following' relation are used essentially.

Counting and measuring. The parallelism requires that there should be a distinction between 'the multiplicity of the horses', i.e. the number counted, and 'the number of the horses itself', i.e. the abstract number. Suppose we count a group of horses and find that there are seven of them. To become 'acquainted with' the one kind of number, is necessarily to become acquainted with the other: for to know that these horses are seven-in-number is just to know that 7 is the number which happens to be the number of these horses. There is just one operation, counting, which leads to this knowledge. But, because of the conceptual distinction between the two kinds of number, the operation has two distinguishable aspects:

(*i*) 'By number we know the multiplicity of the horses': in order to count the horses, we have to set up a one-one correspondence between the horses and an abstract series, namely 1, 2, 3, . . . of numbers. Whatever words we use (if we use any) in counting is irrelevant: the numbers are being, as it were, applied to the collection of horses from outside, and are therefore being treated as abstracts.

(*ii*) 'By the one horse we know the number of the horses itself.' In order to be able to set up the one-one correspondence, we have to know what constitutes a single horse, and to use this knowledge repeatedly.

So the one-one correspondence is two-sided: it requires independent knowledge of (*i*) the abstract number series; (*ii*) the concept of a single horse; and in linking horses and numbers we get knowledge about both at once.

These two aspects of counting, as *Metaphysics* X.1, $1052^b18-1053^a35$ shows, are assimilated by Aristotle to analogous aspects of measuring. Apart from the length to be measured, we have to have a re-applicable unit-measure (cf. 'the one horse') and an abstract number series. There is again a one-one correspondence, between (potential) parts of the length and abstract numbers.

Measuring change by time and time by change. There are certain difficulties in transferring this theory to temporal measurements: the problems of where to find, and how to apply, a re-applicable unit-measure. On these see esp. on 223^b12 ff. (and above on 220^b5 ff.). Assuming such a measure is available, the procedure ought to be analogous to that of spatial measurement. Once again there is a one-one correspondence between (potential) parts of the change and abstract numbers. This can be seen as equivalent to a one-one correspondence between (potential) parts of the change and times expressed as numbers of units. The time (say 'five hours') defines the change in that it specifies its time length; but the time is itself defined by change, in that we reach the result 'five hours' by finding five unit changes of one hour.

(So far as this goes, it does not indicate the need for 'abstract time lengths', over and above the abstract number series, though it suggests that it might be psychologically convenient to work with them.)

The 'following' relation as explaining mutual measurement. At the end of the section, $^{b}24-32$, Aristotle attempts to explain the results so far in the light of the 'following' relation (see on 219^{a}10 ff.). There are two distinct claims: (1) that the quantitative or metric aspect of time is derived from that of change, and that of change from that of (spatial) magnitude; (2) that the mutual measurability of time and change is derived from that of change and spatial magnitude.

(1) From a spatial metric, via the natural mapping (described in the note on 219^{a}10 ff.) it is possible to construct a measure of 'quantity of change'. Using, next, the second natural mapping, it is possible to construct a measure of time. The difficulty is that there is no guarantee that that all measures of time constructed in this way will agree. In other words, there is no guarantee that any pair of simultaneous changes will maintain the same relative proportions of quantities of change throughout all their possible sub-stretches. And, in fact, we know that, for Aristotle, some changes proceeded at a uniform rate, some involved acceleration (see, e.g., *Physics* V.4, 228^{b}15–229^{a}6; *de Caelo* I.8, 277^{a}27–9); these included *natural* changes.

We cannot, therefore, suppose that the metric of time may be derived in this way from *any* change. Rather there must be paradigm changes which 'set the tempo': which are of necessity uniform. In devising measures of time the procedure, now as in Aristotle's day, is in fact to choose a paradigm change or set of paradigm changes, which are relatively undisturbed by external forces, and to define time in terms of such changes. For Aristotle the paradigm changes are the rotations of the celestial spheres, which are of necessity undisturbed by any anomalies. On the role of the rotation of the outermost sphere in particular see on 223^{b}12 ff.

Since times are not tied exclusively to single particular changes (220^{b}5 ff.), it is allowable to derive their structure from paradigm changes.

(2) Given the metrical correspondences as described, it is obviously possible to measure any one of the continua—spatial, magnitude, change, time—by measuring any of the others, provided that the changes are of uniform rate.

220^{b}32. The rest of the chapter discusses 'being in time'. A shorter and less satisfactory treatment is at 222^{b}30 ff. Some motivation can be found in Plato. The *Parmenides* contains arguments (141^a-^e, 151^e-152^a, 155^c-^d) about the consequences and preconditions of 'being in time' or 'participating in time'. The *Timaeus* rejects tensed statements about eternal substance, on the grounds that 'what is always unchangingly the same cannot well either be becoming older or younger through time, or at any time have become so, or now have become so, or be about to become so in the future' (38^a3-5). Aristotle has an interest in investigating the relationships between being in time, being affected by time, and being changeable or unchangeable. He holds that there are everlasting and at least essentially unchanging substances and other items: God, celestial substances, species, numbers, necessary truths. In particular the relationship between God and time is unclear. *De Caelo* I.9, 279^a $12-28$ suggests that God is outside time because outside the changeable universe. But in *Metaphysics* XII.6 ff. God is an activity which goes on in time: God has a 'way of life' (*diagōgē*) (1072^b14), is 'always in a good state' (1072^b24-25), and thinks 'throughout all time' (1075^a10). Aristotle is also concerned (so Annas (2), $105-6$) to show that his account of time can handle all the idioms which seem to presuppose a self-subsistent time.

The present section discusses 'being in time' generally, giving three possible senses:

(*a*) *Being when time is* (221^a10, $19-26$). Since we can make tensed statements about anything that 'is when time is', it seems likely that this is Aristotle's version of Plato's 'participating in time'. His answer to Plato's *Parmenides* arguments is therefore implied by $^a19-26$ here: *this* sense of 'being in time' is so weak that it indicates no real relationship whatever between time and what is thus 'in time'. In particular, if we say, as Plato does, that what is in time 'grows older', the 'growing older' need not be a real change of the thing in itself.

'This is accidentally so' ($^a23-24$): that any two things exist simultaneously is a fact accidentally true about either, and implying nothing about how they are in themselves. 'The other is a necessary consequence' ($^a24$): the consequence is that, if X is in time, there must be a time measuring X. The necessity here, in order to secure the contrast, must be *de re*: it must be in X's essence that it is in time and is measured by time.

(*b*) *Being an aspect of time* (221^a12-13, $14-16$). 'An aspect of time' literally 'something of time': see on 210^b32 ff.

(*c*) *Being measured by time* ($220^b32-221^a9$, 13, $^a16-18$). In spite of the long preamble, this is not clearly defined. It is not clear either what it is for X to be measured by time or for X's being to be measured by time. One possibility is just that X lasts for a finite time: but this would still give only a rather external relationship. It seems conceivable that X might happen to last for only a finite time and yet have only an inessential relationship to the world of time and change; conversely, X might last throughout all time and yet be essentially subject to change. These points can be weakened if X's 'being' is given the interpretation of 'essence' (rather than the weak one of 'duration'). 'X's being is measured by time' will then mean that it is of X's essence that it lasts only a finite time: to be X is (*inter alia*) to last only a finite time. The connections between this condition and being subject to essential change have yet to be elucidated: see on next section.

If X lasts only a finite time, there is time before and after its existence, so that it is surrounded by time. (And this, for Aristotle, just means that there is a set of changes which in total last longer than X: it is not necessary to introduce any universal time.) For the guarantee that there will be change before and after any finite time-length see on 222^{a}24 ff., 223^{b}12 ff.

221^{a}26. Consequence of the definition. On being surrounded by time, see on previous section. On the potential infinity of number see on III.6 and 7. On 'surrounding' as giving the primary sense of 'in' see on 210^{a}14 ff.

The effects of time. Aristotle's remarks are amplified at 222^{b}16–27; the passages may be conveniently taken together.

(*a*) Which changes are cases of time's action? One necessary condition seems to be that the change should not be wholly explicable in terms of the action of forces *external* to the thing changed; so 222^{b}24 'a thing may cease to be even though it is not changed (sc. from outside) at all.' In *Physics* VIII, however, Aristotle (in arguing towards the 'unmoved mover') insists that everything that changes does so because acted on by something else (ch. 4, cf. *Physics* VII.1). These two positions are not inconsistent. A closed system may be so constructed that, even apart from external forces, it will cease to exist as such, after some time, because of the natural interactions of its own constituents; and will, even before that, degenerate in various ways. Aristotle's prime examples are from living beings, human and animal; they are not totally closed systems, but their environment is not responsible for their ageing and their death (unless this is from non-natural causes, including disease), which is due to the *natural* failure of the cooling system (*On Life and Death*, 478^{b}24–8, 479^{a}7–^{b}7). It is of course true that this failure in turn has causes, and environmental ones: *Gen. et Corr.* II.10, 336^{a}31–^{b}24 tries to explain all natural coming-to-be and ceasing-to-be by the variable motion of the sun, though the explanation is incomplete and open to obvious objections (see Joachim, 253–62). But in the last analysis it is clear that the decay of the system is 'built-in' and natural. The 'action of time' is seen, if at all, in natural degenerations of living beings.

(b) At 222[b]25–7 Aristotle insists that such changes are not literally produced by time acting as an agent: that would indeed imply a conception of self-subsistent time such as Aristotle wishes to exclude. Yet at 221[a]30–[b]3 he nevertheless gives some explanatory force to the notion of the 'action of time'. The substantive point being made here is that whatever lasts for only a finite time must be 'acted upon by time', in the sense explained, and conversely. Behind this point is, first, the thesis that lasting for a finite or for an infinite time are always essential properties of things, and there can be nothing which is 'half infinite' in the sense of lasting from all time and then stopping, or beginning and then lasting for all time. Moreover, what is essentially subject to ceasing to be has a natural life span, fixed by its essence, which it (on average) will not greatly exceed or fall short of. (For all this see the difficult discussion at de Caelo I.10–12.) Accordingly, what lasts for a finite time is essentially such as to last for a finite time only, and, since there are no discontinuities in nature, it is essentially such as to suffer natural degeneration in at least the last part of its career. But why should not something everlasting equally be 'acted upon' by time? This question may conveniently be subsumed under a wider one: why is 'the action of time' confined, as it seems to be, to (1) irreversible and (2) degenerative changes (3) of perishable things?

(c) Why is the action of time irreversible? We can imagine an essentially closed system which was capable of self-regeneration, i.e. which in spite of recurrent periods of decay could always transform itself back into its 'best' state. Such a system would be potentially everlasting and therefore, for Aristotle, necessarily everlasting. Time could not be said to have any long-run effect on it; but it would seem, by definition, that the action of time is what has a long-run effect. The periods of decay would, in such a system, not be periods of genuine decay (cf. de Caelo I.10, 280[a]11–23 on the cosmic cycles of Empedocles and Heraclitus). So time's action is by definition irreversible. (It is a further question whether or not there can be, for Aristotle, self-regenerating closed systems: animal species, which must certainly have long-term fluctuations in numbers (owing to long-term, large-scale, changes in the earth's surface), are perhaps an example.) It is clear that this kind of irreversibility is not, in itself, anything like an anticipation of the 'irreversibility of time' in any of the senses in which it has been suggested by modern philosophers or physicists that time is irreversible. (But see further below under (d).)

(*d*) Why is the action of time *degenerative*? Some justification is offered at 221^b3: 'Change brings about the removal of what is originally there', and at 222^b21: 'alteration, in itself, is productive of removal from a (previous) state.' These remarks are true but not adequate, since change also brings about the presence of a new state, and so might equally well be seen as creative. A more substantial point is suggested at 222^b22–4: 'nothing comes to be without its being changed in some way and being acted upon [*paschein* is to be read here instead of *prattein*: see note on p. 209], but a thing may cease to be even though it is not changed [sc. from outside], and this is above all what we usually call ceasing to be—by the agency of time.' The suggestion is that the irreversible change of a closed system is necessarily for the worse, and indeed destructive of the system as such. Here there is a distinct likeness to the Second Law of Thermodynamics. Aristotle has a theory which assimilates all qualitative change (and so far as possible, all change) to the diffusion of heat; though he does not work out the connection anywhere, it would be natural for him to suppose that in a closed system opposed forces would cancel out or be extinguished by their opponents over time and a uniform state would eventually prevail. Here, then, there appears to be implicit something like a remote anticipation of the time-irreversibility in statistical mechanics. (Compare Joachim, 267, on *Gen. and Corr.* II.10, 337^a7–15.)

(*e*) Why is there no action of time on everlasting things? Aristotle has a series of metaphysical doctrines sufficient to exclude this possibility. The action of time could not produce an everlasting change, because there is no such thing apart from the essentially repetitive celestial revolutions (*Physics* VIII.8); nor an infinite series of finite changes, since such a series must be cyclical (*Gen. et Corr.* II.11, 337^a34–338^a17) and so admit no long-run effects; nor a finite number of finite changes, since these could not be due to the thing's intrinsic constitution (it would be inexplicable why they occurred just when they did, and in general potentialities of what is everlasting cannot go unrealized for an infinite time: on the connection between time and modal concepts here see esp. Hintikka).

(*f*) Some final remarks. There is more, and more coherence, in the metaphysical background than appears from the brief references above. Thus (1) the same set of ideas about time and modality underlies both the 'life span' thesis of (*b*), and the impossibility of once for all or non-cyclical changes in what is everlasting, mentioned in (*e*). So there is a connection between the notion that time acts destructively on perishable things (because their perishing is intrinsically pre-determined and therefore time in sum has the long-run effect of taking each of them out of existence—'in the long run

we are all dead' (J. M. Keynes)), and the argument that God and the
universe must be essentially unchanging, which supplies the last step
in the answer to Plato's problem—time cannot act *at all* on everlasting things. These logical links between time and modality have
their roots in Aristotle's ideal of scientific explanation, coupled with
the requirement that the universe should be explicable as a whole.
And (2) the Aristotelian theory of change, which produces a natural
'time direction' (since Aristotelian changes cannot be read backwards, and since closed systems always degenerate) is part of, or at
least harmonizes with, Aristotle's teleological vision of the natural
world. For a consequence of the thesis that closed systems
degenerate is that non-degenerating systems are not closed. Of the
changes which go to produce an animal, and in particular a human
being, in its *best* state, all require an 'input' from outside the matter:
the father's shaping agency and the sun's heat in sexual generation,
the sun's heat in spontaneous generation (*Gen. Anim.* III.11, 762ᵇ
13–16) and in everything else (see (*a*) above), nourishment in
growth and physical development, instruction and sensory input in
psychological development. And this point has a teleological significance for Aristotle: the highest good for everything perishable,
notably human beings and animals, being to participate, so far as they
are naturally capable of it, in the best life, that of God. On this
vision see Joachim's note (Joachim, 255–6) on *Gen. et Corr.* II.10
336ᵃ14–18. The pattern of natural change, as worked out in *Gen.
et Corr.*, involves a continuous downwards diffusion of perfective
changes, derived from God's continuous input of energy via the
celestial rotations. There are, in the sublunary world, counter-
balancing degenerative changes, explained by the imperfection of
sublunary things, and attributable to no one force, strictly speaking;
it is these that are called, in an illuminating metaphor, the actions
of time.

221ᵇ7. Rest: the definition to which Aristotle refers is at 202ᵃ4–5.
What is unchangeable is necessarily everlasting and not in time,
according to both this and the previous sections. What is not everlasting is necessarily both changeable and in time, according to both
sections. Hence 'unchangeable' implies 'not in time' and 'not in time'
implies 'everlasting'. But in Aristotle's universe there are certainly
things which are everlasting yet changeable: e.g. the celestial spheres,
which move; animal species, which increase and diminish in number;
the earth, which changes its surface conformation. 221ᵇ3–5 has laid
it down that these *qua* everlasting' are not in time, and their changes
are not long-run, irreversible, degenerative ones. But their changes
can still be measured, and so, according to the present section, they

too will be measured by time '*qua* changing'. But presumably they are not in time in the strong sense, that 'their being is measured by time', because it is not of their essence to change in the ways indicated.

221^{b}23. 'Things that are not' and time. This section is strangely cavalier, lumping together past existents, future existents, and possible and impossible states of affairs. It can hardly be taken as a guide to Aristotle's mature thought about such matters; more likely it is a first sketch based on a collection of problematic cases of 'things that are not'. Compare the similarly indiscriminate treatment of 'falsehood' at *Metaphysics* V.29.

'Time is a measure in itself of change': because what are counted are changes in the first instance (if they were periods of rest we could not be sure that any time had elapsed), and because the unit is given by a unit change (see on 220^{b}14 ff.). On 'in itself' as opposed to 'accidentally' see on 203^{b}30 ff.

Things that 'sometimes are and sometimes are not' can last only a finite time in total: see on 221^{a}26 ff., under (*e*).

CHAPTER 13

222^{a}10. This brief account of 'the now' is similar to that of chapter 11, to which it apparently refers. Most likely it is a residue of an early draft. It noticeably fails to mention the 'before and after in change'.

The persisting present is the now considered as linking past and future. The unrepeatable instant is the 'now' considered as a potential divider of time. Aristotle claims that the relationship between them is sameness in number but not in being. So the persisting present is identical (same in number) with each instant in turn; this is difficult, unless we suppose that 'being instant J' is a 'phased sortal' and in this case the relationship is that which is described at 219^{b}9–28 by other means. (See, for 'phased sortals', on 219^{a}14 ff.) Then the persisting present can be instants, J, K . . . in turn, just as a human being can be 'this embryo', 'this baby', 'this boy', . . . etc., in turn. There is no 'sameness in being', since *being this baby* is different from *being this boy*; on sameness and difference in being see on 202^{b}5 ff.

The underlying sameness of the persisting present is here derived from an analogy with 'mathematical lines'. The analogy is the same as that which is present implicitly at 219^{a}14 ff., 219^{b}9 ff.; see also on those sections for the 'ubiquitous point'. Here, and at *Gen. et Corr.* I.2, 317^{a}2–17, Aristotle is a little more explicit. The 'ubiquitous point' is an unlocalized potentiality for division; localized points are actual or potential particular divisions. For the analogy cf. also 220^{a}4–11; but 220^{a}12 ff. are not here relevant.

222^{a}24. 'At some time' represents a single Greek word, *pote*.

(1) Why does Aristotle assume that any event that occurs 'at some time' must occur at a finite time-distance from the present? Aristotle's restrictive doctrines about the infinite suggest an explanation. Suppose event B were an infinite time-length later than event A. Then the interval AB would have been traversed, when B happened; but an infinite cannot have been traversed (cf. III.4, 204^{a}2–7). (The infinity of all past time has not been traversed because there was no starting-point; in any case it is dubious whether this infinity is more than potential: see Introduction, 3 and 6.) Hence a bounded interval must be a finite one.

(2) How does Aristotle rule out the possibility of cyclic time? He points out, rightly, that in cyclic time some instant would be both beginning and end of the same time interval, and seems to think this would be evidently self-contradictory; but it can hardly be shown self-contradictory without the assumption that 'before-after' is a linear relation, which is what is at issue.

(3) How does Aristotle rule out the possibility of 'beginning' and 'ending' time? Two arguments are suggested: (*a*) There is no beginning or end of change, so neither is there of time. For independent arguments to show that there is no beginning or end of change see *Physics* VIII.1. (*b*) The 'now' is always both beginning and end. This looks question-begging, but perhaps the argument intended is the one given at *Physics* VIII.1, 251^{b}19–23: the 'now' is by definition a mean or link between past and future.

(Aristotle does not consider the possibility of a metrically bounded time with no first or last moment; but argument (*a*) would take care of this too.)

(4) Sameness and difference of changes and times. See on 220^{b}5 ff., for the point that sameness of changes implies sameness of times. The implication can be derived from the identity-conditions for changes (*Physics* V.4, 227^{b}21 ff.), but also from the fact that it is changes that are counted in counting times. The reverse implication is not strictly true, since different changes may occupy the same time. But they have to be simultaneous changes, which is not in question here.

222^{b}7. The Greek words discussed are *ēdē* ('just'), *arti* ('recently'), *palai* ('long ago'), and *exaiphnēs* ('suddenly'). Aristotle's procedure is curious: he forms *ad hoc* nouns from these adverbs, and then defines the first three as parts of time, and the fourth as something changing in a certain manner. For 'suddenly' cf. Plato, *Parmenides* 156^d, where also 'the suddenly' makes an appearance. Is this section a relic of Academic exercises in definition?

222^{b}16. See on 221^{a}26 ff.

222^{b}27. A coda appropriate to the end of the discussion of time, and presumably surviving from an early draft.

CHAPTER 14

222^{b}30. This section compares badly with the careful discussion of 'being in time' at 220^{b}32 ff. It is presumably part of an early draft. It seeks to show only that 'every alteration and everything that changes is in time' and uses a dubious argument related to the ideas of chs. 11 and 12. The steps are:

(1) 'The before accompanies every change', because every change, i.e. every species of change, can be faster or slower;

(2) The before is defined by reference to the now (the cases of past and of future are considered separately);

(3) The now is in time;

(4) The before is in time; (From (2) and (3).)

(5) Every change is in time. (From (1) and (4).)

223^{a}16. *Where time is.* Time measures rest as well as change (221^{b}7 ff.); but if it is, in itself, a measure of change, it should be where and only where change is going on, as here suggested. The presence of time implies at least the possibility of change at *de Caelo* I.9, 279^{a}12–16.

Time and the soul. 'If there were no soul' must be understood as 'if the universe were such that it was impossible for there ever to be any soul in it'—as appears from the next sentence: 'if it is impossible that there should be something to do the counting'.

It might be thought that a general doctrine about realization of possibilities in time lies behind this claim. In places Aristotle certainly seems to hold that what is always a possibility must sometimes be realized; for an attempt to show that Aristotle held this generally see Hintikka, ch. V. But Hintikka's claim is intrinsically implausible, and the state of the evidence does not suggest Aristotle had a settled position of such a kind.

More likely is that a particular theory about numbers and counting is involved. This conclusion is supported, not undermined, by the parallel passages at *Categories* 7, 7^{b}33–8^{a}6; *Topics* V.9, 138^{b}30–37; *Metaphysics* IV.5, 1010^{b}30–1011^{a}2; *de Anima* III.2, 426^{a}15–26. All but the *Topics* passage refer to the case of sense-perception. The primary objects of sense-perception, the 'sensibles' (*aisthēta*) such as colours and tastes, have no existence independently of perception; whereas the 'substrates', i.e. the material bodies which are called 'perceptible by sense' derivatively, do so exist. So there is a sense in which 'something sense-perceptible' could exist even if there were no perceivers (*Categories* 7) and a sense in which this is false (*Metaphysics* IV.5, *de Anima* III.2).

A similar theory about counting can be extracted from Aristotle's remarks here and elsewhere (see Additional Note A). There are two kinds of 'countables' viz. the concrete totalities and the abstract numbers. If there were no soul, the abstract numbers could not exist, since they are created by the mental operation of abstraction. The concrete totalities would still exist but would not be countable.

(The *Topics* V.9 passage does not quite fit this analogy; it is about the non-applicability of 'breathable' to air in a world containing no breathing animals. The conclusion, however, that the underlying object (air) would not be breathable, is on all fours with the others).

In spite of the *Topics* passage, it therefore seems likely that Aristotle's point is more than just the banal one that, in a world where nothing can count, nothing can ever get to be counted. It is, rather, that such a world would lack the primary objects of counting, viz. the abstract numbers. The effect is to cast doubt on the independent existence of numbers and quantities, not just time-measurements. In view of Aristotle's generally 'down-to-earth' attitude, particularly towards the objects of the sciences, this may be found surprising. But while Aristotle is insistent that mathematics is 'about the real world', he is much less straightforward about the status of 'mathematical objects': see Additional Note A. For Aristotle's motives for anti-realism about time-measurements in particular see Introduction, 3(*c*), and on 218^{b}21 ff.

The supposition of a world containing change and temporal succession, but no soul and no time, is presumably suggested by Plato's *Timaeus* and the debates about its interpretation: see *Timaeus* 30^a, 52^d–53^a, 69^b and Vlastos (2) and (3).

On 'the before and after in change' and its relation to time; see on 219^{a}14 ff., 219^{b}9 ff. On time as a number of *nows*: see on 220^{b}5 ff.

223^a29. Time is 'without qualification, a number of continuous change' (^a33–^b1). It is obscure why this should need stating after the account given in chs. 11 and 12.

The latter part of this section, ^b1–12, is also odd. For the topic in general see on 220^b5 ff. The discussion here is not helpful. In particular it is left quite obscure why change must be simultaneous in order to have the same time; and time is treated straightforwardly as analogous to an abstract number.

223^b12. Certain gaps in Aristotle's theory of time, as presented in chs. 11 and 12, can be filled by the existence of a standard, universally observable, uniform, and everlasting change. (*a*) For time-measurement to be always possible, there must be a uniform change going on at any period. (*b*) For comparisons of non-overlapping times to be possible, the same uniform change must continue over any arbitrarily long interval. (*c*) The problem of the identity of simultaneous 'nows' can be solved, if all 'nows' are derived from the same standard change. (*d*) The everlasting continuity of time needs an everlasting change to guarantee it.

All these requirements are supplied, for Aristotle, by the circular motion of the outermost celestial sphere carrying the fixed stars. In *Physics* VIII an elaborate structure of argument leads to the conclusion that this revolution is the only uniform and everlastingly continuous motion. The present section depends on the theory of *Physics* VIII.

Uniform change. Uniformity of change is discussed at *Physics* V, 228^b15–229^a6. One necessary condition is that the speed of change should be constant. This, of course, involves a reference to a time standard; but in *Physics* VIII it is implied that the primary circular motion must be uniform because there is no source of variation (260^a17–19), so that its uniformity can be known without recourse to time-measurement. At *Physics* VIII, 265^b11–16 it is argued that no other kind of change can be uniform, which implies the remark in this section that only motion can be uniform.

In this section, Aristotle, of course, also assumes that there is a uniform circular motion, as argued in *Physics* VIII and *De Caelo* II.6.

The primacy of uniform circular motion. For time-measurement the most convenient standard is an undisturbed uniform periodic motion (the oscillations of a pendulum or the vibrations in a quartz crystal). This is Aristotle's point, except that he holds that the periodic motion has to be circular, in saying that it is such motion of which 'the number is most easily known'.

For more general remarks on 'primacy' of uniform circular

motion, see *Physics* VIII.7, 260^{a}20–261^{a}27; 9, 265^{a}13–27; *de Caelo* I.2, 269^{a}19–^{b}13.

(On the problem of 'dividing up' mentally, for counting, a uniform uninterrupted motion see on 220^{b}5 ff.)

Time as a cycle. An exercise of a kind Aristotle always seems to enjoy is an elucidation and explanation of popular ideas in terms of Aristotle's own doctrines. Here (223^{b}21–224^{a}2) there are three linked notions:

(*i*) Time is the revolution of the celestial sphere: see on 218^a 30 ff.;

(*ii*) Human affairs form a cycle, i.e. a cyclical pattern: described as a common saying. Cf. the (pseudo-Aristotelian) *Problems* XVII.3, 916^{a}18–39. Aristotle himself believed that in the sublunary world the only important series of changes were cyclical (including long-term changes in human civilizations): see esp. *Gen. et Corr.* II.11, and Joachim, 270–7.

(*iii*) Time is a cycle: unattributed, but linked with (*ii*). Cf., e.g., Herodotus, I.207.2, and the Pythagoreans mentioned by Eudemus (fr. 88 Wehrli, Simplicius *Phys.* 732, 26) who held a strong doctrine of sempiternal recurrence.

Aristotle's concluding point, ^{b}33–^{a}2, aims to explain why time is so thought of: it is difficult to separate what is measured from what measures it, so that time is thought cyclical because it is measured by cyclical changes.

224^{a}2. See on 220^{b}5 ff.

ADDITIONAL NOTES

A. ARISTOTLE'S PHILOSOPHY OF MATHEMATICS

1. Introductory

In mathematics A. found his prime examples of theoretical science. In the *Posterior Analytics*, which treats of the structure of all sciences, the examples are mostly mathematical. It is likely then, that A. had a fairly well-worked-out philosophical position on the nature of the mathematical sciences. But we do not find any full-dress exposition; A.'s thoughts are given, in passing, in a number of places.* The nearest approaches to a set discussion are at *Metaphysics* XIII.3 and (on a restricted front) at *Metaphysics* X.1—2.

This note assumes that the evidence enables us to recover A.'s philosophy of mathematics more or less complete, and that it can be understood as largely determined by its conjunction of: (*a*) a keen interest in what actually goes on in mathematical thinking: in how theorems are discovered, known, and used; (*b*) a general conception of theoretical science, as elaborated in the *Posterior Analytics*; (*c*) philosophical realism about the truths of the sciences; (*d*) anti-Platonism, and (*e*) finitism. But the Note does not aim to supply detailed argument in favour of the interpretation here adopted, either on fundamental or on minor points.†

2. Realism and anti-Platonism

The most important single fact about A.'s conception of mathematics is that it is determinedly *realist*. Mathematics, on this view, is like any other science concerned with how things are in the actual world, and its truths are true in virtue of the way things are in that world.

But with equal determination A. is *anti-Platonist*, in that he opposes Plato's attempt to introduce, as part of reality, a realm of

---

* Most of the relevant passages are presented in English translation, with useful discussion, in Heath (3). For *Metaphysics* XIII see Annas (1).

† I hope to publish a longer version elsewhere. For help with the preparation of this Note, I am indebted to Christopher Peacocke and Charles Parsons.

'separated' or 'self-subsistent' mathematical objects (numbers, geometrical figures) existing in independence of the ordinary everyday world. A. has therefore to hold that the truths of mathematics are derived from the way that actual physical objects are in the actual ordinary world.

How derived? A first sketch might go as follows. For arithmetic, we start from the activity of counting and from numbers as predicates of sets. (On the problems about counting see below, sec. 12.) With these as given, the prototypes of addition, subtraction, multiplication, and division are found in the real world. A collection of two sheep, amalgamated with a non-overlapping collection of three sheep, yields a collection of five sheep. Six collections, non-overlapping in pairs, of five sheep each, yield a collection of thirty sheep, and so on. It turns out to be irrelevant what sort of things we are counting: sheep, horses, pebbles, or whatever it may be. So long as unambiguous counting is possible, the results are always and everywhere the same. This important truth is the basis of arithmetic, and appears in it as the requirement that the binary operations mentioned are unambiguously defined on the natural numbers.

Together with this truth we may harvest the elementary arithmetical truths evinced in such situations, e.g., '2 + 3 = 5'. There are even higher levels of generality, reached in A.'s view by induction and generalization; e.g., the truth that for any two numbers a, b, $a + b = b + a$.

For geometry, we start from the spatial configuration of actual physical objects. The physical operations underlying geometry are the dividing-up and the putting together of solid bodies, and (secondarily) of the surfaces, lines, and points that bound them. It is on the divisibility of physical solids that the constructibility of points, lines, surfaces, and solids in geometry rests; and on the possibility of putting one body up against another that the metrics of lines and angles rest. Just as in arithmetic, geometrical truths are derived by induction and generalization from what goes on in the real world. And the possibility of geometry (which A. takes for granted must be the three-dimensional Euclidean geometry) rests upon the uniformity of the results found by experience.

This sketch deliberately leaves open the questions (a) of the *ultimate* status (in metaphysics or epistemology) of the truths of mathematics; (b) of the nature of the entities, such as numbers and geometrical figures, that appear in them. These questions, particularly (b), will be raised in secs. 5 and following.

3. Finitism: arithmetic

Finitism has now to be incorporated into this way of thinking about mathematics. For metaphysical reasons, A. rejects the possibility of an actual completed infinite (see, in general, Introduction, sec. 3). If then the 'abstract numbers 1,2,3 . . . which appear in the truths of arithmetic are to be respectable entities at all, they must at any time be finitely many. At the same time, as emerges from III.6 and 7, A. for good realist reasons wishes to allow a potential infinity of numbers. Given a physical body, we can in principle divide it, A. holds, as many times as we wish (only not so as ever to *complete* infinitely many divisions). So, if numbers are to be always available for counting collections, there must be a possibility of going beyond any number actually reached.

This potential infinity of numbers suggests that an account of number-theoretic truth, in Aristotelian vein, might be adequately represented by the device of a set of 'possible worlds' with the semantics devised by Kripke. Thus, we might require that, for each natural number n, there was a possible world Wn containing just the natural numbers up to and including n. Then number-theoretic truth could be defined via the notion of truth in a Wn.* Roughly, within any Wn, ordinary number-theory is relativized to take account of the restricted contents of that world. Then the modal operators '□' and '◇' (or 'L' and 'M', which will be used here) are introduced in a standard way as meaning 'in every Wn' and 'in some Wn'. The worlds are assumed to be all mutually accessible, so that the underlying modal logic is that of Lewis's S5. What results as 'arithmetic' is a set of truths valid in every world, and therefore beginning with a necessity-operator. Most differ from familiar analogues only by the insertion of a modal operator or two, with perhaps also some existence-assumptions. For example: instead of the $(x)(Ey)(y > x)$ of ordinary non-finitist arithmetic, we get the finitist $L(x) M(Ey)$ $(y > x)$. Instead of $(x)(y)(x + y = y + x)$, we have $L(x)(y)(z)$ $[(x + y = z) \leftrightarrow (y + x = z)]$. There are also truths with no classical analogues, most notably $L(Ex)(y)(x \geqslant y)$ or 'there is always a greatest number'.

The point of giving this model is to show that A.'s intentions can be embodied in a consistent system with a very natural interpretation, and one close to A.'s own ideas. For A., instead of 'possible worlds' we should speak of 'possible states of the world'.

The truth $L(Ex)(y)(x \geqslant y)$, if A. is a realist, ought to be derived from some fact about how the world is. But this is not the sort of

---

* For this kind of construction see Parsons (2), 162 f. n.11.

truth that can be extracted from experience alone; the discussion of the infinite in III.4−8 makes clear that it is, for A., derived from metaphysics, though it is a truth about the real world for all that.

4. Finitism: geometry

The finitism can be put into geometry on fairly similar lines. But there is a complication or two. There is, for A., a double finitism necessary. First, in any possible world-state there are permitted to be only finitely many points, lines, surfaces, and three-dimensional figures in actual existence (here 'points, lines . . .' refers to actual, physically real bodies and their limits). Correspondingly, when we abstract from physical bodies, in any possible world-state there will be only finitely many of the corresponding geometrical objects. In particular, there will be only finitely many points on any line. Here again, there is a *potential* infinity; every geometrical line can always be divided, which means that, for any line that exists in any possible world-state, there is a possible world-state in which that line is divided in a particular ratio.

Secondly, A. has cosmological reasons, rooted in metaphysical considerations, for holding that the world-system, which contains everything in the universe (other than itself) that is spatially extended, is not only finite in extent but necessarily of the particular extent it is: no contraction or expansion is possible. Here then there is not even a potential kind of infinity. Since geometry is tied to the real facts of the world, it would seem that it cannot admit, not only infinitely long lines but even arbitrarily long ones. This would impose an irritating limitation on Euclidean geometry. (On finitism and geometry, see on 207^b27 ff.)

5. Mathematics is straightforwardly true

It has been shown how mathematics is supposed to be related to the actual world as A. conceives of it. Since the relation is a little indirect, it might be—for all that has been said so far—that A. thought mathematics was a useful device for representing and manipulating truths about the world, but not itself literally true. On this view, for example, such a statement as '2 + 3 = 5' will be a short convenient way of exhibiting a general truth about countable substances, but if taken literally, as stating a relationship between 2, 3, and 5, not true, because there are no such entities as 2, 3 or 5.

This view is not acceptable as an interpretation of A. For A. insists that, in the sciences including mathematics, the first principles and what follows from them are necessary *truths*. Just how they are supposed to be reached and known is indeed a problem. But they *are* known, by *nous* (*An. Post.* II19, 100^{b}5–15). This alone seems to exclude their being anything less than literally true. And the suggestion that mathematical objects do not exist is denied at *Metaphysics* XIII.3: '. . . it is also true to say without qualification that mathematical objects exist, and are such as they are said to be' (1077^{b}32–34, translation after Annas).

Against these passages must be considered another which may raise doubts.

So if one posits objects separated from what is incidental to them, and studies them as such, one will not thereby falsely assert any falsehood, any more than if one draws a line on the ground and says it is a foot long when it is not a foot long; for it is not in the premisses that the falsehood lies. The best way of studying each thing would be this: to separate and posit what is not separate, as the arithmetician does and the geometer. (*Metaphysics* XIII.3, 1078^{a}17–23, translation after Annas.)

The example is of a geometer who draws a diagram in the sand and says 'let this line be a foot long' or something similar. A. admits that a falsehood is involved, but it is one that does not enter into the reasoning, and indeed it is not in any ordinary sense asserted at all. The geometer, in saying 'let this be a foot long' is not really asserting or assuming that *the line in the sand* is a foot long: he is, rather, asserting that the abstract line about which he is talking, and for which the line in the sand stands proxy, is a foot long. The actual diagram is no more than an aid to study (cf. *Post. An.* I.10, 76^{b}39–77^{a}3; *Prior An.* I.41, 49^{b}33–50^{a}4; *Metaphysics* XIV.2, 1089^{a}20–26). And A. remarks that using representative objects in this way is a good way to study; but he does not say that the truths being studied are truths about representative objects, and the whole point of the example is that they are not.

6. What are mathematical objects?*

Mathematics then, contains straightforward truths about mathematical objects. Mathematicians find it convenient to speak and think as as if the objects of their study were Platonic mathematical objects, existing in separation from the ordinary world. But according to the passage just considered, such Platonic objects could be only fictions, entertained (if at all) for the purposes of representation. Hence, actual mathematical objects must be not separated: they must be to be

---

* From this point on, the Note is much indebted to the important paper of Mueller, though it does not wholly accept Mueller's conclusions.

found in the ordinary world. The difficulty is to give a convincing account of A.'s theory of what they are.

A. regularly groups numbers, and mathematical objects generally, with *ta ex aphaireseōs legomena*: 'things so called by abstraction'. The only examples A ever gives of such things are all mathematical objects (unless they are mathematical *truths* at e.g. *Post. An.* I.18, 81^{b}3). It is natural to look to *Metaphysics* XIII.3 for elucidation. Here it is said that the mathematician (*a*) is concerned with particular properties of *physical* objects; but (*b*) considers the bearers of these properties *only* as such, not as physical; and (*c*) 'posits' them as existing simply as bearers of such properties. The last stage is discussed with the example already quoted: it is clear, therefore, that what results from the 'positing' is not a mathematical object, but only a representative fiction. But it is equally clear that physical objects are not mathematical objects either, nor, even, are physical objects considered in a certain way. This horse-considered-as-a-unit cannot be identical with the number 1 for obvious reasons.

The *Metaphysics* XIII.3 account is, therefore, puzzlingly incomplete. An attempt to supply the deficiency seems to be made by a remark at the end, which in the context reads like a lame addition: '. . . geometers talk about existing things, and they are existents: for "existent", may be either "actually existent" or "existent in a matter-like way (*hulikōs*)"' (1078^{a}29–31). Not much can be made of this by itself; but it is the only straightforward clue to emerge from the passage. Otherwise it would seem that we have to suppose that at stage (*b*) above, when the mathematician concentrates on the specifically mathematical properties of actual things, he switches to considering, or perhaps even *creates* by the act of so considering, special mathematical objects.

The dilemma that threatens A. here is only a special case of one that threatens him constantly. It arises from his joint adherence to the principles that 'substance is form' and that it is actual individual things that enjoy the primary kind of existence. In the case, for instance, of a horse, it is individual actual horses that *are* in the truest sense; what they have in common, the form of a horse, is the substance of each and might therefore be in some sense 'more real' than the individual, yet it never leads an independent existence of its own and is irrevocably entangled in matter. This creates the paradox that what the science of zoology studies (the forms of the animals of different species) are things less capable of independent existence than what the science of zoology cannot study as such (individual animals).

It is a paradox, but it is not a downright contradiction, or at least A. seems to manage to prevent it developing into one. In the case of

181

mathematical objects too, it must be assumed that A. kept the theoretical situation tense, but static. In one place he says outright that 'mathematics is about forms' (*eidē*): 'For mathematics is about forms, for its objects are said of any underlying subject: even if geometrical objects are said of some underlying subject, still it is not as being said of an underlying subject that they are geometrical objects' (*Post. An.* I.13, 79ª7—10: translation after Barnes).

The provisional conclusion, then, is that mathematical objects exist in some way analogous to the way in which forms exist. They cannot, then, be found existing apart from their material incarnations. For this reason they may be said to exist 'in a matter-like way': i.e. never on their own, but realizing their potentialities in a series of actual individuals.

7. Mathematical objects: the problem of existence

A problem now arises about the conditions for mathematical objects to exist. To state it first in terms of numbers. Not *all* the natural numbers 1,2,3 . . . can exist at any one time, by the finitist principle. But if not, what determines just which numbers exist at any given time? And how can it be guaranteed that there will always exist enough numbers for the arithmetician's work to be possible and meaningful?

Since mathematics is tied to the real world, the natural first try is to say that the number 6 (say) exists if and only if a collection, six-in-number, of actual things exists, i.e. if and only if there are at least six distinct identifiable things in the world. But this would seem to mean that a mathematician cannot possibly think about numbers greater than *n*, where *n* is the number of actual things in the world at the time. This is implausible; but if mathematicians can think about arbitrarily large numbers, either all numbers that can be thought of pre-exist, in which case infinitely many numbers exist, or numbers are called into existence by the mathematician's thinking of them.

Similar problems arise in geometry. The geometer would be lucky ever to encounter a perfectly spherical physical body; but there are such things—the celestial spheres. But to suppose that there exist in nature perfectly cubical, regularly dodecahedral, or regularly icosahedral bodies (for example) is implausible. Yet geometers successfully talk about the corresponding geometrical figures. Once again it would seem that the only consistent position is to suppose that the mathematical objects are 'created', independently of the physical world, by the mathematician's thought.

This position can be supported both from 223ª21—29 (see on that passage) and from the side of A.'s psychological theories. A.'s theory of thinking includes the principle that the intellect (*nous*) becomes the objects of thought. This principle seems to license the inference that, for example, when a geometer thinks of a 1,000-sided regular figure, such a figure exists in his intellect; or that when an arithmetician thinks of the number 1,729, there is a collection of 1,729 distinct particles of something in his intellect.

There are obviously difficulties with this sort of theory. By convenient choice of notation, a mathematician can easily reach the contemplation of what by everyday standards are vertiginously large numbers, and reason about them with perfect clarity. Likewise, it is implausible to suppose that a geometer can have a billion-sided figure in his intellect and impossible that he should have a line two miles long in it. Moreover, it cannot be sufficient just to have the corresponding sort of collection or object in the intellect: 1,729 particles might be construed as two collections (of 1,000 and 729 particles respectively), and so on. These objections suggest that what is present to the intellect is not so much an exemplification of the mathematical object as a symbolic representation of it: a view which might be licensed by A.'s formula that the mind 'receives the form without the matter'.

On this line, the only easy stopping-point is the position that, for mathematical objects to exist, it is sufficient, and necessary, for them to be thought of. This guarantees the mathematician the existence of all the objects he will ever need, though at the price at severing the direct link with the ordinary material world. There is still an indirect link, since creation of mathematical objects must proceed according to the laws of mathematics, which are derived from the material world as explained above.

Moreover, mathematical objects must themselves have some sort of matter, since A. all along insists that they are not 'separated' in the way Platonic Forms were supposed to be. (So too *de Anima* III.7, 431^{b}12–17.) This matter will be whatever serves as matter to the objects of the intellect, and is to be identified with the 'intelligible matter' (*hulē noētē*) several times mentioned by A. (On intelligible matter, see below sec. 8.)

To make mathematical objects in this way dependent for existence on minds, is not necessarily to make the *truths* of mathematics mind-dependent. For the truths *might* all have the hypothetical form 'If numbers x, y, z . . . exist, such that $P(x, y, z$ . . .$)$ etc., then . . .'. This is unlikely to be A.'s account, however, and indeed he insists that the mathematician must postulate, or prove, the existence of his objects, as an essential part of his science (*Post. An.* I.10, 76^{a}31–36). But A. does not say whether sciences, and the truths they contain, would exist potentially even if there were no minds in the universe. He does imply (223^{a}21 ff.) that mathematics would in some sense have no application to the ordinary world in the absence of minds, meaning apparently something genuinely anti-realist about mathematical truths in the ordinary world (see on 223^{a}16 ff., and, for related considerations about individuals and substance, Woods).

The equivalence between the possibility and the conceivability of the existence of a mathematical object is sufficient to explain the passages in *Physics* III (203^{b}22–25, 207^{b}7–15, 208^{a}14–22) which express the potential infinity of numbers by saying 'they do not give out in thought' (on this see on 208^{a}5 ff.).

8. Intelligible matter

'Intelligible matter' (*hulē noētē*) is mentioned by A. only in *Metaphysics* VII and VIII (VII.10, 1036^{a}9–12; 11, 1036^{b}32–1037^{a}5; VIII.6, 1045^{a}33–^{b}7). It clearly has the function of supplying something corresponding to ordinary matter in the matter-form analysis of mathematical objects. At 1036^{a}11 A. calls it 'present in sensible objects, but not in so far as they are sensible'. This is explicable on the abstractionist view that the mathematician 'considers sensible objects but not *qua* sensible'. In so doing, it has been argued above, he *creates* mathematical objects in his intellect. These have 'intelligible matter', i.e. are made out of the (passive) intellect itself in some way. But to say that intelligible matter is 'present in sensible objects' is to suggest that it exists *outside* any intellect, and many commentators have identified it with space, or pure extension (cf. on 207^{a}15 ff.): this identification is attractive.

In fact, there need be no conflict between the two interpretations of intelligible matter. It can be present, potentially, in sensible objects in just the same way that mathematical objects themselves are. As such, it can be identified with 'space' or 'extension', which A. does not recognize as having any substantial existence. It comes to be present actually (so far as any matter is ever actually present) when the mathematicals come to be actually, out of sensible objects, in the intellect.

ADDITIONAL NOTES

B: ARISTOTELIAN DYNAMICS

The following Note expresses a (partly) rather unorthodox view of
the subject. Within the limits of the available space, I have tried to
indicate the evidence on which the view is based, and to disarm the
more obvious objections, but I have not been able to consider com-
peting views. For other treatments see the works listed under
Carteron, Drabkin, and Owen (7), to all of which I am much
indebted. Collections of many of the relevant texts, in English
translation and with useful commentary, are found in Heath (3) and
in Cohen-Drabkin.

1. Did Aristotle envisage a mathematical science of motion?

For Aristotle it is the business of the physicist to study scientifically
change in all its aspects. So motion certainly falls under physics. But
it does not follow that Aristotle held that there was anything much
to be said about motion in particular, still less that what could be
said must take a mathematical form.

The grounds for thinking that Aristotle did, in fact, think that
there could be a mathematical science of motion are provided by
evidence of two distinct kinds: (a) general statements about applications of mathematics to physical sciences, with examples; (b) statements of what appear to be general laws relating physical quantities
in a mathematical way.

(a) Aristotle on applied mathematics

The texts are: *Post. An.* I.7, 75^b14-17; I.9, 76^a4-25; I.12, 77^a40-
$^b3$; I.13, 78^b34-79^a16; I.27; *Physics* II.2, $193^b22-194^a12$; *Metaphysics* I.8, 989^b31-33; XIII.3, 1078^a5-17; on these see Barnes
(1), 151-5. It is clear that Aristotle in these passages envisages
empirical sciences which are heavily dependent on mathematics;
they are said to be subordinate to the corresponding branches of
mathematics, and such explanations as they can provide are derived
from mathematics. Examples given by Aristotle include optics,
dependent on geometry, harmonics (the theoretical study of musical
pitch-relationships), dependent on arithmetic, and 'mechanics'. In
the first two cases, we can see what is meant: surviving works of
optics and harmonics show that these sciences consisted in straightforward applications of geometry and number-theory respectively—
and little else. The inference is that 'mechanics' too, was, in essence,
just an application of some branch of mathematics: at 76^a24, geometry is specified and at 78^b38 this is specialized to 'solid geometry'.

185

But what did 'mechanics' comprise? To judge by the surviving *Mechanical Problems* (probably by an early Aristotelian) it did indeed cover both elementary statics and elementary dynamics. How, then, does Aristotle suppose that its demonstrations can be reduced to those of geometry? The most likely explanation is that (unlike Plato) he was prepared to accept as 'geometry' the study of the behaviour through time of geometrical objects. That this is so is made probable by the parallel case of astronomy. Aristotle regards 'empirical' astronomy as entirely dependent on a branch of mathematics which he calls 'astronomy' (*astrologikē*) simply (78^{b}39), or 'mathematical astronomy' (79^{a}1). Now, astronomy as a branch of pure mathematics cannot be anything other than what Eudoxus had pioneered in Aristotle's own time: the study of the behaviour through time of mathematical models of the heavens. These studies were drawn upon by Aristotle himself in *Metaphysics* XII.8, where he distinguishes astronomy from other branches of mathematics by the fact that it alone studies 'perceptible substance' (1073^{b}5–8). This distinction need not be taken as Aristotle's final word, *Metaphysics* XII being probably a very early work. The *Post. An.* and *Metaphysics* XIII passages show that 'mechanics' was also supposed to be derived from a branch of geometry. The probability is, therefore, that for sublunary motions too, Aristotle envisaged a kind of geometry which set up models of physical objects and studied their behaviour in time.[1] Aristotle nowhere insists that the objects of mathematics *must* all be considered by mathematicians as timeless and unchanging; if he had done so, it would have contrasted oddly with his readiness, in philosophical analysis, to derive the properties of time from those of geometrical lengths (see on IV.10–14; and Additional Note A). (*Metaphysics* I.8, 989^{b}31–2 shows only that astronomy was then the only recognized application of mathematics to the study of moving objects.)

(b) *Mathematical laws of motion in Aristotle?*

In addition to the general remarks about applied mathematics, there are several passages which seem actually to use mathematics in the discussion of sublunary motions. Here we must distinguish:

  (*i*) statements that suggest, but do not specify, a mathematical relationship linking physical quantities;

  (*ii*) statements that specify a definite mathematical relationship (usually a proportion). The texts may be grouped as follows:

---

[1] There is an isolated report ascribing the origins of mathematical mechanics to Archytas (active *c*.400 BC): Diogenes Laertius 8.83.

A. Relationships between the amount (or 'power' or 'strength'), of an agent and the amount or the 'weight' of the body acted on (or resistant to action), or the amount or time or speed of its change.

(*i*) Non-specific: *de Caelo* I.7, 275^b18-21; I.8, 277^a33-^b5; I.11, 281^a7-27; II.6, 288^a27-33, 288^b12-14; III.6, $305^a 9-13$. *Mot. Anim.* 4, 699^b16-17.

(*ii*) Specific: *Physics* VII.5, $249^b27-250^b7$; VIII.10, $266^a 12-^b27$; *de Caelo* I.7, $274^a33-275^b4$; III.2, 301^b1-16.

B. Relationships between the amount of interacting agents (in 'powers' or 'strengths' or 'motions') and the result of the interaction.

(*i*) Non-specific: *Physics* III.5, 204^b13-19, 205^a1-7; VII.2, 244^a7-11; *de Caelo* I.4, 271^a22-30; II.1, 284^a24-26; II.10, 291^a32-^b10; IV.5, 312^b7-14; IV.6, 313^b16-21; *Gen. et Corr.* I.10, 328^a23-^b14; II.4, 331^a20-^b36; II.7, 334^b20-30; *Meteorologica* I.3, 340^a13-17; I.4, 342^a22-28; *Mot. Anim.* 3, 699^a32-^b11; 4, 699^b14-26.

C. Relationships between the 'weight' or bulk of a body and the speed of its (natural) motion:

(*i*) Non-specific: *Physics* V.4, $228^b28-229^a1$; *de Caelo* I.8, 277^a27-33; II.8, 290^a1-2; II.13, 294^a12-17; III.5, $304^b 13-19$; IV.1, 308^a29-33; IV.2, 308^b15-28; IV.2, 309^b12-16; IV.4, 311^a19-21.

(*ii*) Specific: *Physics* IV.8, 215^a25-29; 216^a11-21; *de Caelo* I.6, $273^b29-274^a16$; III.2, 301^a22-^b1.

D. A relationship between the density of a medium and the speed of a body moving (naturally) through it:

(*ii*) Specific: *Physics* IV.8, $215^a25-216^a11$.

E. Acceleration and deceleration of moving bodies:

(*i*) Non-specific: *Physics* V.6, 230^b24-25; VIII.9, 265^b12-14; *de Caelo* I.8, 277^a27-29, 277^b5-8; II.6, 288^a19-22; III.2, 301^b16-30.

What these generalizations mean, and with what intention the *specific* mathematical relationships are put forward, are obscure and controversial questions. If we could take the statements at face value, they would show that Aristotle held particular mathematical theories about relationships (A), (C), and (D) at least. But it is not certain that the specific statements can be taken at face value, and this doubt causes doubt in turn as to how seriously the non-specific statements are meant. Are they allusions to precise mathematical laws? or generalizations from which Aristotle hoped that precise mathematical laws would be discovered? or simply approximate statements which Aristotle did not think could be improved on?

187

A closer examination of the specific mathematical statements provides a first division: some of them are advanced in an expressly hypothetical way; some on the other hand, are put forward flatly with no obvious indications of reserve. There is, therefore, a prima facie case, here too, for supposing that Aristotle envisaged a mathematical dynamics, and thought that it had at least begun to exist. But the proof that this is so will be complete only if we can make sense of all the generalizations listed, as part of a nascent dynamics—and this is not a straightforward business.

2. Aristotle's concepts of 'speed', 'power', 'strength', 'weight', and 'preponderance'

In interpreting Aristotle's dynamics, it is particularly important not to assume that the technical terms are straightforwardly equivalent to their 'obvious' modern translations. What can be assumed, at least, is that they are terms of which the meaning is not very far removed from ordinary experience. But they must be studied in the context of his theories.

What Aristotle calls 'speed' is essentially what ordinary people would call 'speed'. As a mathematical quantity, it is defined as a ratio of distance to time. Though ratios were not treated as numbers, there is evidence to suggest that the Greek mathematicians of the fourth century were able to operate freely with ratios, just as if they were numbers. Aristotle's 'speed' then, is the average speed over a period of time, defined by a ratio between two numbers (given suitable units of distance and time). But Aristotle is incapable of defining instantaneous 'speed'; indeed, he argues in *Physics* VI that it makes no sense to attribute motion to a body at an instant (VI.3, 234^a24-^b9). This is an important limitation. It does not mean, of course, that Aristotle is incapable of defining increase of 'speed', or acceleration; we can observe increase of Aristotelian 'speed', during a motion, by observing the distances covered during successive units of time. But it is not easy thus to define any definite *quantity* of acceleration, and Aristotle never tries to do so. Moreover, proportions between 'speeds' and, for example, 'weights' or 'powers' will have to be interpreted carefully (see below, sec. 3).

The concepts of 'power' (*dunamis*) and 'strength' (*ischus*) are used by Aristotle in connection with the action of agents on physical bodies. 'Power' is the same word (in Greek) as 'potentiality' and it is clear that the 'power' exerted by the agent is thought of as the expression of its potentiality for bringing about change. It is clear too that Aristotle was willing to consider a 'power' or equivalently its 'strength', as a physical quantity. If we accept the proportionality suggested by *Physics* VII.5, 249^{b}27 ff., the 'power' exerted in a motion is a ratio of the weight of the body moved, *times* the distance moved, to the time taken; i.e. the product of the weight and the 'speed'. (Hence, if we are to look for approximate equivalents within Newtonian dynamics, the 'power' is not the force, but the amount of momentum imparted to the moving body, which is equal to what physicists call the *impulse*, the integral of the force over the time of its application. But, of course, this is only a convenient rough guide, at best, to what is going on; Aristotle had no conception of the mathematics underlying Newtonian theory.)

The concept of 'weight' (*baros*) is, equally, not quite straightforward. Here, of course, Aristotle had an everyday conception from which to start, namely, that of weight as determined by the balance. The 'balance-weight' for ordinary objects obeys the law of additivity: if, in terms of *any* unit, objects A and B have weights of X and Y units respectively, then A and B together weigh X + Y units. This is a truth of physics, not of logic or of mathematics; it expresses the fact that balance-weight (or gravitational mass) is a scalar quantity and can sensibly be represented by a number. Given this everyday quantity, it would be surprising if Aristotle had abandoned it without explaining what he was doing. We should assume, therefore, that in *de Caelo*, where Aristotle discusses 'weight', he is trying to explicate the everyday concept of 'balance weight', possibly to extend it and refine it scientifically, but not to abandon it. (The complications arising from the correlated notion of 'lightness' and the notion of 'relative weight' can be ignored for the purposes of this Note.)

In fact, Aristotle defines 'heavy' (*barus*, corresponding to *baros* 'weight'). To be heavy is to have a natural tendency to move downwards, i.e. towards the centre of the universe. This suggests that weight is a kind of 'power': the potentiality for moving naturally downwards. The explanation of the tilting of a balance is that the weights in the two pans both exert 'power' in trying to move themselves downwards; but that the heavier weight has greater 'power' and therefore overcomes the resistance created by the lighter one.

A term sometimes used by Aristotle is 'preponderance' (*rhopē*). It is not quite clear that he regarded it as a technical term. It derives from the behaviour of the balance (which is said to 'incline', *rhepein*) and so might be expected to mean, like 'weight', a tendency to move downwards.

3. Aristotle's law of falling bodies

It is natural to begin consideration of Aristotle's dynamical generalizations with what he says about freely falling bodies ((C) above in the list), since the fall of heavy bodies and the ascent of light ones are the two natural motions in the lower cosmos. The difficulties, too, of understanding are here particularly great. If we can produce a coherent account of what is going on here, we shall be well on the way to understanding Aristotle's ideas on dynamics as a whole. Among the texts listed in sec. 1 above, under C (i), there is a well-defined group from the *de Caelo*, which form a natural starting-point: II.8, 290^{a}1–2; II.13, 294^{a}12–17; IV.2, 308^{b}15–28 and 309^{b}12–16; IV.4, 311^{a}19–21. These texts, all alike, state that the 'greater' a body is, the more quickly it moves in its natural upward or downward motion. The texts also have in common that they treat this phenomenon as *a matter of common experience*, which can be easily appealed to as such, or casually alluded to, without more ado. They all eschew a mathematical formulation. The first problem, then, is: what is the phenomenon referred to by these texts?

One conceivable explanation is that it is simply the behaviour of weights on a balance. Aristotle often conceives of a motion as being the resultant of two motions (see relevant passages, in sec. 1, under B and sec. 6 below). He might, like the author of *Mechanical Problems*, have interpreted the sinking of the heavier weight in terms of the prevailing of its 'greater speed' of fall. But this would have been an interpretation, not the phenomenon itself. In any case, in the texts mentioned there is no sign that Aristotle has a balance particularly in mind, and one of them expressly talks of letting bodies drop from a height (*de Caelo* II.13, 294^{a}14).

The *only* reasonable explanation of these texts, therefore, is that they refer to the observable differences in the velocities of fall through air and water, owing to resistance, of bodies of various sizes. Very small specks of solid matter, or very small drops of water, fall slowly or not at all through air; through water the differences due to resistance are noticeable even with larger lumps of, say, earth or metal. An objection to this interpretation: in air, at least, a difference between velocities is *not* observable when we reach solid objects of even moderate size. So it is not *obvious*, as Aristotle claims, that the larger object *always* falls faster, beyond any limit of size. But in these passages he is citing it only as a generalization immediately exemplified by ordinary experience (and backed up, perhaps, by the behaviour of balances).

This interpretation will probably serve for *de Caelo* III.5, 304^{b}13–19 as well; and, of the other 'non-specific' passages, one is obscure (*de Caelo* I.8, 277^{a}27–33). (Two others, *de Caelo* IV.1, 308^{a}29–33 and *Physics* V.4, 228^{b}28–229^{a}1, which introduce a *logical* relationship between weight and speed of fall, will be considered later.)

190

It is now possible to approach the difficult passage in *Physics* IV.8, 215^a25-29, and 216^a13-21. Here again, there is a direct appeal to observed fact: 'we *see* . . .' is stated, with emphasis, twice: 215^a25 and 216^a13. So it is natural to suppose that here, too, the phenomenon appealed to is the same. What has given rise to doubt, or, if the interpretation above is accepted, to despair or indignation, is the fact that Aristotle here appears to claim a precise proportionality between the volumes or weights of the bodies and their speeds. For 216^a13-16 reads: 'We see that things which have a greater preponderance of heaviness or of lightness, other things being equal, move through equal distances faster, following the proportion which the magnitudes bear to one another.' What the crucial magnitudes are, here, is not certain: the 'preponderance of weight' (cf. 215^a28 'the excess of weight') might be the excess bulk, or the excess weight, or possibly the excess specific gravity. The point is, however, not at present important, for on any reading the statement is crassly at variance with ordinary experience, *provided we suppose that an exact proportion is being said to hold.*

The question is, then, whether the words 'following the proportion' (*kata logon*) do indeed assert an exact proportionality. It is clear from other instances of these words that they do not always do so: quite frequently they mean nothing more than 'as might be reasonably expected, given the proportion or analogy which exists': so e.g. often in the biological works (passages listed by Bonitz, 437^b14-24). In places where Aristotle certainly wishes to assert an *exact* proportionality, he does *not* use *kata logon*, but uses *ana logon* or speaks of *analogia* or of the identity of one ratio with another.

That it is not an exact proportionality that Aristotle intends here may be suggested by the argument itself. For at 216^a17-20 he suggests that the *only* reasons why one body should fall faster than another are (*a*) shape (here excluded from consideration, by the *ceteris paribus* clause at 216^a14); or (*b*) the greater ability of its bulk or 'preponderance' to cut through the resisting medium. This suggests very strongly that Aristotle has here in mind what is obviously the case; viz. that air offers less resistance than water or a solid body, and so does less to differentiate between bodies as regards their velocity of fall. For Aristotle's aim here is to exhibit the void (if it can exist) as a limiting case, in which all bodies fall equally fast.

What Aristotle is claiming, then, is that larger bodies fall more quickly than smaller ones, *ceteris paribus*, and that there is *some* functional relationship, not an exact proportion, which determines the ratio of the 'speeds' from the ratio of the weights, for any given medium—the speeds being more sharply distinguished, the more resistant the medium is.

Two objections may be made here: (1) If this *is* the argument, why does Aristotle regard it as a *reductio ad absurdum* that all bodies fall at equal speed in a void? Most probably because, on the hypothesis which he is attacking, which is that of the Atomists (see on 214^{b}28 ff.), there is void everywhere. So bodies would 'naturally' fall at the same speed everywhere, which would abolish all practical differences of weight (except on the balance) and therefore (in Aristotle's view) all differences between natural places. (2) If there is no exact proportionality here, what becomes of the exact proportionality stated at 215^{a}29–216^{a}12? If the same body's speeds through (say) air and water are in a proportion which is constant for *every* body, how is it that two bodies which are almost equally fast through air have very different speeds through water? For the moment, it is enough to say in answer that the exact proportionality of 215^{a}29–216^{a}12 is stated in a very tentative way, as if it were a merely illustrative assumption; especially 215^{b}6–7: 'let the speeds have the same proportion one to another as that in which air differs from water . . .'. (This is not ultimately a complete answer; see below, sec. 5.)

We have seen, then, how many of the passages on falling bodies can be explained merely in terms of observation and intelligent straightforward inferences from observation. But there still remain two passages in the *de Caelo* which resist the interpretation so far developed; these are *de Caelo* I.6, 273^{b}29–274^{a}16 and III.2, 301^{a}22–^{b}1.

These two passages have in common, not only that they introduce an exact proportionality between weights and distances or times, but that they make no appeal to experience, and that, instead, they appeal to the existence of the proportionality to prove some further point. It will not do, however, to claim that the purpose of the mathematical relationships here is merely 'dialectical' or 'illustrative'. It is true that the arguments do not absolutely demand the existence of a simple proportionate relationship. But they do demand the existence of *some* definite functional relationship between weights of bodies and distances travelled in a given time (or times taken over a given distance). And Aristotle introduces the proportionalities with no indication, in these cases, that they might be merely tentative or illustrative. He must, therefore, consider them to be in some sense *true*. But they are, on the face of it, incompatible with the other passages as so far interpreted. This is the final, and most serious, difficulty in the whole subject.

The solution that I propose for this difficulty invokes the distinction made by Aristotle (see sec. 1(*a*)) between mathematical physics and 'mechanics' conceived of as an empirical study. It is clear that the texts on falling bodies so far considered belong to mechanics: they are modest generalizations from experience. But at *de Caelo* I.6, $273^b29-274^a16$, it is equally clear that, whatever Aristotle is talking about, it is not actual physical bodies. This becomes obvious once the whole context, $273^b26-274^a18$, is read. His aim, indeed, is to prove that there can be no infinite physical body. He has already proved that, if there were such a thing, it would have infinite weight. In this passage he finishes the proof. But not by proving directly that no physical body can have infinite weight; instead he argues (*a*) there can be no such thing as an infinite weight; *therefore* (*b*) there can be no such thing as a physical body having infinite weight. What is to be made of this curiously round-about procedure? It indicates, at least, that Aristotle does not think that his discussion applies directly to physical bodies—otherwise he would have no need to be so circuitous. So he must be consider-ing weights *in abstraction from* physical bodies. And the business of abstracting from physical realities is what, for Aristotle, is the essence of mathematics.

At *de Caelo* III.2, $301^a22-{}^b1$, it is not quite so obvious that the argument abstracts from physical reality. The word 'body' (*sōma*) is used, though this can apply to geometrical (solid) figures as well as actual bodies. But there is certainly some abstraction, since actual bodies accelerate in falling, whereas Aristotle's proportion between weights (or volumes) and distances travelled makes no allowance for acceleration, but implies a *uniform* speed of fall.

The general explanation of the exact proportionality, then, is that Aristotle thought it was valid in abstract, mathematical physics but not in empirical mechanics. It still remains to show that this was an intelligible view for him to take.

Here we may start from one of the two remaining passages of those listed under C., namely *de Caelo* IV.1, 308^a29-33. This is a *definition* of 'relatively light (er)': that is relatively lighter, 'than which the other (of two bodies having weight and equal in volume) moves downwards naturally faster'. Here, lightness, and corre-spondingly heaviness or weight, is tied by definition to speed of natural movement. Correspondingly, (absolutely) 'heavy' is defined as 'moving downwards', that is, by its nature and if nothing prevents it. So it is natural, as already suggested, to see weight as a poten-tiality or 'power' for moving that (body) of which it is the weight. But bodies, *qua* bodies, resist the action of a 'power' upon them. And actual bodies moving downwards have, in addition, to contend with the resistance of the medium. So there are two levels of abstraction from actual bodies: (1) if we simply abstract from the medium, we consider, in effect, motion in a void. Here the moving power of the weight is counteracted by the 'inertial' resistance of the same weight, so that all bodies fall with equal speed. (2) If we further abstract from the 'inertial' properties of the body, i.e. from the body itself as perceptible, we leave only the weight 'in itself', i.e. the power to move downwards. All 'abstract weights', having no other distinction, must move themselves downward at speeds in proportion to their quantities, there being no resistance, and weight being by definition the power of moving downwards. This presupposes (*i*) that 'powers' are proportionate to speeds, other things being equal, (*ii*) that 'powers' are resisted, in actual bodies, in proportion to the weights of those bodies. But just those proportions are embodied in *Physics* VII.5, 249^{b}27–250^{b}7 (on which more below, sec. 4).

On the view just advanced, Aristotle operates with a conception of 'weight' which is the same throughout, and is equivalent to 'balance weight' in his theory, though not *defined* in terms of 'balance weight'. Moreover, the theory would allow him to claim that the behaviour of weights in a balance was *directly* determined by their behaviour as abstract weights. For, *ex hypothesi*, the behaviour of the balance is determined *instantaneously*, before any actual motion has occurred. Hence no resistance, either by a medium or by the bodies' inertia, need be taken into account.

It may be objected to this solution that it involves supposing that at *de Caelo* I.6 and III.2 Aristotle switches without warning to abstract considerations. To which it may be replied that Aristotle often introduces abstract mathematical arguments in the *de Caelo*, without signalling them. In these places he is discussing abstract points: 'can there be an infinite weight?' and 'need naturally moving things have weights?' Of course, he is ultimately concerned with the real world; but he thinks that what holds in the real world is best understood by means of abstract reasonings yielding explanations.

4. Aristotle's law of 'powers' and their effects

On the view that is being developed, Aristotelian dynamics, though hampered by the lack of the differential calculus, is both a good deal more sensible and rather more subtle than has usually been supposed. Essential use has already been made, in sec. 3 above, of the generalization about 'powers' and their effects enunciated at *Physics* VII.5, 249^{b}27–250^{b}7. This is, I suggest, the cornerstone of the edifice, much as is Newton's Second Law in Newtonian dynamics. The present section surveys the texts listed in sec. 1 above, under (A). Many of the 'non-specific' (A) passages call for no particular comment; they simply state or imply that greater 'powers' imply and/or are implied by greater effects (measured by the amount, or the speed, of the change, or the amount of the body changed). But *de Caelo* I.7, 275^{b}18—21 (an infinite body cannot be moved by a finite 'strength') is an abstract inference requiring some definite mathematical relationship. As for the 'specific' (A)-passages, the two in *de Caelo* occur in the same sort of abstract contexts as the 'specific' (C)-passages in *de Caelo*. In one of them, the proportionality is stated as an assumption; in the other it is assumed correct. But in both it (or some other definite mathematical relationship) is required by the argument. In both cases, Aristotle is at the first level of abstraction, disregarding the effects of the media, but including (since the argument demands their existence) the 'inertial' effects. *Physics* VIII.10, 266^{a}12—^{b}27 is very similar: again, infinite quantities are being discussed, and a definite mathematical relationship is demanded by the arguments; again, only the first stage of abstraction is allowed by the very questions at issue.

The most general statement of the law, as already remarked, is at *Physics* VII.5, 249^{b}27—250^{b}7. This chapter[1] may be divided up as follows (after Heath):

(*i*) We may always regard (in every case of change) the 'power' of the agent, the amount of the changing thing, the amount of the change, and the duration of the change as quantities. Say 'power' A moves amount B a distance of C in a time D; then:

(*ii*) A moves $\frac{1}{2}$ B a distance 2 C in time D;

(*iii*) A moves $\frac{1}{2}$ B a distance C in time $\frac{1}{2}$ D;

(*iv*) $\frac{1}{2}$ A moves $\frac{1}{2}$ B a distance C in time D;

(*v*) but it does *not* follow that:

$\frac{1}{2}$ A moves B a distance $\frac{1}{2}$ C in time D, (or any similar fractions of A and C) for $\frac{1}{2}$ A may not move B *at all* (and similarly any power less than A).

(*vi*) but if A moves B, and E moves F, the distance C in time D, it does follow that A + E moves B + F a distance C in time D.

(*vii*) The same inferences hold, and fail to hold, in all species of change. At the points (*ii*), (*iii*) and (*iv*), and (*vi*) the justification given is that 'it is proportionate'; and it is clear that Aristotle has a general law of proportionality in mind. In fact, from his rules (*ii*), (*iii*), (*iv*), and (*vi*) we can deduce that, in all cases where movement occurs, the proportion of the amount moved to the 'power', is equal (in suitable units) to the proportion of the time to the distance. This applies in all cases of change, *mutatis mutandis*. The effects of the medium are neglected, but 'inertial' effects are not.

The 'inertial' or 'threshold' proviso is that it does not follow,

[1] An English translation in Cohen-Drabkin, 203—4; another in Heath (3), 142—3.

from the fact that power A can move amount B, that power C can move amount D, where A/B > C/D; though it does follow when A/B ≤ C/D. The explanation of this is, presumably, that every body at rest has an initial resistance which must be overcome before *any* movement occurs. That interpretation is confirmed by *Mot. Anim*, 3, 699^{a}32–^{b}10 and 4,699^{b}14–17, which state explicitly that 'there is a certain quantity of strength and power, in accordance with which what stays still does so', and that, if the moving power is less than the 'staying power', no motion will result. Further, that this 'inertial power' is proportionate to *weight* (^{b}15–17). It is wrong, of course, to bring in the modern conception of inertia (which is resistance to acceleration, not to motion); but, with that caveat, 'inertial power' seems a good label.

Physics VII is, admittedly, a very early work. But there is no reason why the proportionality stated in *Physics* VII.5, should not have remained, as indeed it deserved to remain, the central generalization of Aristotle's dynamics. There is no reason why it should not have led him (but for such handicaps as the doctrine of natural motion and the denial of void) in the direction of Newtonian physics, since (as already mentioned) it admits of a Newtonian interpretation.

5. Aristotle's law of the resistance of media

Physics IV.8, 215^{a}29–216^{a}11 is the only discussion of the effect of the medium on the motion. But the general law can be seen as an immediate consequence of 'inertial power'. The medium has to be moved out of the way, which, even if at rest, it will resist. If, as in *Mot. Anim*. 4, the 'inertial power' is proportionate to the weight, it is reasonable that the speed through the medium, other things being equal, should be proportionate to the amount of the medium shifted in a given time, and that this should be inversely proportionate to the 'inertial power' per unit volume, i.e. to the *density* of the medium.

The exact proportionality is, therefore, in accordance with the general theory of the effects of 'powers'. But, as remarked above, it does not agree with experience. This need not have embarrassed Aristotle, since it is manifestly based on an abstraction. The reasoning above assumes that the *whole* of the moving body's motive 'power' is devoted to overcoming the resistance of the medium. But that cannot be correct, since the moving body has also continually to overcome its own resistance to motion. In other words, the discussion at 215^{a}29–216^{a}11 abstracts completely from the physical properties of the moving body itself, apart from its weight. In fact the moving object is nowhere in this passage called a 'body' (cf. *de Caelo* IV.6, 313^{b}16−21, on which see sec. 6 below).

6. Aristotle on the resultant of two 'powers' or two motions

The texts collected under B. in section 1(*b*) above are a miscellaneous set, concerned with cases in which two conflicting 'powers' are simultaneously at work, or two different motions are being inflicted on one and the same body. True to his conceptual scheme, Aristotle assimilates the latter cases to the former: where there are 'powers' there are (virtual) changes, and where there are motions there are 'powers' being applied.

In the very notion of virtual changes, which do not get expressed straightforwardly, there is a logical difficulty for Aristotle's philosophical analysis of change (see Introduction, sec. 2(*f*)). In mechanics, however, he clearly feels free to operate with them; perhaps he regarded them, as he regarded mathematical abstractions generally, as a kind of useful fiction (see Additional Note A). And, of course, it is essential to any mathematical mechanics worthy of the name that there should be laws of composition of motions and/or forces and the like.

The cases considered are of various types:

(*i*) *One body, two different motions*: *de Caelo* I.4, 271^{a}22−30; II.1, 284^{a}24−26; II.10, 291^{a}32−^{b}10; IV.5, 312^{b}7−14; *Meteorologica* I.4, 342^{a}22−28. In *Meteorologica* I.4, Aristotle correctly applies the 'parallelogram of velocities' to the case of an upward motion compounded with a slightly oblique downward motion. In *de Caelo* I.4, he simply speaks of the faster motion 'overcoming' the slower one, and so too in II.10, with a reference to 'the mathematicians' (i.e. Eudoxus and his followers in mathematical astronomy, who used compounded motions). *de Caelo* II.1 and IV.5 are equally non-specific: the faster motion determines the outcome.

(*ii*) *One body, motion vs. inertial resistance*: *Physics* VII.2, 244^{a}7−11; *de Caelo* IV.6, 313^{b}16−21; *Mot. Anim.* 3, 699^{a}32−^{b}11; 4, 699^{b}14−26. In the *Physics* and *de Caelo* texts, the situation is that one 'power' is acting so as to divide up a solid or semi-solid object, either by pulling or by pushing. The *de Caelo* passage takes up again the case of fall through a medium: the condition for any fall to occur is that the 'power' derived from the weight should exceed the 'power' of resistance tending to keep the medium together. (Here the resistance of the body's own weight can be neglected since it is an instantaneous condition.) The *Mot. Anim.* situation is that of a 'power' pushing at a body which is at rest: as stated in *Physics* VII.5, there is a 'threshold effect' and a minimum power required to shift the body at all. The passage implies a version of Newton's Third Law, that action and reaction are equal and opposite. The fact that the earth's 'inertial power' is less than that of the whole heavens is presumably deduced from the assumption that the weight of the earth is less than the presumed weight of the heavens.

(*iii*) *Two bodies mutually interacting: Physics* III.5, 204^b13-19, 205^a1-7; *Gen. et Corr.* I.10, 328^a23-^b14; II.4, 331^a20-^b36; II.7, 334^b20-30; *Meteorologica* I.3, 340^a13-17. These texts deal with the mutual action of the elemental constituents, and contain no precise mathematical relationships, only the notion that the stronger 'power' overcomes the weaker, and consequently, that the 'powers' in the lower cosmos must be, in sum, in balance at all times.

7. Aristotle on the impact of a moving body

Two places in *Meteorologica*, II.8, 365^b28-33 and III.1, 370^b9-10, imply a common-sense point: the impact of a body on other bodies increases with its speed. Little thought, in fact, is needed to see the need for a concept something like that of *momentum*, in explaining the observed facts about impact: neither speed nor weight alone is decisive, but both are important. Did Aristotle have such a concept? If we look again at the passages relating to the impact of a falling body on the medium, we find that *de Caelo* IV.6, 313^b16-21 is carefully vague: 'the weight has a certain power, in accordance with which it is moving downward', while *Physics* IV.8, $215^a29-216^a11$ says nothing about possible variations in the body's power to divide the medium. But at *Physics* IV.8, 216^a17-20, it is said that the body divides it 'by preponderance' (*rhopē*), referring back to 'preponderance of weight or lightness' (216^a13-14). This was earlier interpreted as simply identical with weight. But it is clear that this passage includes projectiles as well as freely falling bodies (216^a20), so that it is natural to ask whether 'preponderance' could not mean 'momentum'. An immediate objection is that a body with greater momentum is not necessarily moving faster; and if difference in weight is ruled out by the *ceteris paribus* clause, then the generalization collapses to a tautology: faster moving bodies move faster. This argument shows that 'preponderance' in its *first* occurrence here, coupled with 'of weight and lightness', cannot mean 'momentum': but in its second occurrence it might do so. (We might translate 'greater preponderance *due to* weight or lightness'.)

Other occurrences of the word *rhopē* in *de Caelo* do not support this suggestion. At II.2, 284^a25 it must be 'virtual downward movement'; at II.14, 297^a28, $^b7$, 10, 14 it seems to be 'downward tendency', as also at III.2, 301^{a}22–3, 24, III.6, 305^{a}25. At IV.1, 307^{b}33 the sense suggested is 'virtual downward movement': it is something that might be considered (wrongly, in Aristotle's opinion) the operation (*energeia*) of the power of downward motion. On the whole, therefore, 'downward tendency' seems correct: it is the 'power' of weight, conceived of as a virtual movement.

Yet the need for a concept corresponding to 'momentum' remains. If Aristotle shows no sign of having one, that suggests a gap in his grasp of the ordinary phenomena. This question is connected with another question: the explanation of the acceleration of freely falling (or rising) bodies.

8. Aristotle on the acceleration in natural motion

The texts are listed under (E) in sec. 1 above. The acceleration of naturally falling or rising bodies is stated as a phenomenon of experience and contrasted with the deceleration in unnatural motion (if left to itself). But no explanation of the phenomenon is attempted, except at *de Caelo* III.2, 301^{b}16–30. Here an explanation is attempted in terms of the medium: only air is mentioned, but water equally has the requisite property, in Aristotle's system, of being relatively both light and heavy. The acceleration of naturally moving bodies is seen as the result of a system with 'positive feedback': The body displaces the air, which in taking up a new position, presses further on the moving body, and so accelerates it further. With unnatural motion the system admits only a 'negative feedback' because there is a continual counteracting tendency. Aristotle hopes to account for the continuance of projectile motion by the same device.

But there is more to it than that. For the cause of the air's being set in motion is the power of the moving body itself to cause movement, as Aristotle explains. The air simply reflects back this power (which we would expect to be proportionate to the momentum; see sec. 7) on to the body itself, *minus* an amount absorbed by the resistance of the air itself. In this way, Aristotle constructs what is in effect a law of inertia: even without the natural movement, a body once set in motion would continue in that state of motion indefinitely, were it not for the resistance of the medium. But the continuance itself depends on the medium, so that it cannot occur when we abstract from the existence of the medium.

In this way Aristotle can provide for acceleration in a given medium, up to a terminal velocity. If the original, natural downward momentum is V and the proportion of momentum lost by the resistance of the medium in the 'recycling' process is always R, then the successive momenta, at suitable intervals, will be V, V + (1 − R)V, V + (1 − R) [V + (1 − R)V], . . . which will tend to the limit V/R. This is only an approximate way of viewing the transaction, since Aristotle has no means of handling continuous changes satisfactorily; but it gives the right kind of result.

The above reasoning depends, of course, on identifying the 'power' involved with the momentum; for the reasons for so doing, see sec. 7 above. If it is right, the 'motive power' of a body is Aristotle's equivalent of the concept of momentum.

9. Final Questions

The above reconstruction of Aristotelian dynamics leads to questions about the system as a whole.

(1) First, how much of a system is it? Does it allow a complete and coherent treatment of the elementary phenomena? Aristotle never attempts such a treatment in the extant works, even in the *de Caelo*, and the impression that is left is one of a series of brilliant improvisations to deal with each phenomenon in turn. There is no sign of a systematic science in the surviving *Mechanica! Problems* either, which must have built on Aristotelian material, and uses Aristotelian ideas. Nor do the works of Aristotle's pupils show much sign of interest in this particular aspect of physics, with few exceptions.

Though the system seems to be coherent so far as it goes, it would necessarily have been much hampered, if any real further development had been attempted, by the lack of a concept of *force*, and (correspondingly) the lack of the differential calculus, which made it almost impossible to handle acceleration and the rates of change of physical quantities.

(2) The historical problem left over is: if the system was as it has been reconstructed above, why are the ancient commentators unaware of the fact? Simplicius could, and did, draw on a tradition of exposition and commentary beginning with the pupils of Aristotle: with Theophrastus, Eudemus, and Strato. It is strange that he (and Alexander of Aphrodisias before him) should have been unaware of the true interpretation of Aristotelian dynamics—unless the pupils of Aristotle had taken no particular trouble to expound or criticize this particular part of their master's physics, in which case understanding of the system could easily have been lost during the decadence of Aristotelian studies after the mid-third century BC. (For the interpretations and criticisms of Alexander, Simplicius, and Philoponus see Cohen-Drabkin, 207−12, 217−23 and Sambursky, ch. 3.)

EXPLANATION OF REFERENCES

1. References to ancient authors

Texts by, or referring to, pre-Socratic thinkers or early sophists are cited from H. Diels and W. Kranz, *Die Fragmente der Vorsokratiker* (6th or any later edition, ed. W. Kranz) Berlin, 1952, 1956, etc. This work is referred to as 'Diels-Kranz' or 'DK'; The references to particular texts follow its system of numbering and lettering.

References to Plato use the titles of dialogues usual in English, and the standard method of reference by the pagination of Stephanus.

References to Aristotle. Some works are referred to by English, some by Latin titles, and some titles are abbreviated, thus:

Prior An. = *Prior Analytics*
Post. An. = *Posterior Analytics*
Gen. et Corr. = *de Generatione et Corruptione*
Hist. Anim. = *Historia Animalium*
Part. Anim. = *de Partibus Animalium*
Mot. Anim. = *de Motu Animalium*
Inc. Anim. = *de Incessu Animalium*
Gen. Anim. = *de Generatione Animalium*
Nic. Eth. = *Nicomachean Ethics*

The references specify number of book and chapter, followed (when the reference is not to the whole chapter) by the usual indication of Bekker pages, columns, and lines. References to books III and IV of the *Physics* usually omit *'Physics'*.

References to other ancient authors follow the system of Liddell-Scott-Jones, *A Greek-English Lexicon*, except that names of authors are not abbreviated.

2. References to modern works

These are by author's name and, where necessary, a number, and are followed where appropriate by chapter or page numbers. The works referred to are listed below. The list also contains some works, not referred to elsewhere in this book, which are useful for the study of *Physics* III and IV.

Ackrill, J. L., (1) *Aristotle's Categories and De Interpretatione*, translated with Notes and Glossary (Clarendon Aristotle Series), Oxford, 1963.

(2) 'Aristotle's distinction between *energeia* and *kinesis*', in: *New Essays on Plato and Aristotle* ed. R. Bambrough, London, 1965.

Annas, Julia, (1) *Aristotle's Metaphysics Books M and N*, translated with Introduction and Notes (Clarendon Aristotle Series) Oxford, 1976.

(2) 'Aristotle, Number and Time', *Philosophical Quarterly* 25 (1975), 97–113.

Anscombe, G. E. M. (1) 'Aristotle and the Sea-battle', *Mind* 65 (1956), 1–15; also in *Aristotle: a collection of critical essays*, ed. J. M. E. Moravcsik, London, 1968; and in: G. E. M. Anscombe, *From Parmenides to Wittgenstein*, Oxford, 1981.

(2) 'The Principle of Individuation',*Proceedings of the Aristotelian Society*, supplementary vol. 27 (1953), 83–96; also in Barnes-Schofield-Sorabji (1), Vol. 3; and in *From Parmenides to Wittgenstein* (see (1) above).

Aquinas, Thomas, *Commentary on Aristotle's Physics*, translated by Richard J. Blackwell, Richard J. Spath, and W. Edmund Thirkel, London, 1963.

Balme, D. M. *Aristotle's De Partibus Animalium I and De Generatione Animalium I*, translated with Notes (Clarendon Aristotle Series), Oxford, 1972.

Barnes, Jonathan, (1) *Aristotle's Posterior Analytics*, translated with Notes (Clarendon Aristotle Series), Oxford, 1975.

(2) *The Presocratic Philosophers*, London, 1979. (2 vols.)

Barnes, Jonathan, Schofield, Malcolm, and Sorabji, Richard, (1) *Articles on Aristotle*, London, 1975.

(2) *Aristotle: a selective Bibliography*, Oxford, 1977.

Bonitz, Hermann,*Index Aristotelicus*, Berlin, 1870.

Bostock, David, (1) 'Aristotle, Zeno and the Potential Infinite', *Proceedings of the Aristotelian Society* 73 (1972–3), 37–51

(2) 'Aristotle's Account of Time', *Phronesis* 25 (1980), 148–69.

Burkert, Walter, *Lore and Science in Ancient Pythagoreanism*, Cambridge, Mass., 1972 (translated from the German by Edwin L. Minar, Jr.).

Burnyeat, M. F. 'Aristotle on Understanding Knowledge', in: *Aristotle on Science: the 'Posterior Analytics'*, (ed. E. Berti) Padua, 1981.

Carteron, Henri, (1) *Aristote: Physique*, texte établi et traduit, Paris, 1926.

(2) *La Notion de force dans le systeme d'Aristote*, Paris, 1924 (part of this, in English translation, in Barnes-Schofield-Sorabji (1), vol. 1).

Charles, David, *Aristotle on Action* (forthcoming, London).

EXPLANATION OF REFERENCES

Charlton, W. *Aristotle's Physics Books I and II*, translated with Introduction and Notes (Clarendon Aristotle Series), Oxford, 1970.

Cherniss, Harold, (1) *Aristotle's Criticism of Presocratic Philosophy*, Baltimore, 1935 (reprinted, New York, 1964).

(2) *Aristotle's Criticism of Plato and the Academy*, vol. 1, Baltimore, 1944 (reprinted, New York, 1962).

Cohen, Morris R. and Drabkin, I. E. *A Source Book in Greek Science*, Cambridge, Mass., 1958.

Conen, P. R. *Die Zeittheorie des Aristoteles*, Munich, 1964.

Davidson, Donald, *Essays on Actions and Events*, Oxford, 1980.

Drabkin, I. E. 'Notes on the Laws of Motion in Aristotle', *American Journal of Philology* 59 (1938), 60–84.

Dummett, Michael, (1) *Frege: Philosophy of Language*, London, 1973

(2) *Elements of Intuitionism*, Oxford, 1977.

(3) *Truth and other Enigmas*, London, 1978.

During, Ingemar, *Naturphilosophie bei Aristoteles und Theophrast* (ed. I. During) Heidelberg, 1969 (Proceedings of the Fourth Symposium Aristotelicum).

During, Ingemar and Owen, G. E. L. *Aristotle and Plato in the mid-Fourth Century* (edd. I. During and G. E. L. Owen), Goteborg, 1960 (proceedings of the First Symposium Aristotelicum).

Evans, J. D. G. *Aristotle's Concept of Dialectic*, Cambridge, 1977.

Fraenkel, Eduard, *Aeschylus Agamemnon* edited with a commentary, Oxford, 1950 (3 vols.).

Frede, Dorothea, *Aristoteles und die 'Seeschlacht'*, Gottingen, 1970.

Frege, Gottlob, 'Uber Sinn und Bedeutung' (English translation, 'On Sense and Reference', by Max Black, in *Translations from the Philosophical Writings of Gottlob Frege*, edd. Peter Geach and Max Black, Oxford, 1960).

Gaiser, Konrad, *Platons ungeschriebene Lehre*, Stuttgart, 1963.

Gautier, René Antoine and Jolif, Jean Yves, *L'Ethique à Nicomaque*, Introduction, traduction et commentaire, 2nd edn., Louvain and Paris, 1970 (3 vols.).

Guthrie, W. K. C. (1) *Aristotle on the Heavens* with an English translation (Loeb Classical Library), London and Cambridge, Mass., 1939.

(2) *A History of Greek Philosophy*, Cambridge, 1962–81 (6 vols.).

Hamlyn, D. W. *Aristotle's De Anima Books II and III*, translated with Introduction and Notes (Clarendon Aristotle Series), Oxford, 1968.

Hardie, R. P. and Gaye, R. K. *The Works of Aristotle translated into English, vol. II: Physica*, Oxford, 1930.

203

Hartman, Edwin, *Substance, Body and Soul: Aristotelian Investigations*, Princeton, 1977.

Heath, (Sir) Thomas L. (1) *A History of Greek Mathematics*, Oxford, 1921 (2 vols.).

(2) *The Thirteen Books of Euclid's Elements* translated . . . with Introduction and Commentary, 2nd. edn. reissued, New York, 1956 (3 vols.).

(3) *Mathematics in Aristotle*, Oxford, 1949.

Hesse, Mary B. *Forces and Fields: the concept of action at a distance in the history of physics*, London, 1961.

Hintikka, Jaakko, *Time and Necessity: studies in Aristotle's theory of modality*, Oxford, 1973.

Hocutt, Max, 'Aristotle's Four Becauses', *Philosophy* 49 (1974), 385—99.

Hornsby, Jennifer, *Actions*, London, 1980.

Jammer, Max, (1) *Concepts of Space*, 2nd. end., New York., 1960.

(2) *Concepts of Force*, 2nd. edn., New York, 1962.

Joachim, Harold H. *Aristotle on Coming-to-Be and Passing-Away . . .* a revised text with Introduction and Commentary, Oxford, 1922.

Jones, Barrington, 'Individuals in Aristotle's Categories', *Phronesis* 14 (1972), 104—23.

Kahn, Charles H. (1) 'Pythagorean Philosophy before Plato', in *The Presocratics*, ed. Alexander P. D. Mourelatos, New York, 1974.

(2) 'Anaximander and the arguments concerning the *apeiron* at *Phys.* 203^{b}4—15', in: *Festschrift Ernst Kapp*, Hamburg, 1958.

Kirwan, Christopher, *Aristotle's Metaphysics Books* Γ, Δ, *and* E, translated with Notes (Clarendon Aristotle Series), Oxford, 1971.

Kosman, L. A. 'Aristotle's definition of motion', *Phronesis* 14 (1969), 40—62.

Lear, Jonathan, 'Aristotelian Infinity', *Proceedings of the Aristotelian Society* 80 (1979—80), 187—210.

Liddell, Henry George, Scott, Robert, and Jones, Henry Steuart, *A Greek-English Lexicon*, A New Edition, revised and augmented throughout . . ., Oxford, 1940.

Mackie, J. L. (1) *Truth, Probability and Paradox: studies in philosophical logic*, Oxford, 1973.

(2) *The Cement of the Universe: a study of causation*, Oxford, 1974.

(3) Review of von Wright, *Journal of Philosophy* 73 (1976), 213—18.

Mansion, A. (1) *Introduction a la Physique aristotélicienne*, 2nd. edn., Louvain and Paris, 1946.

(2) 'La physique aristotélicienne et la philosophie' *Revue neoscolastique de philosophie* 39 (1936), 5—26.

Mansion, S. *Aristote et les problemes de methode*, Louvain, 1961 (Proceedings of the Second Symposium Aristotelicum).

Mellor, D. 'In defence of dispositions', *Philosophical Review* 83 (1974), 157–81.

Miller, Fred D. (1) 'Did Aristotle have a concept of identity?', *Philosophical Review* 82 (1973), 483–90.
(2) 'Aristotle on the reality of time', *Archiv fur Geschichte der Philosophie* 56 (1974), 132–55.

Moravcsik, J. M. E. 'Aristotle's Theory of Categories' in: *Aristotle: A collection of critical essays*, ed. J. M. E. Moravcsik, London, 1968.

Mourelatos, A. P. D. 'Aristotle's Powers and Modern Empiricism', *Ratio* 9 (1967), 97–104.

Mueller, Ian, 'Aristotle on Geometrical Objects', *Archiv fur Geschichte der Philosophie* 52 (1970), 156–71 (also in Barnes-Schofield-Sorabji (1), vol. 3).

Nussbaum, Martha Craven, (1) *Aristotle's De Motu Animalium*, Text with Translation, Commentary and Interpretive Essays, Princeton, 1978.
(2) Review of Hartman, *Journal of Philosophy* 77 (1980), 355–65.

Owen, G. E. L. (1) *Aristotle on Dialectic: The Topics*, ed. G. E. L. Owen, Oxford, 1968 (Proceedings of the Third Symposium Aristotelicum).
(2) 'Logic and Metaphysics in some earlier works of Aristotle', in: During-Owen (also in Barnes-Schofield-Sorabji (1), vol. 3).
(3) 'Tithenai ta Phainomena', in: Mansion, S.; and in Moravcsik.
(4) 'Inherence', *Phronesis* 10 (1965), 97–105.
(5) 'Plato and Parmenides on the Timeless Present', *Monist* 50 (1966), 317–40 (also in Mourelatos (ed.) *The Presocratics*: see Kahn (1)).
(6) 'Aristotle on Time', in: *Motion and Time, Space and Matter: Interrelations in the History and Philosophy of Science*, ed. P. Machamer and R. Turnbull, Columbus, Ohio, 1976 (also in: Barnes-Schofield-Sorabji (1) vol. 3).
(7) 'Aristotle: Method, Physics and Cosmology', in: *A Dictionary of Scientific Biography* ed. C. C. Gillespie, New York, 1970.

Pacius, Julius, *Aristotelis . . . naturalis auscultationis libri viii . . .* commentariis illustravit, Frankfurt, 1596.

Parsons, Charles, (1) 'Mathematical Intuition', *Proceedings of the Aristotelian Society* 80 (1979–80), 145–68.
(2) 'Ontology and Mathematics', *Philosophical Review* 80 (1971), 151–76.

Penner, Terry, 'Verbs and the identity of actions', in: *Ryle*, ed. G. Pitcher and O. P. Wood, New York, 1970.

Ross, W. D. (Sir David) (1) *Aristotle's Physics*, a revised text with introduction and commentary, Oxford, 1936.

(2) *Aristotle's Metaphysics*, a revised text with introduction and commentary, Oxford, 1924 (2 vols.).

(3) *Aristotle's Prior and Posterior Analytics*, a revised text with introduction and commentary, Oxford, 1949.

(4) *Aristotle Parva Naturalia*, a revised text with introduction and commentary, Oxford, 1955.

(5) *Aristotle De Anima*, edited with introduction and commentary, Oxford, 1961.

Sambursky, S. *The Physical World of Late Antiquity*, London, 1962.

Schoedel, Peter, *Aristoteles' Widerlegungen der Zenonischen Beweisgange*, Gottingen, 1975.

Schofield, Malcolm, (1) *An Essay on Anaxagoras*, Cambridge, 1980.

(2) 'Did Parmenides discover Eternity?', *Archiv fur Geschichte der Philosophie* 52 (1970), 113–35.

Solmsen, Friedrich, *Aristotle's System of the Physical World*, Ithaca, N.Y., 1960.

Sorabji, Richard, *Aristotle on Memory*, London, 1972.

Strang, Colin, 'The physical theory of Anaxagoras', *Archiv fur Geschichte der Philosophie* 45 (1963), 101–18 (also in: *Studies in Presocratic Philosophy*, vol. 2, edd. R. E. Allen and D. J. Furley, London, 1975).

Taylor, A, E. *A Commentary on Plato's Timaeus*, Oxford, 1928.

Taylor, C. C. W. 'States, Activities and Performances', *Proceedings of the Aristotelian Society*, supplementary volume, 39 (1965), 85–102.

Vlastos, Gregory, (1) 'The physical theory of Anaxagoras', *Philosophical Review* 59 (1950), 31–57 (also in: *Studies in Presocratic Philosophy*, vol. 2, edd. Allen and Furley; see Strang).

(2) 'The Disorderly Motion in the Timaios', *Classical Quarterly* 33 (1939), 71–83 (also in: *Studies in Plato's Metaphysics*, ed. R. E. Allen, London, 1965).

(3) 'Creation in the Timaeus: is it a fiction?' in: *Studies in Plato's Metaphysics*, ed. Allen; see Vlastos (2).

(4) 'On Plato's Oral Doctrine' in: G. Vlastos, *Platonic Studies*, Princeton, 1973.

von Wright, G. H. *Causality and Determinism*, New York, 1974.

Wedberg, Anders, *Plato's Philosophy of Mathematics*, Stockholm, 1955.

West, M. L. *Hesiod Theogony* edited with Prolegomena and Commentary, Oxford, 1966.

White, Nicholas P. 'Aristotle on Sameness and Oneness', *Philosophical Review* 80 (1971), 177–97.

Wieland, Wolfgang, (1) *Die Aristotelische Physik*, 2nd. edn., Göttingen, 1970.
(2) 'Das Problem der Prinzipienforschung und die Aristotelische Physik', *Kant-Studien* 52 (1960—1), 206—19 (English translation in Barnes-Schofield-Sorabji (1), vol. 1).

Wiggins, David, *Sameness and Substance*, Oxford, 1980.

Wolfson, Harry A. *Crescas' Critique of Aristotle: problems of Aristotle's Physics in Jewish and Arabic philosophy*, 2nd printing, Cambridge, Mass., 1971.

Woods, Michael, 'Substance and Essence in Aristotle', *Proceedings of the Aristotelian Society* 75 (1974—5), 167—80.

Zabarella, Jacobus, *In libros Aristotelis Physicorum commentarii*, Venice, 1601.

The following appeared after work on this volume had been completed:

Lear, Jonathan, 'Aristotle's Philosophy of Mathematics', *Philosophical Review* 91 (1982), 161—92.

Waterlow, Sarah, *Nature, Change and Agency in Aristotle's* Physics, Oxford, 1982.

Williams, C. J. F., *Aristotle's de Generatione et Corruptione*, translated with Notes (Clarendon Aristotle Series), Oxford, 1982.

LIST OF DIVERGENCES FROM THE TEXT OF ROSS

The Greek text presupposed by the translation and notes is that of Ross (1), except as specified below. In each case, the proposed change from Ross's text is followed by a brief justification of the change. (Ross's text follows the MS tradition, unless the contrary is stated.)

201^{a}12–13. Exclude τοῦ ἀντικειμένου. It is clear that the words αὐξητοῦ καὶ φθιτοῦ are intended to function as a single predicate.
201^{b}7. Read αὕτη for αὐτή. Better sense, and equally consonant with the tradition.
202^{a}7–9. Exclude διὸ ἡ κίνησις . . . πάσχει. First clause has no relevance, and διὸ is therefore unexplained. Second clause is pointless repetition.
202^{b}26–28. Exclude ἔτι δὲ γνωριμώτερον . . . ἰατρεύσις. A bad attempt at a general explanation, disrupting the thought of the section, and in which τοῦ δυνάμει ποιητικοῦ καὶ παθητικοῦ is an illogical expression.
203^{b}6. Read ὡς ἀρχῇ for ὡς ἀρχήν. The latter does not give the sense required by the argument.
204^{a}6. Exclude ἡ πέρας. Unnecessary and without parallel in the context.
205^{a}7–8. Exclude δεῖ δὲ . . . σῶμα ἄπειρον αἰσθητόν (the last three words already excluded by Ross). Redundant, and κατὰ παντὸς is oddly expressed.
206^{a}7. Read ἑκάστου for ἕκαστον. The six 'dimensions' are not themselves limits, but are each of them limited. The small change restores this sense and the parallelism in thought with what precedes.
207^{a}11. Exclude οἷον τὸ, and punctuate so: ὥσπερ δὲ τὸ καθ' ἕκαστον, οὕτω καὶ τὸ κυρίως ὅλον, οὐ, etc. The traditional text is inexplicable, since οἷον should introduce an example. The correction is easy.
211^{b}17. Read ὡς ὂν διάστημά τι for διάστημα, ὡς ὄν τι. A slight awkwardness of thought and expression is removed.
212^{b}1–2. Punctuate so: ἄνω μὲν καὶ κάτω, οὐ κύκλῳ δέ, ἔνια, rather than as Ross. The change gives an easier sense.
212^{b}10. Read ἐφ' ὃ for ἐφ' ᾧ. The latter gives no good sense. (The proposed reading is an ancient variant with support among MSS and ancient commentators.)

213^{b}5–6. Exclude οὐ γὰρ ἂν δοκεῖν εἶναι κίνησιν. Illogical or redundant here.

213^{b}24. Exclude καί. The word is pointless here. (There may well be a more deep-seated corruption here, since the expression is still awkward. Aristotle may have written something like ὡς ἀναπνέοντι, καὶ τοῦτο εἶναι ὃ διορίζει, etc.)

214^{b}6–9. Transpose the parenthesis ἀπορίαν . . . ὡς ἔστιν to after (^{b}9). As it stands the remark interrupts the thought.

216^{b}16. Read παρά (conjectured by Ross) for περί. The received text gives no acceptable sense.

216^{b}26. Exclude ἀέρα καὶ ὕδωρ. The words are out of place in a general statement.

219^{b}12. Read μετρεῖ (the reading of the MSS and the ancient commentators) for ὁρίζει. Ross adopted a conjecture of Torstrik on insufficient grounds.

219^{b}19. Read ἡ στιγμή (or perhaps ᾖ στιγμή) for ἢ στιγμή. One or other of these readings is required by the sense of the passage. They were suggested by Owen (6), 22 n.32.

220^{a}21–22. Restore to the text, unchanged, the sentence of the traditional text obelized by Ross: ᾖ μὲν οὖν . . . ἀριθμός. Ross's grounds for doubt are insufficient; the sentence can be understood; see Notes.

221^{a}17. Exclude τῷ χρόνῳ. Makes no sense, and best taken as an attempt to gloss ἐν ἀριθμῷ.

222^{b}16. Exclude μεταβολὴ . . . ἐκστατικόν. Pointless here, and a doublet of 222^{b}21.

222^{b}23. Read πάσχειν for πράττειν. The latter gives no intelligible sense.

223^{b}2. Read ὥσθ' (conjectured by Ross, possibly read by Philoponus) for ὧν. The latter is intelligible but inexplicably clumsy.

224^{a}1. Read μετρούμενον for τῷ μετρουμένῳ. The MSS and Philoponus have τὸ μετρούμενον; Ross adopted an unnecessary conjecture of Torstrik. Something must be changed, but the minimal deletion of τό gives satisfactory sense.

224^{a}1. Read ἀλλ' ἢ μέτρον ἢ πλείω μέτρα for ἀλλ' ἢ πλείω μέτρα. The latter leaves a logical gap, and the change is easy.

GLOSSARY

ἀίδιος everlasting
αἰσθάνεσθαι perceive
   αἰσθητός perceptible (by sense),
      object of (sense)-perception
   αἴσθησις (sense-) perception
   ἀναίσθητος imperceptible
   ἀναισθησία failure to perceive
αἴτιος responsible (for)
   αἴτιον reason, explanation
   αἰτία reason, explanation (ex-
      planatory factor, $203^b12–13$)
ἀκολουθεῖν follow (see on 219^a10
   ff.), accompany
   παρακολουθεῖν be a consequence
      of
ἀλλοιοῦσθαι change qualitatively Intrans.)
   ἀλλοίωσις qualitative change
   ἀλλοιωτός admitting of qualitat-
      ive change
ἀνάγκη necessity
   ἀναγκαῖος necessary
ἀναιρεῖν exhaust
ἀντεστραμμένος, -ως inversely corre-
   sponding/proportionate, in
   inverse correspondence
ἅμα together
ἀπεῖναι be absent
   ἀπουσία absence
ἁπλοῦς simple
   ἁπλῶς without qualification, un-
      qualifiedly
ἀποκεκριμένος distinct
ἀπόστασις distance
ἅπτεσθαι touch, be in contact with
   ἀφή contact (noun), touch (noun)
   ἁπτός tangible
ἀριθμός number
ἄρτι recently
ἀρχή principle, beginning, starting-
   point
ἄτομος indivisible

αὐξάνειν increase (in size)
   αὔξη, αὔξησις increase (in size)
      (noun), extent
   αὐξητός admitting of increase
   συναυξάνειν increase together with
   (αὐτός)
   καθ' αὐτόν, -ήν, -ό, -ά in (respect
      of) itself/themselves (see on
      203^b30 ff., 209^a31 ff.)

βάρος heaviness, weight
βίᾳ forced, by force (see on 214^b28)
   βίαιος forced

γένος genus
   συγγενής of the same kind
γίγνεσθαι come to be, become
   γένεσις coming-to-be
   γενητός admitting of coming-to-be
   ἀγένητος not admitting of coming-
      to-be
γνωρίζειν become acquainted with
   γνώριμος familiar, easily known

διαιρεῖν divide (off/from)
   διαίρεσις division
   διαιρετός divisible
   ἀδιαίρετος indivisible
   εὐδιαίρετος easily divisible
διάνοια mind
διαφορά difference (see on 224^a2)
διϊέναι traverse (verb)
   διεξιέναι traverse (verb)
   ἀδιεξίτητος untraversable
   διέξοδος traverse (noun)
(διϊστάναι)
   διεστηκέναι be extended
   διάστασις extension, dimension
   διάστημα extension (dimension
      209^a4)
δύνασθαι be able, be capable of
   δύναμις power, potentiality

δυνάμει *potentially, in potentiality*
δυνατός *possible, potential, being in potentiality*
ἀδύνατος *impossible*

εἶδος *form, kind ((Platonic) Form,* 209^{b}34)
ὁμοειδής *homogeneous, of the same form*
εἶναι *be, exist*
　τὸ εἶναι *being* (noun)
　τὸ τί ἦν εἶναι *the 'what it was to be'* (see on 202^{b}5 ff.)
　ὅ ποτ(ε) ὄν (ἦν) (see on 219^{a}14 ff.)
　οὐσία *substance* (*being* 218^{a}3, 221^{b}31)
(ἕκαστος)
　καθ᾽ ἕκαστον *in a particular case*
ἔλλειψις *deficiency*
ἐμφαίνεσθαι *present itself to view*
　παρεμφαίνεσθαι *be apparent in addition*
ἐναντίωσις *opposition*
ἐνδέχεσθαι *be possible, be capable of*
ἐνεργεῖν *operate*
　ἐνέργεια *operation*
　ἐνεργείᾳ *in (actual) operation*
　ἐνεργητικός *such as to operate (on)*
ἑνότης *union*
ἕνωσις *unification*
ἐντελέχεια *actuality*
　ἐντελεχείᾳ *actually, in actuality*
ἐξαίφνης *suddenly*
ἕξις *state*
ἐξιστάναι *displace, remove*
　ἐκστατικός *productive of removal*
ἐξωτερικός *untechnical* (see on 217^{b}29 ff.)
ἐπακτικῶς *inductively*
ἐπιστήμη *science*
ἔργον *product*
ἐτεροίωσις *qualitative change*
ἐφεξῆς *next*
ἐχόμενος *adjoining*

ᾗ *qua*
ἤδη *just*
ἠρεμεῖν *be at rest*
　ἠρεμία *state of rest*

θέσις *convention, position*
θίξις *contact*

ἰδέα *(Platonic) Form*
ἴδιος *special*
　ἴδιον *speciality*

καθαίρεσις *reduction*
καθόλου *general(ly), universal(ly)*
κατηγορεῖν *predicate* (verb)
　κατηγορία *category*
　κατηγόρημα *occupant of a category*
κενόν *void*
κινεῖν *change (transitive verb), produce change*
　κινεῖσθαι *change* (intransitive verb), *move, change position*
　κίνησις *change* (noun)
　ἀκινησία *not being changed* (noun)
　κινητός *changeable*
　κινητικός *productive of change*
　ἀκίνητος *unchangeable (immobile* 205^{a}13, ^{b}7 *unchanging* 221^{b}12)
　ἀμετακίνητος *which cannot be moved around*
κοινός *common (general* 208^{a}31)
κόσμος *world-system*
κύριος *basic*
　κυρίως *in the primary sense*

λόγος *reason, definition, proportion, reasoning, argument, account*
　ἐν λόγῳ *to be reckoned (as)*
　λογικός *formal* (see on 202^{a}22)
　λογικῶς *formally*
　ἀναλογία *proportion*

μανός *rare*
　μάνωσις *rarefaction*
μάτην *to no end*
μέγεθος *magnitude* (see on 202^{b}30 ff.)

μεθίστασθαι *change position*
  μετάστασις *change of position*
  ἀντιμεθίστασθαι *replace*
  ἀντιμετάστασις *replacement*
μένειν *be at rest*
  μονή *being at rest* (noun)
μέρος *part*
  κατὰ μέρος *in particular*
  μερίζειν *resolve into parts*
  μεριστός *resoluble into parts*
  ἀμέριστος *irresoluble into parts*
  ὁμοιομερής *with like parts*, (*homoeomery* 203^{a}21, see ad loc.)
μεταβάλλειν *alter*, (*move* (*about*) in IV.1–5)
  μεταβολή *alteration*
μεταληπτικός *participative* (see on 209^{b}6 ff.)
μετέχειν *participate* (*in*)
  μεθεκτικός *participative* (see on 209^{b}17 ff.)
μετρεῖν *measure* (verb)
  μέτρον *measure* (noun)
  μετρητός *measurable*
  ἀναμετρεῖν *measure off*
  καταμετρεῖν *measure out*
μονάς *unit*
μόριον *portion, part*
μορφή *form*

νοῦς *Mind* (Anaxagorean), *intellect*
  νοεῖν *think, take thought, conceive* (*of*)
  νόησις *thought*
  νοητός *intelligible, object of thought*
  νοητικός *relating to thought*
νῦν *now*

ὄγκος *bulk, volume, extended body*
οἰκεῖος *proper*
ὅλος *whole*
  τὸ ὅλον *the whole, the universe*
ὁμαλής *uniform*
ὁμώνυμος *homonymous, so called by homonymy* (see on 202^{a}21 ff.)
ὁρατός *visible*
  ἀόρατος *invisible*

ὅρος *boundary*
  ὁρίζειν *mark off, bound, define*
  ὁρίζεσθαι *define*
  ὡρισμένος *definite, bounded, defined*
  ἀόριστος *indefinite*
  ἀφωρισμένος *distinct*
  διορίζειν *be a boundary between, distinguish, define, determine*
  διόρισις *distinguishing* (noun)
  διορισμός *definition*
οὐρανός *heavens, world*

πάλαι *long ago*
πανσπερμία *hodge-podge* (see on 203^{a}16 ff.)
παρώνυμος *derivative* (see on 207^{b}1 ff.)
πάσχειν *be acted upon*
  πεπονθέναι *have as a property*
  πάθος *property* (217^{b}26 *being acted upon*, 202^{a}24 *modification*)
  πάθημα *quality*
  πάθησις *being acted upon* (noun)
  παθητικός *passive*
  ἀπαθής *not capable of being acted upon, impassive*
  ἀπάθεια *not being acted upon* (noun)
πέρας *limit* (noun)
  περαίνειν *limit* (verb), *reach a limit*
  πεπεράνθαι *be finite*
  πεπερασμένος *finite, limited*
  ἄπειρος *infinite*
  ἀπειρία *infinity*
  ἀπεράντως *infinitely*
περιέχειν *surround* (218^{a}12–13 *include*)
περιίστασθαι *change position around*
  ἀντιπερίστασις *cyclical replacement*
πλῆθος *multiplicity*
πλῆρες *full, plenum*
ποιεῖν *act* (*upon*), *do, make*
  ποίημα *product of action*
  ποίησις *acting upon* (noun)
  ποιητικός *active, productive* (*of*)

ποιόν qualification (see on 200^b26 ff.)
ποσόν quantity (see on 200^b26 ff.)
ποτέ at some time
πρᾶγμα (actual) thing, object, affair
πρός τι relative
προστιθέναι add
    πρόσθεσις addition
πρότερον καὶ ὕστερον, (τὸ) (the) before and after (see on 219^a 14 ff., ^b9 ff.)
πυκνός dense
    πυκνοῦσθαι be condensed
    πύκνωσις condensation

ῥοπή preponderance (see on 215^a24 ff.)

στερεῖν deprive
    στέρησις privation
    στερητικός privative
στιγμή point
στοιχεῖον element
συμβαίνειν happen, turn out, result, work out
    συμβεβηκέναι happen to be true (of), be an accident (of)
    συμβεβηκώς accident(al)
    κατὰ συμβεβηκός accidentally
συνέχειν make continuous, link together
    συνεχής continuous, continuum
    συνέχεια link
σύνθετος composite
συστοιχία column (of correlated opposites; see on 201^b16 ff.)
σῶμα body
    σωματικός corporeal
    ἀσώματος incorporeal

τέλος end
    τέλεως complete
    τελειότης completeness
    τελευτή end
    ἀτελής incomplete
τόδε this (see on 200^b26 ff.)
τόπος place

ὕλη matter, material, material cause

ὑπάρχειν be present (in) (210^b11 be)
    ὑπάρχοντα facts
ὑπερέχειν exceed
    ὑπεροχή excess
ὑποκεῖσθαι be taken as true
    ὑποκειμένον underlying subject (223^a1, given)
ὑπολείπειν give out
ὑπομένειν persist
ὑποτιθέναι posit (as subject)

φέρεσθαι move (intrans.), be in motion
    φορά (loco)motion
    φορητός admitting of locomotion
    ἀντιφέρεσθαι move in the opposite direction
    κυκλοφορία circular motion
    μεταφορητός which can be carried around
    περιφορά revolution
φθείρειν destroy
    φθείρεσθαι cease to be
    φθορά ceasing-to-be (noun)
    φθαρτός admitting of ceasing-to-be
    ἄφθαρτος not admitting of ceasing-to-be
φθίσις decrease (noun)
    φθιτός admitting of decrease
φύσις nature, kind of thing
    φύσει by nature, naturally
    κατὰ φύσιν natural(ly)
    παρὰ φύσιν unnatural(ly)
    πεφυκέναι be (by nature) such (as to), be the kind of thing (to)
    φυσικός natural, student of nature
    φυσικῶς naturally, in accordance with natural science
    φυσιολόγος natural philosopher
    συμπεφυκέναι be fused
    σύμφυσις fusion

χρόνος time
χώρα space
χωρίς separate (adj.), in separation
    χωρίζειν separate (verb, trans.)
    κεχωρισμένος separated

213

χωρισμός *separation*   ψυχή *soul*
χωριστός *separable*
ἀχώριστος *inseparable*

INDEXES

I. INDEX OF PERSONS

Academy, Early (*see also* Plato) 63, 147, 172
Ackrill, J. L. xxii, 57f., 63, 90, 136, 201 f.
Aeschylus 77
Alexander of Aphrodisias 200
Anaxagoras xix, 7, 12, 31, 74 f., 81
Anaximander 8, 76, 80
Annas, J. xxxix, 73, 165, 176, 180, 202
Anscombe, G. E. M. xxii, 202
Aquinas, Thomas xi, 202
Archytas 186
Atomists, Early (*see also* Democritus, Leucippus) xxxiii, 123 f., 129 f., 135, 137, 192

Balme, D. M. 202
Barnes, J. 67, 75, 77, 104, 182, 202
Bonitz, H. 100, 108, 118, 138, 202
Bostock, D. xxi, 202
Burkert, W. 73, 202
Burnyeat, M. F. 202

Carteron, H. xxxv, 185, 202
Charles, D. O. M. xiv, xvii, xviii, 203
Charlton, W. 203
Cherniss, H. xxxii, 73, 203
Cohen, M. R. 185, 195, 200, 203
Conen, P. R. 203

Davidson, D. xvii, 203
Democritus 7, 31, 74 f., 137
Diels, H. 201
Diogenes Laertius 186
Drabkin, I. E 185, 195, 200, 203
Dummett, M. A. E. xxv, 70, 203
During, I. 203

Einstein, A. xxxi
Empedocles 74, 167
Euclid 93–5, 132
Eudemus 175, 200
Eudoxus 95 f., 160, 186, 197
Evans, J. D. G. 203

Fraenkel, E. D. M. 77, 203
Frede, D. xxii, 203
Frege, G. 69 f., 203

Gaiser, K. 203
Galileo xxxiv, 130
Gautier, R. A. 203
Gaye, R. K. 203
Gorgias 100, 109
Guthrie, W. K. C. 130, 203

Hamlyn, D. W. 203
Hardie, R. P. 203
Hartman, E. xviii, 204
Heath, Sir T. L. 73, 84, 95 f., 160, 176, 185, 195, 204
Heraclitus 11, 70, 167
Herodotus 175
Hesiod xxviii, 21, 101
Hesse, M. xv, 204
Hintikka, J. xxii, 60, 77, 83, 98, 168, 172, 204
Hocutt, M. 96, 204
Homer 49
Hornsby, J. xvii, 65, 204

Jammer, M. 204
Joachim, H. H. 64, 97, 100, 122, 167–9, 175, 204
Jolif, J. Y. 203
Jones, B. 57, 204

Kahn, C. H. 73, 204
Keynes, J. M. (Lord) 169
Kirwan, C. 75, 85, 104, 108, 204
Kosman, L. A. 60, 204
Kranz, W. 201
Kripke, S. 178

Lawrence, G. J. L. xvii
Lear, J. xxv, 83, 204, 207
Leucippus 31

Mackie, J. L. xiii, xv, 204
Mansion, A. xxxiv, 204
Mansion, S. 205
Melissus 16, 32 f., 86, 124
Mellor, D. xiii, 205
Miller, F. D. xviii, 205
Moravcsik, J. M. E 57, 205
Mourelatos, A. D. P. xiii, xxxiv, 205
Mueller, I. 180, 205

Newton, Sir I. xxxi
Nussbaum, M. C. xviii, 205

Owen, G. E. L. ix, xxviii, xxxv,
    xlii, xliv, 57, 60, 91, 111, 154,
    185, 203, 205, 209

Pacius, J. xi, 205
Parmenides xxiv, xliv, 16, 86, 109
Paron 51
Parsons C., 176, 178, 205
Peacocke, C. A. B 176
Penner, T. xiv, 63, 205
Philoponus xi, xxxiv, 200, 209
Plato xi, xxvi, xxviii f., xxxi f., xxxv,
    xliv, 7, 15, 23, 56, 63, 78 f., 85,
    88, 89, 96, 99 f., 102, 104 f., 106,
    109, 121, 126, 134, 138, 140,
    141, 165, 169, 172, 173, 176,
    183, 186, 201 (see also Index
    of Subjects)

Pythagoreans 6 f., 10, 32, 63, 78,
    86, 124, 125, 141, 175

Ross, Sir W. D ix, xi, 72, 83, 114, 115,
    120, 134, 138, 142, 206, 208 f.

Sambursky, S. 200, 206
Schoedel, P. xxi, 206
Schofield, M. xliv, 75, 202, 206
Simplicius xi, 103, 135, 175, 200
Socrates 72
Solmsen, F. xxxv, 206
Sophists 45, 72, 154
Sorabji, R. R. K. 142, 202, 206
Strang, C. 75, 206
Strato of Lampsacus 200

Taylor, A. E. xxxii, 206
Taylor, C. C. W. 206
Thales 76
Themistius 115
Theophrastus 200
Torstrik, A. 209

Vlastos, G. 75, 173, 206
von Wright, G. H. xiii, 206

Waterlow, S. 207
Wedberg, A. 73, 206
West, M. L. 101, 206
White, N. P. xviii, 206
Wieland, W. ix, xxxiv, 111, 207
Wiggins, D. R. P. 71, 148, 207
Williams, C. J. F. 207
Wolfson, H. A. 207
Woods, M. J. 79, 184, 207

Xuthus 38, 135

Zabarella, J. xi, 207
Zeno of Elea xxi, xxiv, xxvi, xliv,
    22, 25, 78, 80, 100, 103, 109, 110

II. INDEX OF SUBJECTS

Above see Place, as terminus of change
Acceleration 187 f., 199 f

Accident(ally)
    accident in itself (203^b30) 9, 77

accidentally) (in itself (211^a12)
    26, 112 f.
Action
    contact necessary and sufficient
        for (202^a3) xv, 64
    form as agent and as transmitted
        in (202^a3) xv f., 64
    'not cut off' (202^b5) xvii, 68
    relation to change (202^a13, 21,
        $^b5$) 65-72
    reciprocal (201^a9, 202^a3) xvi,
        60 f., 64 f.
    and being acted on, whether the
        same (202^a13, 21, $^b5$)
        65-72
    'active', 'passive' and relatives
        (200^b26) 58
    of time (211^a26, 222^b16) xlvi,
        166-9
    virtual xvii, 197
    resultant of two actions 187,
        197 f.
    proportional to amount or power
        of agent 187, 194-6
    agency, theory of xiii, xv f.
Actuality
)(potentiality
        in classification of change
            (200^b26) 56-8
        in definition of change (201^a9,
            27, 201^b5) 58-60 61 f.
        and ambivalence of forms
            (201^a19) 60 f.
        of agent and patient 66
        of being and of the infinite
            (206^a9, $^b12$); see Be,
            Infinite
    See also Operation, Potentiality
Agent, Agency see Action
Air
    supposed infinite (203^a16, 205^a8)
    neither heavy nor light (205^a8)
    thought to be nothing or in-
        corporeal (212^a2, 213^a22)
        123 f.
    experiment to show strength of
        (213^a22) 123 f.
Alteration
)(change (200^b26) 55

Archimedes, Axiom of (206^b3) 84
Arithmetic see Counting, Mathe-
    matics, Number

Be
    different uses of 'be' (200^b26,
        201^a9, 203^b30, 206^a9)
        56 f., 77, 82 f.
    'that which is' and categories
        (200^b26) 57
    'the what it was to be' (202^b5)
        70
    'the what is it' (210^b32) 112
    'that being which it is' (219^a14,
        $^b9$, 220^a4) 148 f.
    the being (of what is in time)
        measured by time (220^b32)
        165 f.
    what is not, and time (221^b23)
        170
Becoming
    reality of xlv, xlvii, 156 f.
    See also Coming-to-be
Before and After
    in place, change and time (219^a14)
        146-9
    and the now (219^a22, $^b9$) 150,
        152-6
    and time (219^b1, 222^b30) xliv-
        xlvi, 150-2, 172
Below see Place, as terminus of
    change
Body
    definition of (204^a34) 79
    three dimensional (204^b10,
        209^a2) 79, 102
    no two bodies in same spot
        (209^a2, 210^a25)
    'all that is, is body' (213^a22,
        $^b30$) 125-6
    tangible (213^b30) 126
    whether infinite (203^a16, $^b15$,
        204^a34, $^b10$, 205^a8, $^b24$)
        79-82
    natural places of see Place
    geometrical or abstract 180-4,
        192 f.

Categories

Categories (*cont.*)
  and classification of change
    (200^b26) 56–8
Cause
  'the four causes' (207^b34, 209^a2)
    96, 103
  agency and causation xiii, xv f.
Celestial Sphere
  motion of, and time (218^a30,
    223^b12) xl f., 141, 174 f.
  whether in place (212^a31) 119–21
Change (*see generally* III.1–3)
  a subject for physics (200^b12)
    55 f.
  opinions of others on (210^b16) 63
  classification of (200^b26) xiv,
    56–8
  definition of (210^a9, 27, $^b5$, 16)
    xiii f., 58–62
  individuation and identity of xiv
  as incomplete operation (210^b16)
    xiv f., 63
  'always different' (219^b9) 154 f.
  persisting present in *see* Before and
    After
  continuity and (200^b12, 219^a10)
    55, 144
  derivative from magnitude
    (219^a10, 14, $^b9$, 220^a4,
    $^b14$) xlii f., 142–5, 147–9,
    154 f., 157–9
  and time *see* Time
  ontological status of (200^b26)
    57 f., 139 f.
  transitive and intransitive uses of
    'change' 65
  and operation of agent and
    patient (202^a21, $^b5$)
    xvi–xviii, 65–72
  in changing thing (202^a13) 65 f.
  not instantaneous 140
  circular motion the primary kind
    of (223^b12) 174 f.
  in itself and accidental (211^a12)
    112 f.
  perception of (218^b21, 219^a22)
    141 f., 150
  how infinite (207^b21, 208^a5,
    222^a24) 91–3, 98, 171

mathematical study of 185–8
virtual xvii f., 197 f.
Coming-to-be and Ceasing-to-be
  species of change or alteration
    (201^a9) 55
  perpetual and cyclical (203^b15,
    208^a5, 223^b12) 96, 168,
    175
Completeness
  'complete' defined (206^b33) 85 f.
  relation to finitude and know-
    ability (206^b33, 207^a15)
    xxiii f., 85–8
  incompleteness of change *see*
    Change
  complete)(incomplete, as termini
    of change (200^b26)
Conceivability
  and existence (203^b15, 207^b1,
    208^a5) 97 f., 182–4
Condensation and Rarefaction
  proved to occur (216^b22) 135
  do not presuppose void (216^b30,
    217^a20) 135–7
  theory of (217^a20, $^b11$) 136 f.
  density and weight (217^b11) 137
Contact
  definition of (211^a23) 114
  being finite and being in contact
    (208^a5) 97
  and location 114
  of agent and patient in change
    (202^a3, 212^b29) xv, 64,
    122
  similars naturally in contact
    (212^b29) 122
)(fusion (212^b29) 122
Continua, Continuity
  definition of 'continuous', and
    divisibility (200^b12,
    207^b1, 21, 34) 55 f., 90,
    93, 96, 144
  division of continua (220^a4)
    157–9
  in magnitude, change and time
    (200^b12, 211^a23, 219^a10,
    220^a4, 222^a10) 55, 113 f.,
    144–6, 157–9
Cosmos *see* World-System

Counting
    analogous to measurement
        (220^b14) 162 f.
    in time-measurement *see* Now,
    and finitude (204^a34) xxiv, 79 f.
    presupposes a mind (223^a16) 172 f.
    uses abstract numbers 89 f., 163
    See also Mathematics, Measure-
        ment, Number

Dense, Density *see* Condensation and
    Rarefaction
Dialectic
    aims and methods of (211^b32)
        ix f., 55, 63, 73, 76 f., 100,
        107, 111 f., 125, 138, 141
Dimensions *see* Place, species and
    differences of
Dispositions *see* Potentiality
Dynamics (204^b10, 214^b28, 215^a24)
    xv f., 129–33, 185–200

Elements
    natural philosophers on (203^a16,
        204^b10, 205^b8) 73–5,
        80
    not singly or jointly infinite
        (204^b10, 205^a8) 80 f.
Essence x, 70, 165 f.
    See also Be

Finite, Finitism
    must there be something beyond
        what is finite? (203^b15,
        208^a5) 76
    finiteness of actual bodies,
        numbers and quantities
        (204^a34) xx–xxvi, 79–82
    finitism in mathematics (207^a27)
        76, 93–6, 178–9
    See also Infinite
'Focal Meaning' xlii f., 91–3, 142
'Following' *see* Change, derivative
    from magnitude; *and* Time,
    derivative from Change
Form
)(privation, and structure of
        change (200^b26, 201^b16)
        58, 63

    transmitted in change (202^a3)
        xv f., 64
    as place (209^a31, $^b17$, 211^b5,
        10) 103 f., 106 f., 115
    ambivalence of *see* Potentiality
    Platonic *see* Plato
'Formal' problems and arguments
        (202^a21, 204^a34) 67, 79
Fusion *see* Contact
Future
    anti-realism about (217^b32) xxii
        f., xlvii, 138–40
    See also Now, Time

Geometry *see* Mathematics

Heavy, Heaviness *see* Place, Weight
Homonymy (202^a21) 60, 68
Ho pote on *see* Be: 'that being which
    it is'

Identity *see* Same
In
    uses of 'in' (210^a14) 107–9
    can anything be in itself? (210^a25,
        $^b21$) 109–10
    being in time *see* Time
    being in number *see* Number
    in itself)(accidentally *see* Accident
    in respect of itself)(in respect of
        something else (207^b21,
        209^a31, 210^a25, $^b32$)
        104, 109 *see also* 'Focal
        Meaning'
Increase
    and decrease, species of change
        (201^a9) 57
    does a thing's place increase with
        it? (209^a2, 211^a12,
        212^b22) 103, 112, 121
    does increase presuppose void?
        (213^b2, 214^b16) 124, 127
Inertia 195 f.
Infinite *(see generally* III.4–8)
    a subject for physics (200^b12,
        202^b30, 203^b3, 30,
        204^a34) 55 f., 72 f., 79
    problems about (203^b30) 77
    earlier opinions on (202^b30,

Infinite: earlier opinions on (*cont*.)
203ᵃ4, 16, ᵇ3, 205ᵇ1,
206ᵇ12, 33, 207ᵃ15)
73–6, 81, 85 f.
prima facie case for existence of
(203ᵇ15, 206ᵃ9, 208ᵃ5)
76 f., 96–8
uses of 'infinite' (203ᵇ30) 77 f.
definition of (206ᵇ33) 86
actual and potential (206ᵃ9, ᵇ12)
xx–xxiii, 82 f., 84 f.
by addition) (by division (203ᵇ30,
206ᵇ3, 12, 207ᵃ33) 78,
84
infinite in magnitude is primary
kind of (207ᵇ1, 21) xlii f.,
91–3
must be a principle (203ᵇ3) 73,
75
as material cause (206ᵇ12, 207ᵃ15,
33, ᵇ34) 86, 96
must be a quantity (204ᵃ8,
206ᵇ33) 73, 78
a property of number and magnitude (204ᵃ8) 78
in magnitudes (203ᵇ15, 204ᵃ34,
ᵇ10, 205ᵃ8, ᵇ24, 206ᵃ9,
207ᵇ1) xxxiii f., 97–82,
84, 90–3
in continua (200ᵇ12, 207ᵇ34)
55 f., 96
in number (203ᵇ15, 204ᵃ34,
206ᵃ9, 207ᵇ1) 79 f.,
88–90
in time (203ᵇ15, 206ᵃ9) 83
in mathematics (203ᵇ15, 207ᵇ27)
93–6, 178 f.
no self-subsistent infinite (204ᵃ8)
78 f.
no infinity of elements (205ᵃ8)
81
formless and unknowable (207ᵃ15,
33) 87 f.
surrounded not surrounding
(206ᵇ33, 207ᵃ15, 33,
ᵇ34) 88
)(whole, complete (206ᵇ33, 207ᵃ15)
85 f.
See also Finite

'Just' (temporal word) (222ᵇ7, 27)
171 f.

Leibniz's Law *see* Same
Light (opposite of Heavy) *see* Place,
Weight
Locomotion
species of change (200ᵇ26,
201ᵃ9) 58
the primary species of change
(208ᵃ27) 99
and place (208ᵇ8, 211ᵃ12,
212ᵃ14, ᵇ29) xxvii f.,
xxx f., 101, 112 f., 117.,
121 f.
natural (205ᵇ24, 208ᵇ8) xxviii,
82
in itself) (accidental (211ᵃ12)
112 f.
rotation as (212ᵃ31) 119 f.
and void (213ᵇ2, 214ᵃ16, ᵇ12,
28, 215ᵃ24) 124, 127,
128–33
of projectiles (214ᵇ28) 130
mathematical science of *see* Dynamics
'Long Ago' (227ᵇ7, 27) 171 f.

Magnitude
uses of 'magnitude' 73
divisible ad infinitum (203ᵃ15,
206ᵃ9, ᵇ3, 12, 207ᵇ1,
208ᵃ5) 76
not infinite in extent (204ᵃ34,
ᵇ10, 205ᵃ8, ᵇ24, 206ᵇ12,
207ᵇ1) 79–82, 84 f., 90 f.
change and time derivative from
(207ᵇ21, 219ᵃ10) 91–3,
142–6
mathematical *see* Mathematics:
mathematical objects
See also Before and After, Body,
Continua, Infinite
Mathematics
philosophy of 176–84 *see also*
Finite
realism about 176 f.
Plato's theory of (203ᵃ4, 206ᵇ12)
73, 176 f.

'universal' 160
applied 185 f.
mathematical objects
  formed by abstraction (219^{b}1)
    151, 173, 180–2, 193 f.
  and 'intelligible matter' 86,
    184
  left and right in (208^{b}8) 101
  whether infinite (203^{b}15,
    206^{a}9, ^{b}3, 12, 207^{a}33,
    ^{b}1, 27, 208^{a}5) 76, 93–8,
    178 f.
  See also Counting, Infinite,
    Measurement, Number
Matter, Material Cause
  as place (209^{b}6, 17, 211^{b}5,
    29, 212^{a}2) xxix, 104–7,
    115 f.
  as space xxxi f.
  infinite as *see* Infinite
  in substantial change (217^{a}20)
    136
  has no particulate micro-structure
    (217^{a}20) 137
  intelligible 86, 184
Measurement
  analogous to counting (220^{b}14)
    162 f.
  of time *see* Now, Time
  by time *see* Time: being in time
Medium
  resistance of (215^{a}24) 130–3,
    189–97
Momentum
  in dynamics 132 f., 198 f.

Nature, Natural
  concepts of xiii f., xxiv, xxxiii–
    xxxv
  a principle of change (200^{b}12)
    55 f.
  natural motion *see* Locomotion
  See also Physics
Now
  uses of 'now' (222^{a}10)
  as instant and as persisting present
    (217^{b}32, 219^{b}9, 220^{a}4,
    222^{a}10) xliii–xlvi, 140 f.,
    148 f., 152–5, 156 f., 170 f.

does not cease to be (217^{b}32)
  140 f.
and past and future 217^{b}32 ,
  220^{a}4, 222^{a}10, 222^{b}30)
  140, 170 f.
analogous to a point, not a part
  of time, not divisible
  (217^{b}32, 219^{b}9, 220^{a}4,
  222^{a}10) 138 f., 152–5,
  158 f., 170 f.
defines and measures time (218
  ^{b}21, 219^{a}22, ^{b}33, 220^{a}4)
  142, 150, 158 f.
and time, interdependent (219
  ^{b}33, 220^{b}32) 157, 165,
  172
See also Before and After, Point,
  Simultaneity, Time
Number
  number-nouns derived from
    number-adjectives (207^{b}1)
    90
  'number counted' and 'number
    by which we count' (219
    ^{b}1, 220^{a}27, ^{b}5) xl, 151,
    160, 176 f.
  abstract
    not self-subsistent (204^{a}8,
      207^{b}1) 78, 89
    created by thought (223^{a}16)
      173, 180–4
    conceivability and existence
      (203^{b}15, 207^{b}1, 208^{a}5)
      76, 88 f., 97 f., 180–4
  sameness and difference of (220
    ^{b}5, 223^{a}29, 224^{a}2) 161
  least (207^{b}1, 220^{a}27) 89 f., 160
  'separated' (204^{a}34) 79 f.
  in counting and measurement
    (204^{a}34, 207^{b}1, 220^{b}14,
    223^{b}12) xxxix f., 89 f.,
    163
  'in number' (220^{b}32)
  time as *see* Time
  See also Counting, Finite, Infinite,
    Mathematics, One

One
  indivisible, in counting and

One: indivisible (*cont.*)
  measurement (207^b1, 220^a27,
    $^b14$) 89 f., 160, 163
  by contact (203^a16, 205^a8) 74
  in fusion (212^b29) 122
  See also Same
Opposites
  as termini of change (200^b26) 58
  correlated pairs of (201^b16) 63
Operation
  and actuality (201^a27, $^b5$) 60 f.
  of agent and patient in change
    (202^a13, 21, $^b5$) xvi–xviii,
    65–72
  change as *see* Change
)(change 63

Passive, Patient *see* Action
Past
  realism and anti-realism about
    (217^b32, 223^a16) xxv,
    xlvii f., 139 f., 156 f., 173
  See also Now, Time
'Phased Sortals' 148 f.; *see also* Be:
    'that being which it is'
Physics
  change, infinite, place, void, time
    germane to (200^b12,
    202^b30, 208^a27, 213^a12)
  earlier students of (202^b30,
    203^a16, $^b3$, 213^a22, $^b2$
    216^b22)
  methods and assumptions of ix f.,
    xxxiii f.
  mathematics in *see* Dynamics
  See also Nature, Science
Place (*see generally* IV.1–5)
  uses of 'place' 99, 126
  a subject for physics (200^b12,
    208^a27, 211^a12) 55 f.,
    99
  opinions of others on (208^b27,
    209^b6, 17) 99 f., 101 f.,
    105 f.
  problems about (208^a27, 209^a2,
    210^a25, $^b21$, 212^b22)
    99 f., 102 f.
  prima facie case for existence of
    (208^b1, 8, 25, 27) 100–2

'everything is somewhere/ in a
    place' (208^a27, $^b27$,
    209^a2) 99
  definition of (211^a23, 212^a2,
    14) 116
  common) (particular (209^a31)
  'kinds of place' (205^b24, 208^b8,
    210^b32, 212^b29) xxxi, 82,
    100 f., 147
  'before and after' in *see* Before
    and After
  as terminus of change
    in general (200^b12, 26, 211
    $^a12$) 56, 58, 112 f.
    natural places and motions,
    above and below (205^a8,
    $^b1$, 24, 208^b8, 209^b17,
    210^b32, 211^a12, 212^a21,
    $^b29$, 214^b28) xxvii f.,
    80–82, 101, 106, 112,
    118, 121 f.
    See also Locomotion
  independent of moving bodies
    (208^b1, 27, 209^b17,
    210^b27, 32) 100 f., 102,
    110–2
  of same size as body (209^a2, 31,
    210^b32, 212^a21) 112,
    118
  'circumscriptive' not 'receptive'
    (209^a31, $^b6$, 17, 210^a14,
    $^b32$, 211^a23) 103, 106,
    108 f., 111, 118, 122;
    see also In
  space-based and extension theories
    of, rejected (209^b6, 17,
    211^b14, 29, 212^a2) xxviii
    f., 102, 115 f.; *see also*
    Space, Void
  and location xxvii–xxxi, 100, 121
  and void (208^b25, 213^a12,
    213^b30) 101, 122 f.,
    125 f.; *see also* Space, Void
  not form of body (209^a31, $^b17$,
    211^b10) 103 f., 103 f.,
    106 f., 115
  not matter of body (209^b6, 17,
    211^b29) 104 f., 106 f.,
    116

does not move or change size
   (209^{a}2, 212^{a}14, ^{b}22)
   xxx f., 103, 112 f., 117 f.
is it a cause? (209^{a}2) 103
in place
   what is in place (211^{a}23,
      212^{a}31, 223^{a}16) 113 f.,
      119–21
   potentially) (in actual op-
      eration (212^{a}31) 120
   is the world-system in place?
      (212^{a}31) 119–21
   is a place in place? (209^{a}2,
      210^{b}21, 212^{b}22) 103,
      110, 121
   is a point in place? (209^{a}2,
      212^{b}22) 102, 121
Plato, Platonism
   on change (201^{b}16) 63
   on infinite (203^{a}4, 204^{a}8, 206
      ^{b}12, 207^{a}15) 73, 78 f.,
      85, 88
   on space and place (209^{b}6, 17)
      xxxi f., 100, 102, 104–6,
      126
   on time 138 f., 140 f., 164, 172
   on mathematics 73, 176 f.
   Forms (Platonic) (209^{b}17) 78,
      99
   'unwritten doctrines' (209^{b}6)
      105
   Aristotle's attitude to xxi, xxxi f.,
      78 f., 102, 176 f.
   passages referred to:
      Parmenides
         138^{a}2–^{b}6   106
            a7–^{b}5   109, 121
         141^{a-e} 165
         145^{a}1   104
            ^{b}6–^{c}7   109
            e1   99
         151^e–152^a 165
         152^{b}2–5   140
            b-c   138
            c-d   165
         156^d 172
      Sophist
         256^d 63
      Timaeus

37^c–39^e (esp. 39^{d}1)   141
38^{a}3–5   165
48^e–52^d 105
49^{a}5–6   105
51^{a}7–^{b}1   105
52^{a}8   105
   ^{a}8–^{d}1   99
57^e 63
Point
   analogous to moving thing and to
      now (219^{b}9, 222^{a}10)
      153–5, 170 f.
   and division of lines (220^{a}4)
      157 f.
   has location but not place (209^{a}2,
      212^{b}22) 102, 121
Possibility
   and actuality, for everlasting ob-
      jects (203^{b}15) 77, 168
Potentiality, Power
   physical powers
      in classification and definition
         of change (200^{b}26, 201^{a}9,
         27) xiii f., 56–60, 61 f.
      in explanation of change
         (202^{a}3) xiii f., xv f., 64
      ambivalent (201^{a}19, 202^{a}31)
         xvi, 60 f., 64
      of elements (204^{b}10) 80
      as quantities related mathe-
         matically (204^{b}10) 80,
         186, 188–9, 194–8
   'potentially as matter' (206^{b}12,
      207^{a}15) 85, 87
   See also Actuality
Preponderance
   in explantion of motion (215
      ^{a}24) 132 f., 189, 198 f.
Present *see* Now
Principle
   uses of 'principle' 75
   infinite as *see* Infinite
Privation
)(form *see* Form
   infinite as essentially (207^{b}34) 96

'Qua'
   function of, in definition of change
      (201^{a}27) 58–62

Quantity
in system of categories (= 'so
much') (200^{b}26, 201^{a}9)
57
change of see Increase
Qualification
in system of categories (= 'of such
a kind') (200^{b}26, 201^{a}9)
57
change of see Qualitative Change
Qualitative Change
species of change (200^{b}26, 201^{a}9)
57
continuum of stages in 143

Rare, Rarefaction see Condensation
and Rarefaction
'Recently' (222^{b}7, 27) 171 f.
Relative
in system of categories (200^{b}26)
58
Rest
definition of (202^{a}3) 169
of the infinite, Anaxagoras on
(205^{b}1) 81
measured by time (221^{b}7) 169 f.

Sameness (Oneness) and Difference
in being, in definition, in primary
sense, simply (201^{a}27,
202^{a}13, ^{b}5, 210^{a}25,
213^{a}12, 219^{b}9) 61 f.,
66, 69–71, 110, 122 f.,
154
other kinds of, and identity 66,
69
and Leibniz's Law 69–71, 110
'the same X', applicability of
(224^{a}2) 161
of numbers and times see Number,
Time
Science
concept of ix f., 176
See also Dynamics, Mathematics,
Physics
'Separate', 'Separated', 'Separable'
uses of 79 f., 89, 106, 111, 116,
124, 126 f., 128 f., 135,
176 f., 180 f.

Simultaneity
= being in same now (217^{b}32,
222^{a}24) 141, 171
are there different times simultaneously? (218^{a}30,
220^{b}5, 223^{a}29) xli, 141,
145 155 f., 160–2, 174
See also Now, Together
Space
Hesiod on (208^{b}27) 101
Plato on (209^{b}6) xxxi f., 105
not admitted by Aristotle (211
^{b}14, 216^{a}23) xxviii–
xxxii, xxv f., 101, 115 f.,
133 f.
See also Place, Void
Speed
concept of 188
laws governing (215^{a}24) 187,
189–200
Strength
as physical quantity see Power
Substance
and predication 73
identical with essence 79
in system of categories (= 'this')
(200^{b}26) 57
in classification of change (200
^{b}26) 57 f.
substantial change (217^{a}20) 57 f.,
136 f.
infinite as (203^{a}4, 204^{a}8) 73, 78
f.
'Suddenly' (222^{b}7, 27) 171 f.
Synonymy 72 see also Same in definition

'This' see Substance
Time (see generally IV.10–14)
uses of 'time' 145, 156
a subject for physics (200^{b}12,
217^{b}29) 55 f., 138
earlier opinions on (218^{a}30) 141,
175
problems about (217^{b}32) 138–41
as change qua numbered, as
number of change (219^{b}1,
33, 220^{a}24, 223^{a}29)
xxxviii–xlii, 150–2, 174

as 'the before and after in change' (223^{a}16) *see* Before and After

not change (218^{a}30, ^{b}9) 141

derivation from change (218^{b}21, 219^{a}10, 22, ^{b}1, 9, 207^{b}21) xlii, 91, 145 f.

'always different' (219^{b}9) 154 f.

continuous and divisible (219^{a}10, 220^{a}4, 24) 146, 157–9

before and after in *see* Before and After

how infinite (203^{b}15, 206^{a}9, 208^{a}5, 222^{a}24) xxv, 76, 83, 91–3, 98, 171

measurement of (220^{b}14, 223 ^{b}12) xl f., 162–4, 174

and the now *see* Now

without beginning or end (222^{a}24) 76, 171

not circular (222^{a}24, 223^{b}12) 171, 175

parts of (217^{b}32) 138

'at some time' (222^{a}24) 171

sameness and difference of (218 ^{b}9, 220^{b}5, 223^{a}29) 141, 160–2, 171 f.

not fast or slow (218^{b}9, 220^{a}32) 141, 160

being in time (220^{b}32, 221^{b}23, 222^{b}30) 164–70, 172

measures change and rest (220 ^{b}32, 221^{b}7) 165 f., 169 f.

action of time (221^{a}26, 222^{b}16) xlvi, 166–9

perception of (218^{b}21, 219^{a}22, 223^{a}16) 98, 141 f.

presupposes mind (223^{a}16) 172 f.

abstract xli f., 156

in mathematical physics 186 f., 194–6 *see also* Speed

metaphysics of, in general xxii, xxv, xlv–xlviii

Together (212^{a}21) 114, 118 *see also* Contact, Simultaneity

'Untechnical arguments' (217^{b}29) 138

Vision
theory of (201^{a}27) 62

Void (*see generally* IV.6–9)
uses of 'void' (213^{b}30) 125 f.

a subject for physics (200^{b}12, 213^{a}12) 55 f., 122

earlier opinions on (213^{a}22, ^{b}2) 123–5

common notions about (213^{b}30, 214^{a}16) 123 f., 125 f.

prima facie arguments for and against (213^{a}22, ^{b}2, 214^{a}16) 124 f.

as space, as receptive xxxv f., 122 f., 126, 133 f.

as place (213^{a}12, ^{b}30, 214^{a}16, ^{b}12) 122 f., 126, 129

'distinct', 'separated', 'inseparable' (214^{a}16, 216^{a}23, ^{b}30, 217^{b}20) *see* 'Separate'

arguments against, in general (214^{b}12, 215^{a}24, 216^{a}23) 128–34, 135 f.

not necessary for motion (213^{b}2, 214^{a}16) 124, 127

makes motion impossible (214^{b}12, 28, 215^{a}24) 128 f., 129–33

explains nothing, is superfluous (214^{b}12, 216^{a}23) 129, 133 f., 135 f.

occupancy of, impossible (214 ^{b}12, 216^{a}23) 129, 133 f.

no distinction of places or direction in (214^{b}12) 128 f.

does not explain differences in density (216^{a}30) 135 f.

not presupposed by condensation and rarefaction (217^{a}20) 136 f.

as limiting case in dynamics (215^{a}24) 130–3, 192

See also Place, Space

Weight
concept of 188 f.

'heavy' and 'light' as termini of change (200^{b}26) 58

and natural motions/places (205 ^{b}24, 208^{b}8) 100 f.

Weight (*cont.*)
    in mathematical laws (215^{a}24)
        130–3, 187, 189–94,
        196
    See also Dynamics, Locomotion,
        Place
Whole
    defined and contrasted with in-
        finite (206^{b}33, 207^{a}15)
        85 f.
World-System
    of fixed finite size (207^{b}1) 85,
        95 f.
    whether contained in anything
        (203^{b}3, 15, 208^{a}5, 212^{a}31,
        213^{b}2) 76, 86
    whether in place (212^{a}31) 110,
        119–21
    in Ionian cosmology (203^{b}15)
        xxxiii, 76
    time thought to be change or
        boundary of (218^{a}30) 141